Books by Gerald Eskenazi:

The Lip: A Biography of Leo Durocher

Yaz *(with Carl Yastrzemski)*

Bill Veeck: A Baseball Legend

A Year on Ice

Hockey

The Fastest Sport

There Were Giants in Those Days

A Thinking Man's Guide to Pro Soccer

Hockey Is My Life *(with Phil Esposito)*

The Derek Sanderson Nobody Knows

A Thinking Man's Guide to Pro Hockey

Hockey for Children

Miracle on Ice *(with others)*

The Way It Was *(with others)*

GERALD ESKENAZI

GANG GREEN

AN IRREVERENT LOOK

BEHIND THE SCENES AT

THIRTY-EIGHT (WELL, THIRTY-SEVEN)

SEASONS OF NEW YORK JETS

FOOTBALL FUTILITY

Simon & Schuster

SIMON & SCHUSTER
Rockefeller Center
1230 Avenue of the Americas
New York, NY 10020

SIMON & SCHUSTER and colophon are registered trademarks
of Simon & Schuster Inc.

Designed by Jeanette Olender
Insert designed by Liney Li
Manufactured in the United States of America

10 9 8 7 6 5 4 3 2 1

Library of Congress Cataloging-in-Publication Data
Eskenazi, Gerald.
Gang green: an irreverent look behind the scenes at thirty-eight
(well, thirty-seven) seasons of New York Jets football futility /
Gerald Eskenazi.
p. cm.
Includes index.
1. New York Jets (Football team)—History.
2. New York Jets (Football team)—Humor.   I. Title.
GV956.N4E797   1998
796.332′64′097471—dc21   98-37878   CIP
ISBN 0-684-84115-0

Acknowledgments

Sports are still compelling.

Those of us who write about games can lose sight of the hold they retain on fans, young and old, and the secure place they keep in our lives. Cynicism because of the foolishness of some and the greed of others is forgotten when a grown man or woman spots Joe Namath at an airport. Or when the Jets win a football game. Or—and this does happen, you know—lose a game.

So it was enormous fun to write this book. Not many newspaper reporters actually get the chance to write 100,000 words about a subject they know and that is fun to describe.

Probably every town or major city has its Jets. To me, the Jets are a metaphor for longing, for the desire to recreate a fond memory that is always elusive. Like most of us, the Jets have to be content with small victories; for many, though, those too are elusive. Still, the sun rises and people get up and go to work. The Jets put on their uniforms and take the field. Who knows? Maybe that's all we should expect out of life.

In looking at this franchise, I had many helpful operatives. Some of them actually played the game, but all had insight into what goes on. One of the most important was Jeff Neuman of Simon & Schuster. Mostly, everyone enjoyed observing. So thanks to:

Joe Namath, leRoy Neiman, Joe Goldstein, Dave Anderson,

Acknowledgments *8*

Frank Ramos, John Schmitt, Bill Mazer, Helen Dillon, Bob Reese, Sammy Baugh, Harold Rosenthal, Walt Michaels, Art Kaminsky, Rich Cimini, Dr. James Nicholas, Steve Serby, Rabbi Myron Fenster, Doug Miller, Ralph Baker, Dan Sekanovich, Barton Silverman, Scott Kerniss, Rick Diamond, Charley Winner, Frank Scatoni, Paul Needell, Bruce Coslet, Pepper Burruss, Joe Klecko, Ron Wolf, Joe Walton, Boomer Esiason, Dick Haley, Janet Pawson, Don Maynard, Curley Johnson, Weeb Ewbank, Mike Kensil, Berj Najarian, Marty Lyons, Richard Todd, Greg Buttle.

This is for—in order of their appearance—Andy Shuster and Anna G. Eskenazi. Each married a child Rosalind and I brought into the world. Then Andy collaborated with Ellen to create Corey, and Anna teamed up with Mark to produce Alexa. As we know in sports, the clock continues.

Contents

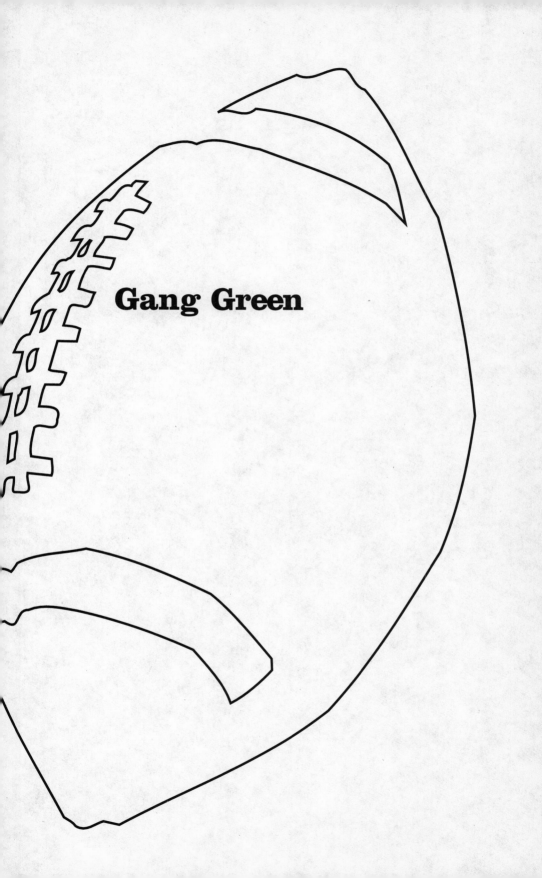

Gang Green

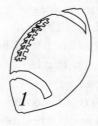

Why?

One summer day in 1997, when the Jets were on the verge of still another new era, Joe Namath reflected on his life since football, since the Super Bowl, since the sixties. Almost 30 years earlier he and his Jets teammates helped define an era, a moment in time that has shone brighter than anything the Jets have done since. He is in his 50s now, a father of two young girls, and he couldn't wait until tomorrow because every day was a new adventure in living with his wife, Tatiana.

So, Joe, I asked, what are your thoughts on what's happened to the Jets in the years since that moment of triumph?

Joe hesitated, then replied, "I can't think of any good reason to discuss my personal reasons why the Jets have done what they do. It's like being an American. You may not like what the government does, but you support it."

. . .

My route to the world of the Jets was different from Joe's. And I get paid to question.

On a beautiful fall day in Brooklyn, back around 1950, I invented the I formation, which helped transform football. It happened on Schenck Avenue, around the corner from my house on Sutter Avenue in East New York, and it was a brilliant success.

Here was its exquisite, yet simple, premise: Three of us lined up in an "I." I took the ball, turned around to my friend behind me, and handed it off. He then also turned and handed it to the guy behind him.

The three defenders in front of us were flat-footed. They lost sight of the ball the instant I turned, and never realized what we were doing. We scored the easiest of touchdowns, which consisted of running to the next manhole cover.

This sensational play worked three or four times, and then someone on the other side got smart. They lined up in a defensive I formation themselves. The I formation, as practiced by us that fall, had been neutralized. Clearly, football was a game of adjustments, a lesson I learned as a teenager. Football life had its yin and yang.

Twenty-five years later, in the summer of 1975, *The New York Times* asked me to become the beat reporter covering the New York Jets. It was an assignment I welcomed enthusiastically. Since that day on the Brooklyn streets where I found my invention smashed, I had taken a casual attitude toward the game; I grew up, loved and lost the Brooklyn Dodgers baseball team, became a sportswriter, and enjoyed success and some small measure of fame writing about the Rangers hockey team. It was an odd sport for me to cover: I had never played hockey on the Brooklyn streets, of course, and the first hockey game I ever saw I wrote about (luckily for me, it had a fight and a gaggle of goals).

But the Rangers had a failing: They could never win a championship. Their last had come in 1940. Every spring, they lost their final playoff game. They were a New York joke. Every year I thought of Sisyphus and Icarus as I summed up the Rangers' season.

Oh, in the cool, crisp Canadian Septembers I used to follow the Rangers up to Kitchener, Ontario, for the start of their training camp. It was exciting and fun and I learned to respect the game and appreciate the hold it had on an entire country. And in time, I came to see the beauty of hockey. I pulled out all the adjectives I had acquired at City College of New York and in reading those writers I respected.

While the Rangers were flailing annually at their fate, the New York Jets had become a celebrity outfit with a showbiz owner and Joe Namath, whose nickname of Broadway Joe was all one needed to know, at quarterback. He was a rollicking sixties counterpart to those other New York icons, the Babe, the Duke, and the Mick—a long-haired quarterback who won a Super Bowl against a team from The Establishment. The Jets were part of a New Wave in sports, a cinéma vérité of jockdom—players who spoke the truth, not clichés, whose actions mirrored the larger society's aspirations, and whose followers were younger and hipper than the buttoned-down followers of the NFL's Giants.

But that was then. The Jets I came to write about were like life as Kafka or George Carlin might have pictured it—only more so. They led an existence based in the everyday reality so many of us faced, one of small victories offset by large losses.

And yet the Jets had stretches of near-stardom: the early 1980s under the oh-so-human Walt Michaels, when the Sack Exchange made everyone bullish on the Jets' future. There was the emergence of the young and gifted runner Freeman McNeil, the breathtaking fluidity of receiver Wesley Walker hauling in a pass thrown by Richard Todd, Namath's successor.

And who could forget the mid-1980s when the team, directed by Joe Walton, allowed Jets fans to renew their dreams: the punishing defense in which linebacker Lance Mehl would tackle a dozen enemy players a game, and when the Who's-He-Turned-Golden-Boy, Ken O'Brien, would rocket the ball to the smooth-as-silk Al Toon.

There were Sundays when the Jets were pro football's best team.

Indeed, if you were a Jets fan in the 1980s, you had one of the better stretches of NFL success—up to a point. They tantalized, they sent players to the Pro Bowl, and then they went nowhere in the postseason.

My good friend Rabbi Myron Fenster, former head of the New York Board of Rabbis, spoke for the many who remained Jets fans no matter their tribulations.

"It's good for the soul," the rabbi explained. "It teaches you about striving and redemption, although I must admit I'm waiting for the redemption a long time."

The Jets had their great moments, even while I was writing about them. On those best Sundays, they energized their youthful fans, who often celebrated as if they were at a circus, not a football game. Going to a Jets game when they're winning is very different from being at a Giants game. For the Giants, there is the sense of watching gladiators; the Jets, though, play in a funhouse, cotton-candy atmosphere.

There was a new vision as the millennium approached, with likely expectations that the team could be good, maybe even great, once again. Hope is all Jets fans have ever wanted, and they may have finally gotten it in a realistic manner. The team even went back to the future as 1998 dawned, reviving the uniform of the Super Bowl era.

But as happiness is made sweeter by the memory of affliction, this is a propitious time to remind the freshly optimistic about the failures of the past. We can begin with that moment in the Seattle Kingdome when I asked the tearful punter, Chuck Ramsey, why he was crying after a loss to the Seahawks.

"How would you feel," he said between sobs, "if the coach told you in front of the entire team, 'I can fart farther than you can punt'?"

How, indeed?

Every year there is the new start for the Jets and their fans, who constitute the largest season-ticket base in sports—77,000 seats sold every game, year-in, year-out. To its credit, Jets management became the last in pro football to require season-ticket-holders to buy tickets for the exhibition games as well. And traditionally, the Jets' ticket prices have been the lowest in the NFL.

So when the team slides, it doesn't hurt fans (in the pocketbook, at any rate) as much to stay away. Every year from the time they moved into Giants Stadium in 1984, 15 percent of Jets ticket-holders never even went to games. By far it was the largest number of bail-outs in sports: 90,000 no-shows who no-show every year; $3 million worth of tickets annually down the drain. That dearth of live fans reached its high (that is to say, low) in the dismal year of 1996, when the 1–15 team chased away more than 200,000 fans who had actually paid for their seats.

With 1997's stunning surprise of a 9–7 team, fans not only turned out in record numbers, they actually stayed until the end, cheering themselves hoarse.

They did that in the final moments of a pre-Thanksgiving victory over the Vikings, and it brought tears to the eyes of the octogenarian owner, Leon Hess. So what if they would be stuck for 90 minutes in the parking lot afterward? This was something many of them had never seen—a winning Jets season (the first in nine years, actually) and a team that didn't fall apart.

Yet, how difficult it must have been almost every other year, when there was the hope in springtime as the college draft took place and the new fresh faces were paraded on the sports pages. Then there was the anticipation and sweat of the summer, when the team was hammered together on the grounds of Hofstra University in Hempstead, Long Island, where the Jets enjoy a fenced-in enclave that includes three football fields, an enclosed bubble in their upbeat new world, and the two-story Weeb Ewbank Hall.

There, a glass case houses the Vince Lombardi Super Bowl trophy, gleaming silver by Tiffany's. It sits there looking like the United States Constitution in its protected case in Washington. Airless, it is preserved against the ravages of time. You know it was once really touched by humanity, but is now so old it is like regarding the bones of an ancient civilization. It is hard to relate to in modern terms.

For close to 30 years, Jets summers have given way to the realities of fall, when the games count and during which time, usually, the first hint of failed promises surfaces. Finally, there is the bleak winter as, locked in failure, hopes wither and die.

I believe the Jets are the most famous bad franchise in sports. But that doesn't mean they are a team that cannot be enjoyed, even loved. The sports world has its lovable losers, teams with a tradition of not getting it right. But none has the cachet of the Jets, who have become famous for being bad.

Let us count the ways:

- Through their first 37 seasons, since their creation in 1960, they were the only team in professional sports without a coach who produced a winning career record during his tenure there.
- Not one player drafted since Joe Namath in 1964 has even been a finalist for the Football Hall of Fame based on a Jets career.
- The Jets are the only football team since the merger of 1970 that has failed to win a division title.
- The Jets are the only team playing in a stadium named for another team.

But these are facts, cold and obvious. What distinguishes the Jets has been the way the club has gloried in the ineffable, the inane, and even the inscrutable:

- Can't find a place to practice? How about the side of the road on the Belt Parkway in Queens, New York? Or even Rikers Island prison, where the fans were frisked.
- How about that wonderful moment during a scrimmage in Easton, Pennsylvania, when Brigitte Nielsen, the six-foot-two-inch blonde actress and ex-wife of Sylvester Stallone, hopped out of her limousine on the sidelines to see her inamorata, Mark Gastineau, practice?
- Even if you have a place to play, why not have the honor of being the first team ever to perform in a game suspended by lightning?
- You say your quarterback Richard Todd has a broken little toe? He got it while watching television at home.
- Johnny Johnson became the first NFL player to run 90 yards from scrimmage—and not score a touchdown. He was hauled down from behind inches from the goal line. It remains the longest play in Jets history and, metaphorically, counted for nothing.
- And even when life suddenly seemed good again in 1997, when the Jets had a chance to make the playoffs in the final game of

the season, they were foiled by the Lions, who intercepted three different passers—two of whom had never thrown a big-league pass before the year began. Those throws were watched from the sidelines by the Jets' putative $25 million quarterback.

All sports is a striving. Few are called, though, to define themselves in the full failure of such striving. This the Jets have done—not intentionally, of course; not maliciously, certainly; but inevitably. For example, when I sat down as the millennium approached to start writing this book, it had been 11 years since the Jets had won more than half their games in a season, nine years since they produced a winning campaign, 28 years since finishing first, and eight years since boasting of a first-string Pro Bowl player.

"If I could only win two games in a row again," cornerback Aaron Glenn said dreamily one day before the 1997 season, reflecting on that golden twin in October 1994.

When a team continues to underperform, year in and year out, it covers itself in that mantle of helplessness. The year before I began this book, the Jets signed Neil O'Donnell, picked up from the Super Bowl Steelers, to the fourth-largest contract in NFL history, a five-year, $25 million package. He played six games before tearing his shoulder. He was warming up before a game for his return, went into a routine backpedal—and tore a calf muscle. End of season.

O'Donnell had been a Jet only a few days when he realized he had joined a team mired in its culture of losing.

"How do I get these guys to stop thinking so negatively?" he asked.

Think of a team with the opposite qualities: baseball's Yankees, for example. Their long-time excellence creates an aura that elevates those who join the team. A rising tide raises all ships, and rising expectations—on the Yankees, on the 49ers, on the Chicago Bulls or the Montreal Canadiens—do the same.

Imagine how difficult it must be for a player—or a head coach—to join the Jets and confront history, and the inevitable comparisons to the past bad times as soon as things turn sour: the inexorable dunking by the news media, the old bugaboos that they are a team without a home of their own, without a recent past, with a history of collapses.

"What's the name of that guy in the cartoons who walks around with the cloud over his head?" wondered one Jet on one losing Sunday in 1996.

"Why does this always seem to happen to us?" lamented Johnny Mitchell, one of their failed number-one draft picks, as the 1994 season slid away with defeat after December defeat.

Shortly after his unanswerable question, Johnny, a boxing fan, spotted me at ringside covering a fight in Atlantic City. He and a friend, portly yet wearing a jogging suit, came over and spoke enthusiastically about boxing.

"So what do you do?" I asked the fat friend.

"Part-time psychic," he replied proudly.

Why, it's enough to make you wonder about the nature of sport, the nature of being a Jet, and of being a Jet follower. Why do these things always happen to them?

This is not a trick question.

2

The Early Days

The Jets were created as the New York Titans in 1960—during the upbeat final days of the Eisenhower administration, when America still flexed its expansionist muscle—and took the field just before John F. Kennedy was preparing to debate Vice-President Richard Nixon. They were in the fledgling American Football League: a raucous, buccaneering loop that was a true rival to the established National Football League. It never aspired to be a vanilla copy; it had balls—both kinds—as well as the two-point conversion and a clutch of good quarterbacks. To help them open up the game with a more exciting passing attack, the AFL even used a ball that was more pointy than the classic NFL ball, a rounder spheroid emblazoned with the nickname "the Duke." (The Duke was the honorific for Giants owner Wellington Mara, whose namesake was the Irish-born Duke of Wellington.) The AFL's ball was designed differently so that its quarterbacks could toss the hell out of it.

The men who began the AFL, megamillionaires such as Texan Lamar Hunt (whose brothers once cornered the silver market in

America) and Detroit industrialist Ralph Wilson, gave themselves a nickname: The Foolish Club.

A famed sports announcer of the day, Harry Wismer, was the incessantly upbeat owner of the Titans. He was also the biggest bullshitter ever created. He once called *The New York Times*, where I had just started as a copy boy. I answered the phones. This was his opening gambit:

"Hello, this is Harry Wismer. Who's this?"

I told him my name. It was unknown to anyone outside of my family and friends and a few people in the office, who were impressed with the way I tore copy paper off the AP machine and got the coffee order right. I had yet to have a byline.

"Jerry," he shouted into the phone, "you're doing a great job!"

His checks bounced, too.

Harry had been a celebrity sports announcer in an era when voices had faces: the days of Bill Stern, Graham McNamee, Ted Husing.

Wismer put himself in that florid pantheon with his broadcasts of Notre Dame football. He had a staccato style made even more dramatic because of his penchant for shouting into the microphone. With his wavy dark hair and sharp features, he also was able to carve a minor career in films, playing sports announcers.

It was a theatrical time for broadcasters of the Wismer ilk. When Harry did a game, that was the reality for the millions of Americans who heard him. There was no television to speak of, and moviegoers had to wait a week before seeing in the theaters what had happened on the field. Radio broadcasters painted pictures to fuel the imagination of the listeners, and in no other sport were there such colorful portraits as in the football broadcasts.

In 1960, Wismer used his personal wealth (which consisted of paper, since it was all in a stock market that was about to plummet) to back the team. Offices? He operated out of his apartment, albeit a huge set of rooms over on Park Avenue, fancy digs that faced a courtyard. Harry had married well twice, first to a Ford, which gave him the chance to broadcast the Detroit Lions games, and then to the widow of one of America's famed Jewish gangsters, Abner (Longie) Zwillman.

It was at his Park Avenue apartment in 1960 that Harry held a press conference to introduce his first coach.

Harold Rosenthal, interpreter of man's foibles on the playing field for the great, departed *Herald Tribune*, was there in his role as reporter. Writers covering the Titans were considered a notch below the Giants' beat reporters.

"We were the shnooks of the beat writers," recalls Harold from his retirement manse in Boca Raton, Florida. "The top guys were writing about the Giants. I was an old baseball writer. Used to cover the Dodgers, then switched to the Yanks. But the football Giants were a great team to get onto. Every Tuesday they had a big press conference and you had steak—your one chance in the week to get a free steak meal.

"Harry used to have a guy with him, Steve Sabo, a kind of a cheerleader. Everything that Harry said, Sabo would interject, just so you wouldn't miss it, 'Hey, that was pretty funny.' He was a short, peppery guy built along the lines of a Hank Stram. He was scouting for talent by reading those 25-cent football magazines."

So Harold was in Harry's apartment, and here's how Harry conducted his first major announcement:

"Harry hired Sammy Baugh, the old Redskins quarterback, as the Titans' first coach. We didn't know that was coming, though. Wismer called us into his apartment, where he had a three-piece band in the living room—guitar, sax, and bass—all dressed in cowboy uniforms. Meanwhile, he was hiding Sammy in the bedroom to come out as a surprise. We were hanging around, next to where one of the girls was working on the tickets. Harry always had tickets around, on the bed, the table, the sofa.

"And Harry says, 'Gentlemen, I want to introduce the new coach of the Titans—Slingin' Sammy Baugh.' And the band struck up 'The Eyes of Texas.' Sammy was so embarrassed. He was from Texas but he was no country boy, and they had him dressed up in a cowboy hat and bandanna."

Sammy Baugh was one of the three or four greatest names in the history of pro football. He was its premier quarterback, slinging for the Redskins in the thirties, forties, and fifties, and also creating punting records. He was less than 10 years removed from his playing days and still had legendary status and aura.

Baugh's arrival was a coup for Harry, who gloried in the surprise celebrity. Once, at a Titans' luncheon, he got up and announced, "Gentlemen, I want to introduce John Roosevelt." And John, one of FDR's five sons, rose, smiled, and shook hands with the puzzled attendees.

Wismer was always mixing fact and fiction, the real celebrity with the phantom. A favorite routine when he was announcing football games on the radio was to spot a senator, say, and call out over the airwaves, "How ya doin', Senator Taft?" when, of course, there wasn't any such person present.

Harry also was bitter—no, paranoid—about the Giants once the Titans were created. He would try to outmuscle the Giants, who played in nearby Yankee Stadium, when he believed they were sabotaging his team. One of his pals, and a part-owner of the Titans, was Clark Clifford, adviser to presidents, Kennedy confidant, and man about Washington.

Wismer called Clifford and told him that the Maras were slashing the tires of cars parked at the Polo Grounds to discourage people from attending Titans games. Clifford, perhaps busy with the Cuban Missile Crisis, couldn't help him with that one.

Despite Harry's business and political connections, he had made a titanic mistake. He invested a disproportionate amount of his money in Brunswick bowling stock, and bowling's boom was about to crash louder than a 10-strike. Harry started scrambling. Before long, the Titans couldn't even pay the taxi drivers who took the players to the games, let alone pay the players.

Still, Baugh got his first-year team to perform at a 7–7 clip, although the average Polo Grounds crowd was about 10,000. These were generous estimates, reminding one of the line uttered by Dick Young of the *Daily News:* Describing an obviously sparse crowd whose numbers were inflated by a press agent, Young wrote, "The game attracted 10,000 fans, 5,000 of whom came disguised as empty seats."

The AFL was created with eight teams, all of which exist today, although some have different nicknames or homes. The Titans played in the Eastern Division with the Buffalo Bills, Boston Patriots, and Houston Oilers. The Oakland Raiders and Denver Broncos made up the Western Division, along with two teams that would eventually move—the Los Angeles Chargers (to San Diego) and the Dallas Texans (to Kansas City, changing their name to Chiefs).

Wismer clothed his Titans in blue and gold and got an infusion of money from ABC, which was the so-called "third" network and still desperately attempting to make inroads on CBS and NBC. CBS, of course, had the highfalutin NFL to showcase. ABC countered with the AFL, and Wismer brokered the deal, signing a five-year television pact for the league. That first year, the entire league received $1,785,000. After the league took out its expenses, the Titans got about $150,000 as their share for the whole season, which came in very handy very soon: the opening game at the Polo Grounds against the Bills attracted merely 5,727 paying customers.

Watching the Titans face Buffalo at the huge and deserted Polo Grounds, Harry sat next to Ralph Wilson, the Bills' fabulously wealthy owner. Wilson looked out with dismay at the crowd of a few thousand as the halftime festivities began. The marching band paraded out to midfield and faced the box where the Wismers and the Wilsons sat. The band started to play "Everything's Coming up Roses."

"So I'm looking at this empty stadium," recalls Wilson, "and Harry turns to his wife and says, 'Listen, hon—they're playing our song!'"

Those were still great days for the cities, and the Jets played in the once-lofty Polo Grounds, deserted just two years earlier by its most famed tenants, baseball's Giants, who fled to the Left Coast to be near their main gate attraction, the Dodgers. The Jets were to remain in Manhattan until one of the outer boroughs beckoned.

Don Maynard at this point was little more than a footnote to history. He had been the Giants' player who returned the kickoff in their 1958 sudden-death overtime loss to the Baltimore Colts. On the Titans, he became the first of many players who were to perform for both New York football teams.

No one was more individualistic or idiosyncratic, or parsimonious. Teammates joked that he lifted towels and toilet paper out of hotel rooms. When he joined the Giants in 1958 as a rookie out of what is now known as the University of Texas–El Paso, he arrived in New York looking like a cinematic stereotype of the Old West. He wore cowboy boots, blue jeans, and sideburns. This was, remember, the Eisenhower Era. He was told to shave off his sideburns.

"No, sir," he said.

And then when he reported in 1959, his all-out running style displeased Allie Sherman, then an assistant coach.

"This isn't a track meet," Sherman told him. "Shorten your strides."

"But I cover more ground in one stride than anybody else does around here in three," he retorted.

The Giants cut him the next day. He went up to play in Canada.

Sammy Baugh, though, knew of Maynard from Texas school days. He was not going to let Maynard slip away.

In the weathered Polo Grounds, Maynard became the franchise's first star as he unveiled uncommon talent. He caught 72 passes for 1,265 yards. The Titans generated little excitement either in New York or around the new league, though. Their top rusher was named Dewey Bohling, and he gained only 431 yards. Al Dorow was the quarterback.

With their stadium just across the river from the big ball yard in the Bronx, some of the Titans actually shared a hotel with some of the Giants and Yankees—the famed Concourse Plaza on the Grand Concourse.

One of Maynard's fellow Texans, punter Curley Johnson, became a Bronxite.

"We got to know Mickey Mantle and a lot of those guys," said Curley. "We'd all end up in the same places. Sometimes we'd go up to the roof of the hotel and we could see them playing a game in Yankee Stadium."

In year two of their three-year history, the Titans posted another 7–7 mark, but as far as the New York fan was concerned, they were just another team out there without any famous faces. The Giants were resurgent under Allie Sherman, their new head coach, and new quarterback Y. A. Tittle. The Giants, after all, were famous; the Titans had players with little or no history.

Indeed, the most heroic figure in the entire new league may well have been its commissioner, Joe Foss. Its founding was only 15 years after World War II, and Foss was still remembered as a flying "ace"—a former Marine general who had shot down 27 Japanese Zeros during the war. He himself had been shot down, crashed somewhere in the Pacific, and according to one story, was saved by a missionary on some island. Foss's name gave some credibility to the AFL.

Foss had been born on a farm in Sioux Falls, South Dakota, in 1916. He took responsibility for his family when he was merely a high-school junior after his father was killed by lightning.

He attended three colleges and joined the armed forces in 1940. He had always wanted to be a fighter pilot. He got his wish, giving as good as he got, for he was shot down four times himself. The real story of that final ditching was that he was forced to float in the Pacific for five hours before he was spotted.

Foss received the Congressional Medal of Honor, became a legislator in South Dakota, and then its governor. Back then, Americans knew the names of their war heroes. Still, he was surprised in 1959 when Wismer and others approached him about leading the new league.

Foss's philosophy was practical: He didn't believe the league could survive by raiding the NFL. Instead, the AFL scoured small southern schools, or checked out Canadian Football League players. The unknown, the unwanted, the overlooked—these were to form the basis for the league and the Titans.

He also had another philosophy: openness. Let the press and the public in. Put a human face on the football gladiator, whose body was hidden from view behind a helmet and armor. He believed in opening the locker rooms immediately after games instead of the "cooling-off" period preferred by the NFL.

"That's how we did it in combat," he explained one day in 1998, just before the Super Bowl in which the Denver Broncos were to revive the old AFL memories with their upset over the Green Bay Packers. "I came down from combat and let the war correspondents talk to the pilots on the wing. They got it right from the horse's mouth."

Still, Wismer didn't always agree with the hero. They argued incessantly. Foss showed up at the Titans' Thanksgiving Day game in 1961 and announced, "There isn't enough room in this league for both of us."

But the two obviously patched up their differences. For who was Wismer's best man when he got married shortly afterward? Foss.

Wismer could be exasperating, especially when money got tight, as Sammy Baugh would learn. Baugh had a two-year run as coach. His teams posted a 14–14 record. Now, a .500 mark is just that— not bad, not too good, either. And yet, in 1997, almost 40 years later, when the Jets made their dramatic move by hiring Bill Parcells as commander-in-chief and dictator-for-life, Baugh's mediocre record still stood as the best career coaching mark any Jets coach had achieved on the club.

He was so competent that Wismer had to get rid of him when the 1962 season loomed. For Baugh wanted to get paid, and his salary of $28,000 was stifling Wismer, who simply stopped paying his coach sometime during the 1961 season.

Harry had hoped his new bride could bail him out of his personal and professional financial problems. But while she had scads of money, she also had children from a previous marriage, who balked at such an expenditure.

So as 1962 began, Sammy made plans for another year in New York, a place so different from Rotan, Texas, where he ran and leased 20,000 acres for cattle ranching. Sammy was coming back, all right—if only to make sure he got paid what Wismer owed him on the 1961 salary.

His two years as Titans coach had soured him on the big city. He came to it embarrassed with the farm-boy image that Wismer attached to him, and then Baugh struggled to get his team to play, when every week was an adventure in finance as well, since no one ever was really sure he'd get paid.

Then one day Sammy picked up a paper and found out that the new Titans coach was Clyde (Bulldog) Turner. Sammy had been fired in the newspapers.

Thirty-five years later, a few days before his 83rd birthday, Baugh sat back in his chair at the ranch and in his laconic Texan style, remembered those Titans days:

"New York, I always had trouble getting around. Harry never

called me, never wrote me a letter that I was fired. Oh, Harry
always had something going. See, he still owed me money, but he
hired Bulldog Turner. What Harry wanted me to do was just not
come out there. But I knew damn well I wouldn't get the rest of
my money because he'd say I didn't report.

"So I called Bulldog—hell, we knew each other for years—and I
said, 'Now, Bulldog, I'm not going to do anything on the club but
I've got to be here to get paid.' Harry could always say he didn't
fire me. It's true he never wrote me, never gave me any sort of
goddamn notification. The son of a bitch would have to fire me.

"Bulldog said, 'Just do anything out here you want to,' and Harry
found me and got it settled."

The money problems had started in the Titans' second season of
1961. "It got so bad, when they started passing out the checks guys
ran to the banks as fast as they could," recalls Baugh. "But I feel
sorry for Harry. If he could have held out for the third year, he
would have got into that new stadium. That Polo Grounds was a
messy place. It was dirty and it looked awful, I don't know how
they got any people to come out." (Actually, Shea Stadium wasn't
ready for the Jets until after their fourth year.)

The way Sammy remembers it, the Titans had "a pretty good
ballclub by the end of the second season." But some of the players
were injured and Harry, desperate to make the playoffs, called all
the players together and told them he'd give everyone a bonus if
they won their last three games.

"Boys," Baugh said after Wismer left, "you heard what he said. I
know you've been worried about your money." The players got so
excited about the possibility of actually being paid that they
banded together just to see if he really would deliver. It was not to
be. Despite the smallest announced Polo Grounds crowd (purport-
edly 9,462 people) in Baugh's tenure, the Titans defeated the Dallas
Texans (soon to be the Kansas City Chiefs), but were clobbered,
48–21, by the Oilers and then 35–24 by the same Texans.

The Titans situation worsened in 1962, naturally. Bulldog Turner
was presiding over a team on which all pretense of bill-paying was
gone. Bill Tackmann, the road secretary, was in theory the money
man; he didn't really have money, but he was supposed to pay

certain bills. As Harold Rosenthal recalls, "He could sign for a hotel and not pay them later—but you couldn't sign for a cab. At least not after you stiffed them before."

Thus came the time the Titans had a game in Oakland and took cabs from their hotel to the stadium. Tips? The cabbies never even got paid by the club for the fares. When the game was over, the cabbies revolted and wouldn't take them back. The players got together, chipped in, and paid for their own cabs, squeezing three and four wide-bodies into one car.

It got so bad in 1962 that the team went to Boston by bus—and after the game, they returned by bus. Unfortunately for the team, the money problems leaked out to the public. It was a sinking ship, and the first to leave usually are the fans.

Actually, the Boston Patriots were in pretty bad shape as well. When they came in for a game in New York, which was played at night, they had a ritual: They'd go to a hotel for the afternoon— but not spend the night. They would return by train after the game. So the players were warned not to turn the covers on the beds; if they did, the hotel would charge an extra four dollars, the same charge as if the player had spent the night. To make sure the players did not mess up the beds, each Patriot had four dollars deducted in advance from his salary. If the hotel charged the team, the player lost his four dollars.

Yet the Titans had crashed New York at a time when there was a void in New York sports. The Dodgers and Giants of baseball had left only two years before the Titans were created. New York, once a three-team baseball town, had only the Yankees, who were becoming, for the first time, boring in their excellence.

"Rooting for the Yankees," someone said, "is like rooting for U.S. Steel." The sixties had begun, and with that the first hints of cynicism toward the grand American traditions and the great old sports teams.

Unfortunately for the Titans, in their third year the Mets were created. They wedged their way into the Polo Grounds in the spring of 1962 and instantly created a cult following that big-league sports had never known before—a wave of fans rooting for lovable losers. Indeed, the worse the Mets played, the more lovable they became. The other big-league teams in town besides the Yankees were the football Giants, the Knicks, and the Rangers. All had their loyal followers.

These four clubs were fought over by seven—count 'em, seven —New York City newspapers: the *Times,* the *Tribune,* the *Post,* the *Daily News,* the *Mirror,* the *Journal-American,* and the *World-Telegram & Sun.* In the other boroughs there were the *Long Island Press* and the *Star.*

Still, the Titans had to scramble for "ink," especially on my paper. The *Times's* sports columnist, Arthur Daley, was a man of habit. Every day I got him a ham and cheese on rye/lettuce and tomato. On meatless Fridays, he switched to just plain cheese. Arthur liked the tried and true. It took him years to concede in print that Cassius Clay had changed his name to Muhammad Ali.

Arthur—whose friendship with the Giants' Jack Mara, co-owner with his brother Wellington, went back to school days—rarely visited the Titans or watched them play. Sundays were his Giants days. Even though the Titans played at home on Saturday nights, Arthur's column for the Sunday paper was written by Friday afternoon, and he was not about to break his personal tradition.

This kind of indifference helped keep Titans fans away. A total of 4,719 attended their first home game of year three. Wismer was left scrambling to sell tickets from his apartment.

His German-born housekeeper used to scream at the mess the flow of visitors made. She didn't even have the kitchen to herself— Harry's PR man, a fellow named Ted Emory, used to keep the mimeograph machine in the kitchen. She'd come in to fix dinner, and Emory would be there running off press releases on the countertop.

It was there that one day Charlie Jones, the silver-haired, silver-voiced announcer, paid a visit.

Jones spotted some tickets for the upcoming game sitting on a big, round table. Harry excused himself to go to the bathroom, leaving Charlie alone in the apartment. Just then someone knocked on the door. Charlie answered it, and two people said they had come wanting to buy tickets. Since Harry wasn't around, Charlie dutifully sold them a pair. Then Charlie looked at his watch. He had to leave. Wismer still was out of the room, so Charlie simply left the money for Harry and went off. If only Harry had been so conscientious about paying people.

While the Titans were limping to a 5–9 record, the Giants captured another division crown, packing Yankee Stadium. The Titans averaged less than one-tenth of what the Giants attracted, and their financial ruin was complete as Wismer ran out of money.

The last two home games of the team named the Titans, just before Christmas in 1962, saw crowds of 4,011 for the Bills and 3,828 for the Oilers. By then, the league had taken over the club. The players' salaries were personally guaranteed by Lamar Hunt. Indeed, before a late-season game scheduled for Denver, the players had threatened not to travel there unless someone could guarantee their paychecks. That's when Hunt stepped in, and the Titans flew to Denver, where only 15,776 fans saw a historic match-up. It was the last game the Titans ever won, and it was a beaut—46–45.

Bulldog's only season as coach had produced a 5–9 record. After three seasons in the AFL, the Titans had impressed no one and had left a legacy that could be enjoyed and chuckled over only decades later.

The season featured one of those moments that, in various forms, helped to undo Titans and Jets teams over the decades. For despite their money problems, the Titans had put together a two-game winning streak for the first time that season. At 4–5, they still had five games remaining to become respectable, maybe even produce their first winning season. Hunt's Dallas Texans were coming into the Polo Grounds.

They came, and they conquered by 52–31. The Titans wound up losing four of their last five games, their head coach, their colors, their name, and their identity.

Almost nothing remains today of the Titans, even in the record books. For despite the obscene number of points the team yielded —423 by the close of business for the season—that's not even a team record. They seemed doomed by the name, the place they played, the forgettable record they made.

No one got a Christmas present.

"The last time I saw Harry, I was coaching Houston and we

played the Jets in New York," recalls Baugh. "And Harry called me and said, 'Could I ride to the game on the bus?' and I said, hell, yes. He sat on our bench the whole first half, then he went up to the press box. He came down a few minutes later and his nose was all bloodied and he had blood all over his shirt. Someone had beat him up. It was the last time I ever saw Harry, all bloodied."

Inevitably, the team wound up in bankruptcy court, where it was rescued on March 28, 1963, by an odd fellowship of men tied together by their love of horse racing.

Their total cost to buy the team they were to rename the Jets: $1 million. Today that franchise is worth about a quarter of a billion dollars. Goodness had nothing to do with it.

3

Weeb

Why "the Jets"? Well, it had nothing to do with the fact that
jet planes were flying over Shea Stadium every 45 seconds
throughout a game; these Jets weren't even in Shea yet. They
had to play 1963 in the Polo Grounds, and then shift to Shea
the following season. The name "Jets" was chosen to celebrate
the fact that this was the jet age, a new age. And anyway, "Jets"
sounded a little bit like "Mets," a team that had become so
popular so quickly.

The new owners were all officials of Monmouth Park, or had
horse racing connections. The most notable (to the general public)
was David A. (Sonny) Werblin, one of America's great impresarios.

Werblin was a founder of Music Corporation of America (MCA)
and turned it into a combination talent agency and production
company—so big, in fact, that eventually the government forced it
to break up, but not before Werblin had given new meaning to the
term "talent agent." He had so many key Hollywood performers
in the 1930s and 1940s that he often controlled the making of a
movie.

If, for example, you wanted Alice Faye, you had to take her husband, Phil Harris, and his orchestra. And his client list included America's superstars: Elizabeth Taylor, for one, and later Johnny Carson.

Sonny knew star quality.

"Joe would light up a room," he liked to say when explaining the importance of luring Joe Namath to join the upstart Jets rather than seeing him go to the NFL.

Sonny, a Jew from Brooklyn, was born on St. Patrick's Day. He gave the Jets their Kelly green and white colors in his honor. There was no marketing consultant to determine team colors, as there would be for the Jaguars and Panthers more than 30 years later, no decision based on potential sale of Jets logos. They wore Sonny's colors. Sonny also rewarded himself with the owner's box, to which he brought a parade of celebrities.

Sonny quickly established an ain't-we-got-fun atmosphere. He was a traveling movie set; he wanted you drinking with him and meeting his coterie of Broadway friends. One thing about Sonny: His nose for stardom led him to make snap judgments about people, and if he had a flaw in sports it was that he equated it on almost every level to show business. That was to work fine with Namath, but it wasn't so fine when it came to his final stewardship at Madison Square Garden and his leadership of the Knicks and Rangers. But that was 15 years in the future; for now, there was a myth to create and its name was Jets.

In a way, the Jets' arrival led to my elevation to reporter. It also said something about the way those of us in the newspaper business looked at the Jets.

One of the rising writers at the *Times* was a fellow named Howard Tuckner. He was always bringing in starlet types to watch him work on rewrite on Saturday nights, when I of course was still stripping the copy machines in my best quick-wristed fashion as a copy boy. Howie seemed to have it all: He was young, a Columbia graduate, barely 30, had a terrific writing style, and had already done some magazine pieces.

A few months after the Titans became the Jets, Howie, somber as usual, came over to me and said bitterly, "Well, you got your wish. I'm leaving. There's going to be a reporter's spot open."

Why would he leave like this, at such a promising time in his career?

"They want me to cover the Jets," he said. "I want the Giants." And he quit.

Too bad for him. He never had a chance to meet Weeb Ewbank.

. . .

On a flight to some football destination in the 1990s, I happened to sit next to John Schmitt. He was the Jets' center for 10 years under Ewbank. I mentioned I was writing a book, and Weeb's name came up.

"I can recite Weeb's speech verbatim. Same speech every year," said Schmitt, beaming at the chance to go into his routine.

"If you're going to fool around," Weeb would advise the players, "do it with an older woman. They don't swell and they don't tell."

That was Weeb. Practical.

Weeb's name, his physical appearance, his folksy way of talking —why, he had to be named Weeb. Nothing else would do. But it all hid an understanding of the game, perhaps even an intensity. Certainly, he knew what drove men. Probably the same things that drove him, even though he was shorter, rounder, and less imposing than anyone around him.

Weeb might get rattled for the moment, but it passed. If there was a problem with the way the team played, he had a folksy response: "I've seen sicker cows than this get well."

Just before the Jets hired him, the Baltimore Colts fired him. They fired him just three years after he had led them to a second consecutive NFL championship. His first title with the Colts came in the famed "greatest game ever played," when they defeated the Giants on Alan Ameche's overtime run. That was the 1958 championship game, the one that historians like to say put pro football on the television map and stamped the title of "legend" on Johnny Unitas. By 1962, though, the Colts were playing .500 ball, and the megalomaniacal owner, Carroll Rosenbloom, fired Weeb and hired his youngest assistant, Don Shula, to run the club.

In some ways, Weeb's situation was like Casey Stengel's on the Mets. He was an older man (Weeb was 56), with ties back to the sport's early days, leading teams to championships until suddenly one day he was declared too old and too irrelevant. But his name value remains, and he hooks up with a new team trying in the worst way to get started.

Weeb was named Jets coach and general manager the same day the team's new name was announced. Wilbur Charles Ewbank—his nickname stemmed from the time a younger brother mispronounced "Wilbur"—came to the club following nine seasons coaching the Colts, and a career of contact with football's greats.

Once again, he was inheriting a losing team. It took him five seasons in Baltimore to produce a champion from a tattered group, but he had helped develop Unitas as a quarterback, and he had helped develop Otto Graham with the Browns, who were the 1950 NFL champions. He knew he'd never get the Jets going until he could find a quarterback for New York.

Despite standing just five foot seven, Weeb had been a quarterback at Miami of Ohio, then had coached under Paul Brown. Before that he was a head coach for 12 years at high schools in Oxford, Ohio—starting way back in 1930—and at Washington University in St. Louis after the war.

The war gave Weeb the chance to move into big-time football when he joined the Navy. He was assigned to the Great Lakes Naval Training Station outside Chicago, where he teamed up again with Brown, his former college teammate, who was the head coach. Great Lakes played a schedule that was among the toughest in the country, facing major college as well as service teams.

Weeb and Brown teamed up again after the war in Cleveland. Under Brown's merciless direction, the Cleveland Browns brought football into a new era of modernity. P.B., as he was known, instituted innovations such as intelligence testing, film analysis, and sideline signal-calling by shuttling in players. Weeb learned, as did many other assistants and players under Brown.

On the Jets, Weeb surrounded himself with a staff of assistants that included Walt Michaels, Chuck Knox, and Clive Rush, all of whom went on to head-coaching careers in the NFL.

"I had a five-year plan in Baltimore," said Ewbank, when asked how long it would take to make the Jets into a contender. "And I don't see why we can't build a winner here in five years."

Weeb never seemed to have enough players or practice time. He

was allowed to dress only 33 players. He was not allowed to practice in the Polo Grounds or, eventually, Shea Stadium whenever he
wanted. Weeb's Jets were always second-class citizens behind the
Mets.

Meanwhile, he fretted about the small roster size. That's why
Michaels suited up for the opening game of the Jets-Ewbank era
in 1963.

"We had four linebackers on the 33-man roster, and three got
hurt," recalls Walt from his Pennsylvania farm, where he has spent
most of the years since the 1982 season. When that campaign
ended, he was fired a week after the Jets came within a game of
going to a Super Bowl.

"Weeb said, 'Where are we going to get a linebacker from?' and
Chuck, who was always kidding, said, 'You got one here who used
to play.' Me. Well, I said, 'At least I'll know where I'm supposed to
line up. I'm the coach.'"

Michaels's coaching salary was $11,000 for the year. Weeb,
though, signed him to a $15,000 player's contract—and prorated
it for one game. "So," recalls Michaels, "I made about $300 for the
game. I played the tight end side. I remember it like yesterday. It
was up in Boston, hot, about 85 degrees. And I was fine until the
end of the game. I hung in there. And then Babe Parilli scrambled
and I was too tired to extend myself. He made a first down."

Those first-year Jets had only two coaches on defense—Walt,
who had been a Cleveland Browns linebacker and coached that
unit and the line, and Jack Donaldson, who handled the secondary.
Rush had the receivers, and Knox had the offensive line and running backs. Weeb handled the quarterbacks.

What about a coordinator?

"None," says Michaels. "We used to meet on Mondays at Weeb's
house in Westchester. We didn't have a facility where we could do
anything at the Polo Grounds. We only had one projector there.
There was a locker room, and nothing else. We bought two more
projectors."

Weeb's personality was very different from that of his mentor,
Brown. "Easygoing and detailed," recalls Walt. "Weeb wasn't fiery.
Chuck, meanwhile, was a very good offensive-line coach. He had

studied players he liked, and created a sort of body-type model for what he wanted."

Weeb's first-year Jets record of 5–8–1 came in the team's final Polo Grounds season. It still was difficult to get excited about the club, although there was an air of anticipation because the team's owners had made a deal to move into brand-new Shea Stadium the following season. Still, the Jets didn't have a widely recognized name.

The quarterback in Weeb's first year was Dick Wood (real first name: Malcolm), a laconic Georgian. There was nothing terribly exciting or New York about him. In his two seasons running the Jets offense, he failed to complete half his passes. Still, Weeb was seeding the team and bringing out the best in players. He knew personnel.

Oh, the team still needed to create some excitement. But it was going to a new stadium, and in 1964 there would be a rookie runner named Matt Snell. There was also Don Maynard, who, toiling in the pass-happy AFL, was overlooked by the football public and the sportswriters. In his first three seasons he snared 171 passes, 22 for touchdowns. He averaged 17 yards a catch, even though his quarterbacks were mediocre, at best. No pass defense, was the established line. The purists perceived his statistics as tainted.

The team that was to be molded into the Super Bowl Jets was not in place yet. In fact, very little was in place.

"Weeb once took us someplace on the bus, and suddenly he says, 'Here's a place,'" recalls Michaels. "And we drove onto the grass next to the highway and put some towels down. We practiced right there. The cops went by and never stopped us. It was right near Shea, but the Mets wouldn't let us in while the baseball season was on."

Weeb recalls that practice, but as usual, he doesn't make a big deal out of it. He didn't make a big deal out of most things.

"I remember the kids came over to watch practice, and I said to one, 'Sonny, will you move your bicycle?' And he said, 'No, it's as much my park as it is yours.'"

Retelling the story, Weeb laughs. No big deal. Not even being kept out of Shea until a third of the season was over, or holding practices in Rikers Island. For as Weeb explains, "We didn't cry about it. I had two world championships and I understood a little bit about what it took to win."

"The funniest thing was how we got to Rikers Island back around 1963 or '64," says Michaels. "We were flying into LaGuardia and passed over a football field, and Weeb said, 'There's a field down there. Let's find out whose it is.' It was on the Rikers Island prison grounds. The authorities said, okay, you can come in—but only if you let our prisoners watch during recreation time."

Thus, the Jets went to prison to train. In the 1960s, you could be busted for marijuana use, and several of the prisoners were musicians who had been arrested for such infractions. They formed a prison band that used to greet the Jets during practice.

The prisoners enjoyed these moments away from the lockup. They could scream and yell and not worry about retaliation by the guards for having broken prison rules.

The Jets began attracting burgeoning crowds to their real games as well. Routinely, 20,000 fans would show up at the Polo Grounds as Weeb's team became competitive. Their new green uniforms gave them a certain dash. They began to execute on the field.

There was also a tragic event that was to underscore the difference between the two leagues: the assassination of President Kennedy.

After the assassination, the AFL quickly called off its games while the NFL decided to play theirs. While the older league claimed that the games would help the country find itself again, the AFL touched a more tender spot by deciding to shutter its gates in respect.

Soon the Jets got more favorable publicity when, in the draft for the 1964 season, they outbid the Giants for Matt Snell, the sought-after Ohio State running back. This was the first time an important player, someone the public recognized, had opted to become a Jet rather than a Giant.

Suddenly, good feeling was taking over. And then the Jets moved into Shea, a spanking-new major-league stadium, to start the 1964 season. It was a palpable change, and a record turnout of 45,000 fans saw the team trounce the Broncos.

But the Jets didn't open their season again at Shea for the next 14 years, and then it took a court order. When the Jets were fortunate enough to get into Shea, they had to use the visitors' locker room, because Shea Stadium was the private domain of the Mets, who were owned by Mrs. Charles Shipman Payson. She was born Joan Whitney, heiress to one of America's great fortunes. Her brother was John Hay (Jock) Whitney, publisher of the *Herald Tribune*, ambassador to the Court of St. James's. She had been crazy about the baseball Giants, and when they left she needed another toy—er, team—to root for. Thanks to her involvement, the Mets came along.

Her liaison on the team was the patrician stockbroker M. Donald Grant, who came from humbler beginnings (his father was a member of the Hockey Hall of Fame in Canada, and M. Donald had started work as a hotel bellhop). New York City wanted a baseball team so much that it gave the Mets free office space in the stadium, free electricity—and even the revenue from the Jets' sales of hot dogs, programs, and parking.

The Mets looked at the Jets with about the same disdain that Donald Trump would exhibit toward a tenant living in one of his rent-controlled apartments. They grudgingly permitted the Jets to put in over the boiler room a coaches' office that Michaels describes as a "dungeon." In the offseason, the coaches used the Jets' Madison Avenue executive offices for meetings; they were allowed into their "home" only at the pleasure of the Mets. Grant made it clear that he hated it when, after a football game, the movable stands that were a feature of Shea's then-modern design scarred his precious grass.

The Jets were permitted to play at Shea on Saturday nights, though, and they packed them in. Sunday had become the day for NFL football, but the AFL was reluctant to take on the Giants head-to-head. When the Giants were on the road, everyone in New York was watching them on television; when they were home, blacked-out on local television, hundreds, if not thousands, of fans would go to motels in Connecticut, or visit friends there, to watch the broadcasts. In fact, there was one motel in Stratford that even hired a marching band for its own halftime Giants festivities. The Giants owned New York as they captured three straight conference titles in the early 1960s. They brought football's first roars of "Defense!" to the game, and fans were enamored of Gifford and Robustelli and Grier and Rote and Conerly and Huff and Tittle.

Over at the *Times*, we began to pay increased attention to the Jets when they moved into Shea, especially after that huge opening-game turnout. Then 50,000 more turned out for the Chargers.

Yet we didn't even have a reporter assigned to write a "follow" story on Sundays. Here were the Jets, with huge crowds, the biggest in the AFL and more than most in the NFL, with Snell a rising star running and catching all over the field, and we didn't give them respect.

In fact, I wound up writing about them from the office on Sunday for Monday's paper, even though I hadn't even gone to the game. I don't mean to imply I wrote about their live game (it is amazing how many people to this day ask me if I or my fellow reporters actually go to the games we write about), but the reporters who were assigned to cover their Saturday night games took Sundays off. For many readers of the *Times*, who didn't get the late Sunday editions with the Jets game story, my piece in the Monday paper was the first they read about their team.

Around noon on Sundays, the Jets' public-relations director, Frank Ramos, would call me. All I knew about the Jets was what I had read in the paper. I was never at their workouts, hadn't been to one of their games; I was a young reporter on rewrite, which meant I rarely left the office for live assignments.

Frank talked me through the maze of statistics that often stifle the enjoyment of the game. And somehow, win, lose, or tie, the Jets always seemed to have done better than the other team by the time Frank was finished talking to me. Even when they lost, Frank had found some bright spots. And always I wrote about the attendance, which was becoming the most significant aspect of the Jets.

Then, on November 8, 1964, there was a breakthrough. For the first time, the Jets and Giants were playing at home the same day. The Jets were playing a Sunday game against the Bills at Shea while the Giants were facing the Cowboys at Yankee Stadium.

The symbolism of this clash was significant. The Jets attracted the AFL's first 60,000-plus crowd, a full house at Shea. The Giants pulled in their usual 64,000. But the Jets really weren't competing for Giants fans since virtually all of those at Yankee Stadium were season-ticket-holders—and the Giants weren't on television.

Still, the 61,929 at Shea made headlines and, more important, gave the public a perception of the Jets' equality, at least in drawing power. Too bad for the Jets at that key moment in their existence that they didn't win: They started a three-game losing streak, in fact, as they wound up a second straight season under Ewbank with a discouraging 5–8–1 won–lost–tied record. But the Jets had established the fact that they could draw, and draw big. They had become a player in the most important arena in American sports, and they had done it without a signature performer.

Snell, the rookie rusher, amassed almost a thousand yards. Maynard was a big-play receiver, Bake Turner caught the ball in a crowd, Curley Johnson could punt, and Jim Turner was a top placekicker—and yet there was no one to coalesce these fine players on offense.

That would change in a big way in 1965.

4

Joe

The first room Sonny Werblin had Joe Willie Namath light up in New York was at Broadway's most famous watering hole, Toots Shor's. Sonny loved the glitter of Broadway, and now he had discovered the Jets' leading man in the quarterback from the University of Alabama. Sonny let his football people worry about Joe's ability to read defenses; at cocktail parties, Sonny knew, people would turn and face the door when Joe entered the room.

In a sense, Sonny played Pygmalion with Joe. This shaggy-haired, laid-back small-town guy with the adopted southern accent was a drawing card, a magnet. And somehow, Sonny had figured that New York was where he belonged. Joe knew it, too.

Toots Shor's was where Hemingway and Winchell and the gossip columnists and all sorts of characters hung out. It was where Shor, an obese former bouncer, used to stage legendary drinking bouts with Jackie Gleason and the writer Bob Considine. Jimmy Cannon often was there with Joe DiMaggio. It was Sonny's kind of place. Sonny, who always had a drink in his hand, appreciated New York, and now he had the player he was convinced could help him break the NFL's hold on football in the American imagination. Why, perhaps even one day his Jets could challenge the NFL for pro football's championship. And Sonny would be there, with his quarterback.

At the bar, Werblin mingled with the sportswriters, bragging how he had made a deal with the rookie for a staggering sum.

Sonny was the prime mover in the AFL's shifting to NBC. In his first year with the Jets, he was still involved with MCA, and that entertainment conglomerate had done the original contract between the AFL and ABC in 1960. Jay Michaels of MCA, whose son, Al, was to become one of the leading sports broadcasters, had been involved in brokering that original deal.

Then in 1964, Sonny's second year with the Jets, he made the deal to put the entire league on NBC, which was seeking a big-time incursion into CBS's pro football dominance. The contract was to begin in 1965, and it brought the AFL a five-year package worth $36 million to be divided among the eight clubs, a fourfold increase over the league's first TV deal.

Now, flush with NBC's money, the AFL could go after college football's best players, especially the quarterbacks. Essentially, Sonny had negotiated the Jets' future with NBC, and that future turned out to be Joe Namath.

How big a factor was Werblin in the scheme of things?

When he retired from MCA to devote full time to the Jets, *Variety*'s page-one story headlined his departure—"Mr. Show Business Retires." He became more of a public figure with the Jets than he ever had been as an agent, even though he was one of the seminal figures in creating television programming. MCA's holdings included Decca Records, Universal pictures, MCA-TV, and a host of stars and recording artists. Not a bad operation for Sonny, the kid from Flatbush whose first foray into showbiz had included guarding the instruments for Guy Lombardo's band.

So this drinking-and-noshing reception at Shor's was hardly unusual for Werblin, although not standard procedure in the world of sports at the time. But as always, Sonny brought a sense of fun to the proceedings. To be around the Jets was to be around something that was a cross between sports and show business.

Something else that was not quite sports business as usual took place that day at Shor's.

Although they hadn't examined Namath, the Jets had been aware that Joe had a knee problem, ever since the fourth game of the season in his senior year, when Alabama played North Carolina State. Joe was more than a passing quarterback at Alabama: He ran, too.

"Bear Bryant called me 'Babe'—as in Babe Ruth," Joe recalls. He could do many things, most of them heroically. Against NC State, this time he ran, and he was caught. He was hauled down by the knee.

"They took me to the hospital and aspirated my knee. Blood was in the fluid, so they knew something was torn, but they never knew what. There were no MRIs then. No arthroscopy. Bandage them up, get the animals ready for the next game."

The day after Joe got out of the Alabama hospital, he was walking somewhat easily when the knee buckled. It buckled five times that week.

"Hurt like hell," he recalled. "Once, it buckled when I was loading the trunk of my car. Or it went in practice. I also hurt it four more times in games that season. I wanted to play, though. I don't think at Alabama they wanted to jeopardize my knee. They just didn't know better."

What most of us knew about Joe Namath was this:

The day after the Orange Bowl, on January 2, 1965, Joe of Beaver Falls, Pennsylvania, and the University of Alabama, signed a contract to play for the Jets. What a coincidence and a coup—to sign him up only a few hours after he was first eligible to talk money. Well, actually, the deal had been done days before.

"You know, Sonny said before Joe's last game, 'We're going to sign him,'" recalls Michaels. "We got hold of a lawyer down in Alabama named Mike Bite. His law firm was Bite, Bite, and Bite. Today it can be told. It's more than 30 years later—we had him signed before his final game in the Orange Bowl. That was against the rules. You weren't supposed to do that. Who cares now? Hey, the government puts out these documents 25 years later, past the statute of limitations."

The amount of money Joe was supposed to receive was so extraordinary by the standards of the times that it made him and the Jets instant national celebrities.

The contract was worth $427,000, over three years. Most sportswriters who reported that figure in the newspapers didn't understand it completely. Remember, football players were the lowest-paid of the big three American sports. Baseball's greatest pitcher, Sandy Koufax, threatened to quit if he didn't get more than $125,000 a year.

Namath's famed $427,000 figure—it took on a life of its own, becoming a benchmark for years—actually was worth considerably less. It included the value of a new car—a blue Lincoln Continental—and the deal was also predicated on various bonuses. If all the bonuses were met, if you figured in the car's list price, well, maybe you came to something like $427,000 over three years.

The money, Namath's ascension, and a deal with the Oilers, who held the AFL draft rights to Namath, all theoretically were done within 24 hours. And who was tutoring the quarterbacks on the Oilers? Former Titans coach Sammy Baugh.

Baugh and the Oilers coveted Joe. "We had the rights to him," recalls Baugh. "He told us he wouldn't play in Houston. He said, 'I'm not playing anywhere unless I can play in New York.' So the Jets traded us the rights to [Tulsa quarterback] Jerry Rhome and we traded them the rights to Joe Namath."

While everyone in Shor's was buzzing about Joe's arrival, Dr. James A. Nicholas was examining Namath's knees in the bathroom and made a stunning discovery.

That was where the Jets learned the truth about Namath's knees.

Nicholas, the Jets' orthopedist and a pioneer in sports medicine, was a confidant, a coach, and a fan whose celebrity patients had included John F. Kennedy and Greek shipping magnate Aristotle Onassis.

Nicholas had been on the surgical team that had operated on Kennedy, who had a back problem stemming from his *PT-109* accident. And it was Dr. Nicholas who discovered that the future president also was suffering from Addison's Disease, a diagnosis that Jackie Kennedy believed saved her husband's life, and for which she remained grateful and close to Dr. Nicholas.

Nicholas had been an original Titan, for Wismer had been under his care and asked him if he'd be interested in joining the club as team physician and surgeon.

"I had been doing research on osteoporosis," remembers Nicholas, "and I thought this would be a good way to learn what effect exercise had on the bone. I could observe it with athletes." Little did he know he would become Namath's medical Boswell.

Everyone at Shor's was having a fine old time when a reporter happened to ask Nicholas, "Have you examined Namath?"

"I hadn't, and I mentioned it to Weeb. He said, 'Go take a look at him.' "

Nicholas and Namath went into the men's room at Shor's. Joe sat on a toilet seat and Nicholas took a look at the knees.

After a few twists and turn of the knee, Nicholas said, "If I had known this before, I would have told Sonny to forget you."

Those Namath knees! One of them wobbled. And that was the first time the Jets realized that they had made a gimpy-kneed quarterback the foundation of their franchise, while outside the bathroom everyone was drinking and toasting the new era.

Nicholas immediately went back to the party.

"I said to Weeb, 'Hope we've got another quarterback. We'll have to operate on this guy,' " recalls Nicholas.

So at the same time the Jets announced the coming of Joe Namath, they also announced that he would be undergoing knee surgery almost immediately.

"He had a very unstable knee," remembers Nicholas, who recites Namath's surgeries as readily as a stat freak can tell you how many touchdowns he tossed in 1966. "The cruciate ligament was bad and we scheduled surgery immediately. I opened the knee as best I could, tightened the knee. We didn't know he'd play—and indeed we had drafted another quarterback, John Huarte from Notre Dame. He was the Heisman Trophy winner but he couldn't throw overhand because of an old shoulder separation. And here's a trivia question for you: Did you know we drafted a third quarterback? It was Bob Schweickert out of Virginia Tech. So the Jets drafted three quarterbacks in 1964 because they weren't sure Joe Namath would sign, or if he'd be healthy enough to play."

But neither Joe nor Sonny nor the Jets nor New York were to be denied the special importance he brought with him. And Sonny gloried in Joe's celebrity status.

Sonny, agent to the stars, allowed Joe his own set of rules, which were different from the others'. Sonny believed Joe should be seen with the movers and shakers, and they should get to know him. So Joe would be out late at one of Sonny's parties—while Weeb had to leave that same party early to check on the players. Well, at least Weeb knew where Joe was—partying with Sonny.

Athletes didn't usually live in Manhattan, but Sonny had Namath move in with Joe Hirsch, the lead writer for *The Morning Telegraph*, which was horse racing's bible. Hirsch might have been a New Yorker, but he had the charm of a southern gentleman and he was up on everything that was going on in the big city. Hirsch's racing connections allowed him to mingle with New Yorkers of a certain tone, and he brought Namath along.

Meanwhile, Joe found his own friends and his own hangouts—Jilly's, for one. There he and Frank and Sammy and Dean would drink late into the night, and Joe would get driven back to the apartment, grab some sleep, and turn out the next morning for practice.

Of course, as Joe's legend on the field grew, as he became the first quarterback ever to throw for 4,000 yards in a 14-game season (which he did in 1967), as he took the field wearing white shoes, sporting long hair, growing a Fu Manchu mustache, wearing pantyhose in a commercial, donning a mink, telling of his white llama bedroom rug—he became a star off the field as well. He was America's Bachelor.

Yet there were always other parts to Joe. He may have been celebrated as a football player, but as he grew up in Beaver Falls, baseball was the game he really loved. He was good enough, in fact, for a Dodger scout named Tom Lasorda to try to sweet-talk him into going to Los Angeles.

"The Cubs offered me $50,000 to sign with them," Joe recalls. "And the University of Alabama offered me a football scholarship. Coach Bear Bryant wanted me to bring Alabama into the 1960s' new passing style. If you had asked me, though, I would have picked baseball. I had an Olds Starfire, a blue convertible, all picked out with part of that Cubs bonus money.

"We had a meeting at home to decide what to do with my future. My folks were divorced, so my father wasn't there. But my mother, Rose, was sitting at the table along with two of my brothers and my sister. My mother was working as a maid for a doctor. We could have done a lot with that $50,000.

"My brother Bob looked at my mother and said, 'Well, Mom, what do you want Joe to do?' She says, 'Well, I want Joey to go to college.'

"Bob pounded the table with his fist and says, 'That's it, Joe. You go to college.'"

Namath recalls the late Bear Bryant with awe, and still refers to him as "Coach Bryant."

"He was a big man and he loomed over us. What added to his mystique was his habit of watching practice from a tower way above the field on the sideline. Sometimes you wouldn't even see him at practice, but you knew he was up there, looking down at you. And he made you respect and fear him. You never wanted to get him angry at you. You didn't want to mess up in class, either, or he'd call you inside his office and make you feel so small. He had his own discipline separate from the school's. If you screwed up, you belonged to him. You never knew what the punishment would be. The physical abuse was as bad as the verbal. I don't mean the Bear hit you; he made you do punishing laps, or stair-climbing. He called it 'My Time.'"

The Bear and Weeb, he says, "were two different people, two different styles of coaching. The sport wasn't the same in the pros. I'm in the exhibition game against the Patriots and I'm standing beside Weeb on the sidelines and Maynard drops a pass, and Weeb says to Don, 'That's a bunch of stuff.' And Maynard says, 'Hell, Weeb, what do you expect for $50 a game?' And that was a bit confusing to me, the way the discipline on the team was different."

Twenty-three days after signing his Jets contract, Joe went in for surgery. Six months later he played in the exhibition game against the Patriots. And in the second game of the season, after sitting on the bench in the opener, he replaced Mike Taliaferro (pronounced "Tolliver"!) in the second quarter against Kansas City. His era really began in Game 3 when a reluctant Weeb, who wanted to break him in slowly, started Joe against the Bills.

The knee was always a concern with Joe. Scramble? Out of the question except once in a while. At those moments, Weeb and everyone else on the bench and in the Shea stands held their breath. But he became a classic drop-back passer, and when it came to surveying the landscape for the deep threat, nobody did it better. His hand held the football, but suddenly it thrust forward like a serpent's tongue and there it would fly. Snell claimed he could hear Joe's passes coming.

Naturally, some veterans were skeptical of the rookie. The money and his personality overshadowed everything. Joe didn't always make meetings on time, and that led to some problems. But Joe was also a groundbreaker; he had a rapport with the black athletes, and sometimes at training camp he'd be the only white player sitting at a table with them. One of his closest childhood pals had been a black youngster, but Joe never made an issue of it. He simply moved easily in the various circles that a football team is composed of.

Like the New York legend of the 1920s, Babe Ruth, Joe had brought the sense of imminence to his game. Something great could happen any moment. But it wasn't only the possibility of the touchdown bomb; it was the possibility that it could all be over for him with one bad hit by a marauding defensive lineman. Joe not only was the most dangerous football player around, he was the most vulnerable.

Whenever a friend or stranger approached him, the first question always was, "How's the knee, Joe?" By the time the Jets went to the Super Bowl, he had undergone surgery a total of three times on both knees—yet never missed a regular-season game.

Despite those medical procedures, his impact on football was immediate and startling. In that very first start against the Bills he heaved the ball 40 times, completing 19 passes for 287 yards and a pair of touchdowns. But the Jets lost. In fact, in his career, the Jets lost more often than they won. He was imposing and indomitable and scary, and yet his insistence on the bomb resulted in this odd fact: He threw more interceptions than touchdowns in his career. He ended his rookie year with 18 touchdowns and 15 interceptions; he would have only one other season in which his touchdowns would exceed his interceptions.

The NFL uses a quarterback-rating system that seems complicated and that few people understand. But quite simply, it factors
in such numbers as touchdowns and interceptions (which offset
each other but which weigh heavily), as well as completion percentage and yards per attempt.

By the time Joe was voted into the Hall of Fame in 1985, he
ranked only 52nd among 67 eligible passers. When the 1997 season
began—20 years after his last game—he ranked 95th of 112. Quarterbacks such as Wade Wilson, Bubby Brister, Lynn Dickey, Doug
Williams, and Eric Hipple rank ahead of him. But with the game
on the line, do you want Eric Hipple or Joe Namath barking out
the signals?

So much for the tyranny of statistics. They told nothing of what
Joe was about.

He was the AFL's rookie of the year in 1965, although the Jets
were 5–8–1, and he quickly followed that up with a starring appearance in the league's all-star game the next season—he was the
only second-year player in the game and was voted its most valuable player. That 1966 campaign marked the first time the Jets had
a .500 season, as they finished 6–6–2. In that .500 year, Joe threw
the ball a pro football record 471 times, 34 a game.

You had to be there when Joe threw. I had not been prepared for
the noise, the excitement, the overall feeling of drama that en-
gulfed a stadium the first time in a game he took the snap and
went into his backpedal. Everyone stood and roared. In stadium
after stadium, all across America, Joe evoked this dramatic reaction. Perhaps only Muhammad Ali riveted an audience the way Joe
could.

In only his second year, the AFL forced the momentous merger
agreement with the NFL. It is impossible to gauge, or perhaps to
overemphasize, the Namath factor in bringing this about. It was
becoming costly to the NFL to bid against a rival league for the
best players. So the leagues agreed to play a championship game
following the 1966 season, and then to actually merge in 1970.

By the time Joe was ascending the Giants were in decline. Arthur
Daley, the *Times's* Pulitzer Prize–winning columnist, reluctantly
agreed to visit a Jets game once in a while. It did not come easily;
the 1960s couldn't end soon enough for Arthur.

With Joe and the Jets becoming famous, they were starting to share the sports pages with the Giants. One day in the office, I noticed that Jim Roach, the sports editor, had tacked a letter to the bulletin board. It was from Giants president Wellington Mara.

It read, if memory serves, "My late brother Jack once told me that if something bothers you, don't keep it in. So I'm writing to express my distress over the coverage of the Giants in *The New York Times*. You have consistently given more space to the Jets."

Roach wondered if that was, in fact, true. So he assigned the Sunday editor, Frank Litsky, the paper's most famous figure filbert, who can instantly translate meters to square feet, or whatever they come out to, the job of measuring the length of every story written that year on the Jets and the Giants. This Frank did with his usual enthusiasm. I remember him taking out his metal ruler and leaning over the bound volumes of the *Times* of months earlier. Frank loved this sort of stuff. A great track and field writer and expert, he even used to keep a chart detailing American and foreign equivalents of measurements.

The result of his painstaking research was . . . the Giants won by a few inches.

Proudly, Roach tacked that information to the bottom of Mara's letter.

The Jets had won a subtle victory, although they didn't know it then. For the decline of the Giants was hastened by moments like this, Wellington Mara admitted to me a decade letter.

I was working on a book about his team's great era, called *There Were Giants in Those Days*, covering the time of Gifford and Conerly, and Tittle and Rote and Robustelli. Mara made a startling admission.

"I think the Jets coming in when they did contributed to our bad years, because we tried to do everything for the short term rather than the long haul—we'd trade a draft choice for a player, figuring he'd give us one or two good years. We didn't want to accept how the public might react if we had a bad year or two or three.

"In other words, it was a question of misplaced pride. The fans would have stuck with us anyhow. They did stick with us through all the bad years. In the past we had been able to fill in—a Robustelli, a Modzelewski, a Walton—we added people like that. That was fine when we had a great nucleus. But after 1963 we kept trying to add without realizing the nucleus wasn't as strong as it had been. Like I said, it was a question of misplaced pride."

That 15-year decline ended with the arrival of general manager George Young, and the Giants' glory flowered again under the coaching reign of Bill Parcells—the very man the Jets were to choose in an effort to pick themselves up from their own low point just before the millennium.

As the Giants became lost in the 1960s, Namath's legend peaked. In 1967, he accumulated 343 aerial yards in the season's finale against the Chargers to become the first quarterback to amass 4,000 yards in a season. That victory also punctuated the Jets' first winning season of 8–5–1, a memory that hardly fades because there have been so few of them. You thought it would never stop, right? Namath was at the helm, all was right with the Jets' world.

This first winning season brought the Jets close to football respectability to match their celebrity status. In fact, at one point the club was 7–2–1. But despite Joe's 60 pass attempts the next game, they fell to the Broncos to start a three-game losing streak. Still, the message of 1967 was clear: The Jets could play football, as well as simply play.

Joe's celebrity status forced the team to develop a whole different way of getting from place to place. Even getting into the chartered airplane was a production because Joe Namath was among those being transported.

You have to understand this about flying with a professional football team: It is different from taking a commercial flight. It is, of course, impossible for an NFL team to fly commercial. There are, first of all, about 50 athletes of uncommon size. According to the league's agreement with the Players Association, the players are entitled to an empty seat between them when they sit in a three-abreast aisle.

There is the phalanx of coaches, several trainers and assistants, front-office officials, physicians, broadcasters. And luggage. An incredible array of equipment and medical-related gear: helmets and pads for each player, hundreds of yards of tape, and dozens of bottles of balms and pills. The gear alone weighs more than 5,000 pounds. Overall, about 85 people travel with the club during the regular season, but as many as 130 may be aboard in the preseason, before the rosters have been trimmed. And when Joe was playing, the team used to allow us reporters to travel with them.

Hundreds of people began to wait for him after every game, and there were always weekly mob scenes. The club's traveling secretary then was a folksy, genial operative named John Free. He was forced to devise ways to get Namath aboard without causing a riot.

Free's most innovative adventure?

"We were playing at San Diego. The locker room opened onto a tunnel, and when I looked down the end of it, I could see hundreds of people waiting at the buses. I knew there was no way I could get Namath out there."

Luckily for Free, he had been dealing with the Namath phenomenon for years.

"I saw a van loading towels. I said to the driver, 'I'll give you $10 if you drive this gentleman out of the stadium.' "

The driver looked at Free and said, "That's Joe Namath. Okay."

Then the driver remembered something. His girlfriend was sitting on the bundles of towels in the back. He told his girlfriend to "come up front with me. Namath can stay in the back with the towels by himself. I don't want you sitting back there with him."

So Namath was spirited out of the stadium in a laundry truck, which drove a few hundred yards away from the buses. When the buses left, they stopped to pick up the quarterback.

Every time the Jets went somewhere, they received a police motorcycle escort—from the airport to the hotel, the hotel to the game, the game to the airport. Cops hung around the hotel. Being around the Namath Jets was like being at a Hollywood party, or getting inside the velvet rope at Studio 54. Free hired local off-duty police for $20 or $25 and those cops loved it. One or two motorcycle cops would be in front of the cortege, another behind, with sirens blaring. Red lights? Traffic jams? It didn't matter. The Jets got through. I once saw a motorcycle cop who was leading a Jets entourage do a handstand on his bike.

Once aboard the plane, Free kept clucking away like a mother hen. One of his jobs was to check on whether someone had gotten on who didn't belong. This actually happened during the Namath years. As players found their seats on a postgame flight from Oakland, Free spotted an unfamiliar face in the crowd. Free didn't say a word; he merely went up to one of the bigger linemen and told him to go sit next to the stranger while Free questioned him.

"I heard you guys were going to New York, and I needed a ride, so I figured I'd get on," the stowaway explained. He was ushered off, but Free did it politely.

So the Jets as a whole were developing the one quality Sonny Werblin prized above all: star quality. The focus of all this public attention, they were achieving some success on the field as well. All that was left for them was to actually reach the playoffs some day, and maybe justify all the hyperventilating around them.

This they did, in a game that shocked the world.

5

Super, Once

In sports, teams are defined by a body of work. Rarely is it merely a single moment that evokes every memory about a club. Think back to, say, the football Giants. Was it only the Bills' Scott Norwood's missed field goal that preserved Super Bowl XXV for them that we lionize? Rather, isn't it all the other fine and great things they had done in championship games—changing sneakers to beat the Bears on a frozen field, or Phil Simms's sharpshooting eye against the Broncos?

And certainly the Yankees had so many championships that Reggie Jackson's three-home-run game isn't the only lingering thought. Nor is Don Larsen's perfect game. The Celtics amassed titles with Bill Russell clambering up the boards and with Larry Bird slinging in an over-the-shoulder bolo. Certainly, the Canadiens have had their share, from Rocket Richard backhanding in the puck to Ken Dryden making outlandish saves.

The Jets are in that pantheon. And they are housed there despite having only one title, one defining image. Because they have never repeated, there is the constant of failed expectations. Unfair, perhaps. Equally unfair will be the criticism of Tiger Woods when he blows a tournament, especially the Masters. It was unfair for the baseball world to compare Doc Gooden forever after with his first two glorious seasons. But this is the nature of sports.

The Jets achieved such fame, such notoriety, became such a product and symbol of their times, that they also became a frozen icon. They can have life breathed back into them only by another great success. In the meantime, they and their fans have had to live with their moment in the sun, which, to keep the astronomical analogy, was a convergence of the Age of Aquarius and the shattering of the old sports verities.

The Jets' Super Bowl had many aspects to it that gave it a theatrical and historic aura. Except for a few former Colts on the Jets, none of them had ever been in a playoff game. Until two weeks earlier, with a victory over the Raiders, the franchise had never seen the postseason.

The NFL has grandfathered the Super Bowl name, but in reality, the first Super Bowl to be called the Super Bowl was the Jets against the Colts. Before then? The first two affairs, won by the Packers, were called "The World Championship Game." In fact, even the tickets (cost: $12) for the Jets-Colts were printed as "Third World Championship Game." It was too late to print the words "Super Bowl" on them because that name had been adopted only weeks before.

The name "Super Bowl" was laughed at by many because it had such grandiose pretensions. Remember, this was a time when America was girding for Woodstock, getting rid of tail fins on its cars, worried about its worldwide image. But a little Texas girl's drawling description of her high-bouncing Super Ball gave her daddy the inspiration. She was Sharron Hunt, and her father was Lamar Hunt, the powerful football figure who was owner of the Kansas City Chiefs. So Super Bowl it was, leading to Super Sunday.

When the Jets and Colts met on January 12, 1969, at the Orange Bowl, the game did not have the grandiloquent roman numeral III just yet. That was not attached to the Super Bowl until the following year. And when that happened, the first three championship games were transformed magically into Super Bowls I, II, and III.

Imagine what Sonny Werblin could have done at the Super

Bowl. But Sonny wasn't a part of the excitement. It was perhaps inevitable that the team's other owners would eventually rebel at Werblin's fame and his 50-yard-line seats. With the team (and Sonny) commanding such a bright spotlight, the others wanted their share of the glory.

Those owners included Leon Hess and Phil Iselin. Hess was one of America's most dynamic businessmen, whose will and political connections (he contributed to everyone running for mayor or governor or senator) had helped him forge an oil empire as head of the Amerada Hess Corporation. He dealt with Middle Eastern potentates and dictators and had one of the great poker faces in American sports or industry. Iselin, a pleasant man who ran a dress business, had sunk some of his money into Monmouth Park, then the Jets. There were also Townsend Martin, who tended to his own personal fortune, and Donald Lillis, a hard-driving, successful stockbroker.

Although the Jets led the league in attendance for four straight seasons under Werblin's presidency, they showed no profit. But they were approaching a bonanza, with the merger just two years away. And early in 1968, the partners gave Sonny a choice—buy them out, or sell to them. Sonny sold.

Lillis in particular was unhappy with the inordinate amount of public attention that had come to Werblin, who most people viewed as the owner, even though his share was virtually equal to the others. After the $1 million purchase, the owners had invested another $500,000, so their money was flowing out early. And then Werblin had spent even more of their money when he went ahead and made that famous record $427,000 deal with Namath! But Sonny didn't stop there. He paid $325,000 to Carl McAdams, $300,000 to Bill Yearby, $200,000 to John Huarte, and $150,000 more to Bob Schweickert. None except Huarte was still with the Jets when the owners made the move.

Those bonuses chewed away at the team's financial success at Shea Stadium, where they sold 51,000 season seats and where their home attendance, counting standing room, averaged 62,434 in a stadium with 60,000 seats.

Typically, Sonny threw himself a bash at Luchow's, the now-defunct landmark German restaurant, to say good-bye to the press.

Most of the people he invited there didn't even realize it was his farewell to football party. He worked the room. He tweaked me good-naturedly when I told him I liked the lox.

"Scotch salmon," he corrected, patting my shoulder.

That move to oust Werblin was Part I of the big change for the Jets—a change that, as this book is being written 30 years later, still influences the team.

The other change? The one not made for a strong man: Lillis's failure to swing Vince Lombardi back to New York from Green Bay. Just a few months before Werblin's ouster, Lombardi stepped down as coach of the Packers in the wake of his second straight Super Bowl triumph.

Lillis often ran into Lombardi at a small Italian restaurant on Third Avenue and had spoken with him several times about coming to the Jets, either as coach or general manager. But Lombardi, who was to stay in Green Bay another year and then leave for a piece of the Redskins, opted not to return to New York. Who knows what might have happened? Maybe not Lou Holtz.

A decade later, the Jets again failed to get another prodigal son, renegade Al Davis of the Raiders, who would consider returning only if they offered a piece of the team. This the Jets, by then dominated by Hess, were not about to do.

In an ironic footnote to the Lombardi search, Lillis explained why he was contacting the gruff but successful coach.

"We want to have a winning team. We haven't got that yet. And we want to make some money," he emphasized.

Lillis didn't live to see the winning team. And although it didn't win much after the Super Bowl, it did make money. It just couldn't combine the two often enough.

We will never know what would have happened to the Jets in the years since if Lillis had survived. He died within two months of taking over, and the benign Phil Iselin replaced him.

Phil was a pleasant man who, if he had a beard, could have played Santa Claus at Christmas parties. In fact, he presided over one of the great parties sportswriters used to enjoy, an annual summertime bash at Monmouth Park for football and horse-racing writers. When older sportswriters talk of how the relationship between themselves and the team has changed, they think of days like that of Iselin's party. (Of course, latter-day club officials bemoan that lost contact too, which led to kinder, gentler reporting. And today's younger writers would be appalled at the often symbiotic relationship that existed then.)

We'd start the day at "21," for breakfast. Then the private buses would roll out for the trip to New Jersey. Waiters on the buses wore white tuxedo jackets and served Bloody Marys and champagne. At the track, we were escorted into a garden penthouselike private-box area where we had our own betting windows.

Before the races, Betty Iselin would walk around with a huge basket filled with daily-double tickets. All the writers' spouses (that is to say, the wives) would stick a hand in and pick out a double ticket.

There was lunch, and a day at the races. In the evening, we'd all go to a private club on the beach for dinner and dancing. At these soirees, Namath would often appear. Once Sonny left, Joe's appearances diminished. Sonny, of course, had been the ubiquitous host. He would be quiet only when his wife, Leah Ray, a former band singer, performed.

He didn't talk much about his show-business contacts. But once, as he discussed his famous clients, Frank Litsky's wife, Arlene, asked him, "Sonny, what's Elizabeth Taylor really like?"

"Short," he replied. "Very short."

The press and the public missed Werblin's presence as head of the Jets. Lillis, though, seemed to be a strong replacement.

"I think Daddy would have devoted more of his time to the Jets," says Helen Dillon, Lillis's daughter, who inherited his 25 percent share. She became the only woman on the board of directors of an NFL team at the time, a position she enjoyed immensely because it allowed her to come to practices on Wednesday with her children, to fly in the bulkhead front seat of their charter plane, and to act as mother hen to 40 big, wealthy young men. She never pretended to know about the workings of football or even to involve herself with hiring and firing. I suspect that management didn't bother her with the details of what was going on, and she probably didn't want to know, either. She was the last of the owners to sell to Hess, who acquired 100 percent of the team by buying her out in 1984.

"My father was tough," she recalled. "He came from nothing. His father was a conductor on the Lehigh Valley Railroad. It was interesting how all the owners came from such varied backgrounds. Dad owned Bowie race track. He somehow got involved with Donald Grant, you know, the fellow with the Mets, and he hooked him up with the guys at Monmouth and then he invested in a football team. But, really, Leon was a self-made man and I believe Phil was, too. Townie, though, came from money. He was a Phipps. His job was handling his money."

Helen latched on to the Jets with some seriousness after becoming an owner. "All of a sudden, there it was. I had been going to the games, but shortly after my father died I was divorced and it was a great filler for me. The kids and I had something to do every week, two girls and a boy. I loved it. I even started a players' wives' association with Randy Beverly's wife. I remember once going out to practice with Amy, and they called practice off. So Dottie Hampton and I went into the locker room and we cleaned it up." Dottie's husband, Bill, the equipment manager, has been with the Jets since their creation.

That 1968 season without Sonny transformed the Jets into something none of the other owners could have imagined. They paid him about $2 million for his 17 percent share. His tenfold profit never seemed enough, though. Sonny was a man who wanted to have a piece of the spotlight: He didn't necessarily want to be in it, but he wanted to see it. He was to recall years later that his greatest thrill in sports came that moment when his horse, Silent Screen, briefly got the lead in the Kentucky Derby as the field turned for home. This happened a year after the Super Bowl. For that instant, with the track announcer calling out that Silent Screen was in front, Sonny's frustrations ended.

In a sense, that race mirrored what he had with the Jets: He got close to the front, but he got shut out in the homestretch. He was passed by other owners. His horse finished fifth.

.   .   .

This is what Sonny missed that Super Bowl year:

The Kansas City Chiefs were some experts' pick to capture the

AFL title, perhaps even good enough to take the Super Bowl. But in the opening game of the 1968 season, the Jets produced a one-point victory at Kansas City. Typically, the Jets opened on the road, as they did every year until 1978, because Shea Stadium was the Mets' playpen. In this championship season the Jets played their first three games on the road.

The Jets won their opener even though the two key running backs, Emerson Boozer and Matt Snell; the gifted, good-hands receiver, George Sauer; and Johnny Sample, the loudmouthed, big-play defender, were all unsigned as the season opened. It is unthinkable today, and yet the Jets started their championship season without all of them.

Emerson Boozer might have become the Gale Sayers of his day. He was a sixth-round choice out of Maryland State in 1966. He was only five-eleven and barely 200 pounds, but midway through his second season he had already scored a pro-football-high 13 touchdowns. He had a twisting style but he also was able to slide off tacklers.

In Game 8 of his sophomore season, two Kansas City Chiefs sandwiched him, and suddenly he couldn't walk. Dr. Nicholas, who operated on Boozer's right knee, said the ligament and cartilage damage was the worst he had ever seen.

Boozer returned in 1968 but his sophomore-season touchdown splurge was merely a memory. Still, he picked up five scores and ran for 441 yards. He had also learned how to become a blocker for Snell. The marvelous slithery skills Boozer had exhibited as a runner were never to be seen again, but instead he became the straight-ahead bruising blocker every team covets.

Matt Snell was the Mr. Inside to Boozer's outside attack. Snell was the first rookie to be selected in Ewbank's regime and the first to be romanced by Werblin's dollars. Snell was the first player the Jets chose in 1964 after his career at Ohio State; the Giants drafted him too, but there were rumors that that was simply to force the Jets to pay him more money. The Giants hoped the Jets would simply run out of cash and go away.

At Ohio State, Snell had been a fullback, a linebacker, and a defensive end at 220 pounds. Ewbank decided on fullback for him, and Snell responded with a rookie season that included 948 rushing yards and 393 more receiving. He was the AFL's rookie of the year.

But like Boozer, he was vulnerable. After three straight seasons finishing among the league's top 10 in both rushing and pass-receiving, he was injured in the 1967 opener at Buffalo. He twisted his knee while running (and without having been hit), and he needed surgery to repair cartilage damage.

He returned to form in 1968 at the age of 27, running for 747 yards. Like Boozer, he became a fearsome blocker. But neither was ever a great runner again.

George Sauer was the team's bookish player. Indeed, he eventually retired young, claiming he wanted to write a book. He wore black horn-rimmed glasses and had long blond hair and a tender manner. His playbook was filled with personal observations.

In his back pocket at one training camp he carried a copy of Camus's *The Myth of Sisyphus*. Presumably, the man condemned to rolling the stone uphill for eternity taught Sauer that it was better to have precise patterns to escape. That was what he was famous for—that, and his hands.

It had been a long journey, but George Sauer, Jr., finally became more famous than his dad, a big man who had been an All-America fullback at Nebraska, had played with the Packers, had coached Navy and Baylor, and was a member of the College Football Hall of Fame. By the late '60s, George Sauer, Sr., was the Jets' director of player personnel—that is, he scouted college players. And one of the best he had acquired was his own son out of Texas.

Johnny Sample was different from the others. He talked a lot, on and off the field. His mouth may have gotten him into trouble in the staid NFL, where he played for the Colts, the Steelers, and the Redskins. Then, he claimed he was "blackballed" by the NFL and became a Jet in 1966 at the age of 29. At six-one and 205 pounds he was bigger than most defensive backs, and he liked to hit big-time, too.

But he enjoyed talking even more. His game, he felt, was based in large measure on getting the other guy's goat. As a second-year player he even baited the great Frank Gifford in the 1959 championship meeting between the Colts and the Giants.

"Hey, Hollywood," Sample shouted at the flanker when they lined up, "You're too pretty to be playing this game!"

"Stop running off at the mouth," Gifford snapped. "You've got a lot to learn, kid."

That's just what Sample wanted to hear. "That's when I knew I had him," he explained years later. "When they get sore and answer you back. They get mad at me and they try to do things to hurt me. They forget their patterns and that's when I accomplish what I want—especially late in the game." Late that game he intercepted a Charley Conerly pass and returned it 42 yards for a touchdown.

But Sample's first tenure under Weeb Ewbank ended in dismay. Ewbank attempted to find him for fumbling a punt, and Sample went home to Philadelphia. A few days later he was traded to the Steelers. After one season, Coach Buddy Parker unloaded him. But three productive seasons at Washington ended when Otto Graham became head coach and didn't like Sample. He was traded to Chicago, but he never played for the Bears; he got into an argument with owner George Halas, and Commissioner Pete Rozelle ruled Sample could go wherever he wanted. He was a free agent, but no one in the NFL wanted him. He returned to Ewbank, who had moved on to New York.

So Weeb was reunited with Sample, and Weeb had his contract contretemps with him and other major players, yet somehow everybody knew it would come out all right. Still, Weeb was functioning as general manager as well as coach, and he was forever having problems getting his players to sign contracts in a timely manner.

The day before the season opened, something of significance happened that offset the ongoing contract disputes. Namath was elected offensive captain by his teammates for the first time. They acknowledged that he was their leader as well as their most important player.

The honor was important to him. In earlier years, his curfew-breaking and his refusal to participate in all the preseason activity were seen as part of a failure to demonstrate the leadership his teammates demanded. But now, following his 4,000-yard season, and with the growing realization that this man was something special, that he played in constant pain, he was named the team's leader.

It was a veteran team coming off that first winning season in franchise history. But it was also Weeb's sixth year with the club. If he didn't win the division, the newly empowered owners were going to look around. Ewbank put in a few new rules—nothing stronger to drink than beer on plane trips, all visitors out of the clubhouse an hour before the game.

Namath had his pass-blocking in place, thanks to Weeb's astute personnel choices. On the line he had Winston Hill and Dave Herman, along with Bob Talamini and a rookie, Sam Walton. Challenging Talamini at left guard was the youngster Randy Rasmussen. The receivers were the whippet Maynard and George Sauer, Jr., whose great hands and precise routes were the complement to the free-spirited Maynard. Snell and Boozer were about to explode as a great running tandem. Pete Lammons was the versatile tight end.

The defensive unit was unchanged except for John Elliott at right tackle, bulked up to 250 pounds.

Namath responded to his election as the new captain by throwing a pair of touchdowns against the Chiefs, and then expertly directing a closing drive that lasted six minutes to keep them at bay.

The Boston Patriots had their own home-field problems, and a week later they were the home-team hosts—in Birmingham, Alabama. The Jets generated another victory with Jim Turner setting a club record with four field goals. That gave him six straight for the season.

And where was Turner practicing to achieve this expertise? Not at Shea Stadium, closed to the Jets, but in an open area of nearby Flushing Meadow Park.

"I didn't have any goalposts to kick at there," he recalled. "I had to aim between a couple of small trees."

Then came a two-point loss at Buffalo, but at least the Jets were coming home.

They were welcomed by the largest crowd in the history of the league, 63,786, who saw Boozer's last-minute touchdown propel them to a victory over the Chargers. That was followed by a loss to the Broncos, but then the Jets generated a four-game winning streak. The Jets become the big story in New York, along with an ascendant Knicks five. But the Jets were transcending the game of football.

A team's heroics were chronicled for the first time in American sports history by an artist, and an outstanding one at that—perhaps the most famous in the country. Certainly, masses who didn't know a Rothko from realism could appreciate leRoy Neiman. He had sketched the Jets from the mid-1960s, and he had become such a fixture around the team that he was there in the locker room when Joe's knees were getting taped at the Orange Bowl—as he had been around on the eve of the Super Bowl when coach Clive Rush did bed-check.

Neiman was the Jets' artist-in-residence. In the old, pre-NFL days, the Medicis kept sculptors and painters on retainers. Now the Jets had their own master craftsman, and something of what we knew and felt about them came from his observations that captured that one second in history when something happened.

These days Neiman is ensconced on Central Park West with a studio below his penthouse that is draped with 14th-century Belgian tapestries. He hauled out his Jets sketches and drawings and watercolors from almost 30 years before, including a folder of Namaths, to show a visitor.

It was Werblin who brought leRoy to the Jets. Neiman had been acclaimed for his work in *Playboy,* and he had chronicled young Muhammad Ali. But fighters had always been surrounded by artists and artistic types. A football team—this was something different.

"Sonny commissioned me to do some stuff," recalls the congenial Neiman. "My work was all over the place then. I used to be in store windows. But nobody was doing sports. Cartoonists never draw live. I was there. I was incessant."

And so he was. Neiman prowled the sidelines, he was with Joe at Bachelors III and at his apartment. He was behind the goal line or he was up in the owners' box.

Once, on the sidelines at Shea Stadium, Neiman put his sketchpad down. It had rained earlier, and the excitable Ewbank, running past him to follow a play, stepped on the drawing with a muddy shoe. Weeb looked down and said, "LeRoy, you're improving."

LeRoy returned to the 1960s as he surveyed the pictures in front of him and the sunlight streamed into his studio.

"This is the night I drew Joe with Tom Jones," he says of a picture dated "11/17/65." That was weeks before Joe completed his rookie season with a victory over the Bills.

"Who knew he'd be such a big star?" says Neiman. He was speaking of Namath, not the singer. "I must have sold 50 Joes over the years. I stopped selling them. I want to collect them."

Then there is a poignant drawing of Boozer, Number 32, trudging to the sidelines, a gladiator returning from battle holding his helmet in one hand and his shoe, knocked off in combat, in the other.

"That's an important drawing," remarks Neiman.

He sorts through the pictures and comes across Weeb. Neiman laughs. "Look what I wrote on this," he says with delight. " 'Like a skipper on a starry night at sea.' Not bad. Not bad."

They are all in front of him, players such as Dave Herman, so scholarly in glasses, but neck and shoulders tensed.

"He used to get worked up before a game. If you were in a doorway and he was coming, he never saw you. You'd go through it with him."

One sheet of paper is almost filled with the torso of a player, as if the page isn't wide enough to contain him.

"Poor Sherman. A tragedy," says Neiman about 300-something-pound Sherman Plunkett, a diabetic who was too heavy to be weighed on the team's scale. "He could never get his weight down, never, no matter what Weeb did. He died without ever realizing his potential.

"Here's George Sauer with short hair," and leRoy is staring at the likeness of a man who could have made NFL history if he hadn't quit at his prime to go off somewhere to write a book. While Maynard was leading the league with his spectacular yards-per-catch average, Sauer, with the gifted hands that could also write, was leading the Jets in receptions.

"Now look at this difference in Sauer. Remember, he cut his hair when his father was there. After his father left, George let his hair grow back. That's when I knew he was coming back to his old form as a player."

Neiman was around Joe with a pad and pencil all the time.

"Joe liked what I was doing because I was the only artist around. I don't know if he ever liked my work. He never complimented me. The kind thing about being around and giving away your pictures is that no one ever insults you."

He used to give away his sketches all the time. "Players would request them and I'd give it to them. These days they buy them. They go through their agents. The fun is gone."

But not forgotten. He remembered how he gave other athletes paintings—"and they'd lose them. I'd give 'em to Joe Louis and they disappeared. Guys would leave them in taxis. 'Hey, give me another one,' they'd say. One day I made a sketch of Hank Aaron. I think he was in Milwaukee then. 'Gee,' he says, 'can you make another one? I'd like to give one to my mother.' "

LeRoy was such a part of the Jets scene that he would be at Namath's apartment, 300 East 76th Street. "There was that famous chandelier of his. It was okay, not that great. Guys used to throw a football around his apartment, and I wrote on the sketch Namath telling them: 'Hey you guys. Careful not to hit my chandelier.' "

There was a sketch of Namath getting a massage, or Namath talking to friends. And there was Namath in a stylized attitude wearing nothing but shorts. In front of him, trainer Jeff Snedeker was on his knees taping Joe's knees. In that pose, Joe looked like a bullfighter being dressed before entering the corrida.

Indeed, Neiman had written below it, "Like dressing the matador."

Asked why he had done so many sketches of Namath, leRoy replies, "It's the same when you're around Ali or Tyson. We're all affected by the guy who makes something happen."

Even at the beginning of Joe's Broadway run, they noticed him. Once, up in the owners' box, Betty Iselin regarded the famous Namath slouch and remarked to Neiman, "Joe's always slumped over. Why doesn't he stand up straight?" To the owners, Joe was almost as much a commodity as a player. He was an object to show off at parties, so why shouldn't he have good posture?

Neiman's Super Bowl III drawings also tell about a game and a way of life that has changed very much. Imagine Parcells allowing a photographer or a painter along on bed-check. Yet there is Clive

Rush at a half-open doorway. Behind it, Namath, in his shorts, has his hand on the door as if just opening it after being roused from sleep.

"He told Clive he just woke up," says Neiman. "I wonder if that was true. Anyway, it was fun to go along on bed-check."

That week, the Jets were allowed to have one guest, whose food would be paid for. But Talamini brought his entire family to the game. He had to pay for most of what they ate.

"I used to bring food to his room," recalls Neiman.

He didn't only work the Jets' side of the room. At the Super Bowl he sketched Earl Morrall and Mike Curtis and Johnny Unitas. In a game at Atlanta, he was fascinated with Coach Norm Van Brocklin, who was smoking a cigarette on the sidelines.

"That's why I did the picture. He had a cigarette in his mouth. The sideline was littered with the butts. Imagine a coach smoking today in a game."

His final years with the Jets included 1974, when he took in a game against the Bills. "That's O.J.," says Neiman. "And here's O.J. on Joe's TV show."

Being around the Jets was fun—"It was like a buildup to something, an ascending. It all tapered off in the 1970s," claims Neiman. "It's still tapering off. People are always lamenting and blaming."

.   .   .

The fun and the outrageousness of those days remain a part of many Jets' lives, for those in and out of uniform—and for those who never put one on. The Jets' game in Oakland during that 1968 season saw such bizarre, nutty, funny circumstances that it became a permanent part of sports lore. The Jets-Raiders affair came to be known simply as the "Heidi" game.

Even today, players have some vague notion that a Heidi game was a pivotal moment in Jets annals. But they don't quite know what it was about. Was it a championship, a playoff, a game to decide the season?

It actually was a midseason game between two clubs that were 7–2 and leading their divisions. The Raiders had already been to a Super Bowl, while the Jets were flexing their muscles following that first winning season.

The Jets and Raiders had always been contentious, and a nasty relationship had brewed for years. The year before, the Raiders' Ike Lassiter broke Namath's cheekbone in the next-to-last game of the season. And then, a few plays later, Ben Davidson, a Bunyanesque character who sported a handlebar mustache, swatted Joe just for fun. But Namath remained in the game.

Later that night, the *Times*'s Dave Anderson was sitting in the hotel lobby. The team was staying on the West Coast since it was going to wind up the season the following Sunday at San Diego. Suddenly, Anderson spotted Namath. Joe was wearing a tuxedo. He went up to the front desk to check out.

"Where are you going?" Anderson asked.

"To Vegas," replied Joe. "We don't have bed-check tonight."

A week later, wearing a special faceguard, Joe produced another big game to get his 4,000-yard season.

But now it was a year later. The photograph of Davidson swinging at Joe was hanging in the Raiders' offices—a proud symbol of the team's violence.

The teams met in Oakland for an unofficial playoff preview, the Jets with their four-game winning streak, the Raiders with three in a row.

Before the game, one of the game officials asked Dr. Nicholas to take a look at his bad back. This Nicholas did, and then promised to return when the game was over to check it out again.

The game turned into a brutal, penalty-laced affair, with players pounding one another and points lighting up the scoreboard. The Jets went ahead by 32–29 on Turner's field goal with 65 seconds remaining. But it was also close to 7 P.M. in the crowded, TV-saturated East. And at seven o'clock eastern time, a made-for-television movie, *Heidi,* the story of the little girl in the Swiss Alps, was scheduled to appear on NBC. It would star Jennifer Edwards, who never made the impact on audiences that Shirley Temple had in the 1930s version. Then again, Shirley Temple never was blamed for preempting a football game.

What harm, thought NBC officials, could there be in leaving the game after a commercial? The Jets were about to win. Someone in the control room calculated that 10 seconds would be sliced from the clock in the kickoff. There wasn't enough time in 55 seconds to make a difference. So the network cut away from Oakland and shifted to *Heidi*.

From his home, Allan B. (Scotty) Connal, the head of NBC Sports, immediately sensed this was not a good idea. He tried to persuade the technicians on duty not to switch from those last seconds of the late-running game. But he couldn't get through to anyone who mattered, and *Heidi* it was.

When the 11 o'clock news went on that night, fans heard for the first time the unbelievable final score: Oakland 43, Jets 32. While they weren't watching, the Raiders had scored 14 points. Raiders quarterback Daryle Lamonica connected twice with running back Charlie Smith, who outfoxed rookie strong safety Mike D'Amato. First, Smith gained 20 yards, with a D'Amato penalty tacked on. The next play, Smith took a swing pass and scampered 43 yards for a touchdown.

Was Weeb nuts playing the rookie against Smith? Weeb had no choice; the veteran Jim Hudson had been ejected for complaining about a penalty called against him. D'Amato was the only safety available.

Now, with 42 seconds remaining, the Raiders led by 36–32. Only a touchdown would win it for the Jets. Then again, with Namath and Maynard and Sauer, it didn't seem impossible. But Earl Christy fumbled the kickoff, chased it back to the 10, lost it again, and watched it slither to the two. From there, a fellow named Preston Ridlehuber, who was never to play another season for the Raiders, scooped it up and ran in for the touchdown. Two scores, nine seconds apart.

No one back in New York knew this, though.

An hour after the game, Weeb telephoned his wife, Lucy, back in New York.

"Congratulations," she told him.

"For what?" said Weeb.

"On winning," she replied.

"We lost the game," said Ewbank.

Of course, Weeb was hardly alone in not realizing how New Yorkers were reacting to what happened. The Jets did not return home after the game because they had a game in San Diego the following week; as was the custom then, with consecutive West Coast games, the Jets simply spent the whole week in California.

So after the game they flew to Long Beach. When the players turned on the late news, they learned that the NBC switchboard in New York had been knocked out of commission by thousands of callers. Some of the outraged fans had actually telephoned the police to find out what had happened.

If fans were irate over not knowing what had happened, imagine how teed off the Jets were, who did. When the game ended, Walt Michaels was still seething over Hudson's ejection. He believed it cost the Jets the game. So did Dr. Nicholas.

They headed for the officials' room. The door was locked. Walt started to bang on it, abetted by the doctor.

"Walt was yelling his head off," recalls Nicholas. "I went along with him. I thought I'd see the official I had examined and give him a piece of my mind and take a look at his back."

Nicholas complained while examining his patient. The next day, the league sent a letter to the Jets telling them that Nicholas was fined $2,500 and Michaels $5,000. The official, who got a free diagnosis, had turned in the good doctor.

"I'm the only team doctor in history ever fined for banging on the door," Nicholas likes to relate to this day.

Walt Michaels is still trying to bang down doors.

The next day, the network's program director, Julian Goodman, issued a public apology for "a forgivable error committed by humans who were concerned with the children."

A noble sentiment, indeed. But nobility gave way to practicality as NBC and the NFL altered their policy. Now, whenever a game is shown in either team's home market, it stays on to the end, regardless of the score. Even if the children will miss a kiddies' movie.

Neither the Jets nor the Raiders lost again in 1968. Both captured their divisions. That pitted them against each other in the AFL Championship Game.

If you want another example of the Jets' paranoia about the Raiders, there was the case of Al Davis and Curley Johnson's kicking shoe.

"I used to tie up my shoe when I kicked off," recalls Curley. That gave him more of an elevated angle to hit the ball, allowing him to send it higher.

"But Al Davis used to call time out before I kicked. He told the officials there were weights in my shoe." Davis was also hoping the delay, and the inspection, would frustrate the edgy kicker.

"They changed the rules on me," says Johnson. "You had to use a store-bought shoe."

Namath seemed oblivious to Davis's machinations. Joe tossed three touchdowns. But the game wasn't clinched until Lamonica and Smith flirted once again with victory. With the Jets leading by 27–23, and slightly more than two minutes remaining, the Raiders penetrated to the Jets' 24-yard line.

On a swing pass, Lamonica tossed the ball toward Smith, who saw the ball roll off his fingers for an incompletion. But Smith was still behind Lamonica, making the pass a lateral rather than a forward pass. It was a free ball, not an incomplete forward pass, and Ralph Baker, whose duty was to cover Smith on that play, scooped up the ball and rumbled toward the end zone. A whistle halted him from scoring; once a lateral touches the ground, it may be recovered, but not advanced. Still, the Jets had possession on their 30. They ran out the clock.

"It was the exact same play where he threw the ball to Smith in the *Heidi* game," Baker recalls. "We were prepared for it. We had seen the film many times. Only this time the ball went behind the receiver."

Baker had another flashback at that instant—to a play that the Patriots had had that season, when they advanced a lateral. Baker wasn't quite sure what the rule was, but this was no time to look it up.

"I decided to pick it up anyway. It was a comical scene. I picked it up and started to run, and then Smith would gallop. Then he'd slow down. Then I'd slow down. It was as if we each had second thoughts about whether I could advance it. I kept running, almost 80 yards. It seemed like an eternity. And then I threw the ball in the stands."

It was another of those instants, when you look at teams that win or lose championships, that turn a franchise around. Who knows what the Jets' future would have been like if the one play had ended differently? Who knows how many bad bounces in future years and decades buried Jets teams that might have achieved the same measure of success?

In the spontaneous celebration that followed the victory, Weeb was lifted onto the shoulders of his players. Photographers recorded the moment with Ewbank's face contorted in tears, presumably tears of joy. They weren't.

"Remember when the players put me on their shoulders?" he was to recount. "Well, some little kid came along and swung on my right leg. It really irritated the hip joint."

Then they weren't tears of joy?

"They were tears, period," he said.

Still, he says even 30 years later of the celebrating players who hoisted him above the crowd, "I understand why players do that —running and jumping and screaming that you see so much in basketball now. Unless you've ever done it, won a championship, you can't appreciate the feeling."

But he had to be outfitted with a cane as a result of that odd mishap, and he limped around for the next two weeks as the Jets prepared for the Super Bowl against his old team, the Colts. Baltimore had dispatched the Browns, 34–0, in the NFL title game.

"I went on crutches for one day and I said, 'This is a bunch of stuff,'" says Weeb, echoing his favorite expression, "and I threw it away." He got a cane instead, but avoided using it as much as possible. Even after the Super Bowl, he didn't walk with one, and it affected him terribly over the years. "I couldn't stand the pain," he admits now. "It was like a toothache." Eventually, he needed surgery on both knees. But that was long into the future.

The Super Bowl week began with a team meeting at Shea Stadium. Ewbank hobbled into the room and warned his players not to say anything inflammatory about the Colts. Already, Weeb had worried about a quotation from Joe in which he had rated the Raiders' Lamonica better than Earl Morrall of the Colts.

"Let me do all the talking," Ewbank commanded the players. How much poorer football history would be if everyone had listened.

The team, complete with wives and children, then flew to Florida, where they would be housed in Fort Lauderdale for the Super Bowl.

Today, there are security forces aboard the team planes. When the Giants won their second Super Bowl, an FBI man went along on the team bus because of terrorist fears. On that Jets charter back then, though, the most fearsome force was Bob Talamini's four children.

Meanwhile, the oddsmaker to the nation, Jimmy (the Greek) Snyder, who called himself a public-relations consultant, established a betting line from his Las Vegas offices: The Colts, he pronounced, were 17 points better than the Jets. "The Jets," he explained, "have a tiger by the tail."

On the flight, Namath spoke to the *Times*'s Dave Anderson, his favorite writer. Joe never forgot kindnesses, and for a long time he never forgot slights. Thus, in later years he refused to talk to the *Post*'s Paul Zimmerman (who became known as "Dr. Z" when he switched to *Sports Illustrated*), or to the *News*'s Larry Fox. Both writers claimed Joe misinterpreted stories or headlines. He banished both of them to listening distance only. They were permitted to poke their heads into his conferences but were not allowed to ask him questions. With Dave, though, Joe was always open and honest.

"Seventeen points?" Joe told Anderson. "If we were allowed to bet, I'd bet $100,000 on this one. I might sound like I'm boasting and bragging, and I am. Ask anybody who's played against us in our league. The Colts are good, but we're good, too."

Namath resolved that the Colts' reputation wouldn't affect him, that their 15–1 won–lost record, including playoff victories, meant nothing. He would go by what he saw on the films. "The one-eyed monster," he called the projector that would unveil the Colts to Joe and the Jets.

Ask Joe Namath about his talking today and he still doesn't understand what the fuss was all about. He was being honest, that's all. Thus, he decided that not only was Lamonica better than Morrall, but John Hadl, Bob Griese, and he, too, were better than any of the quarterbacks in the NFL.

As the team bus headed for the hotel in Fort Lauderdale, as the police escort ushered it past the swaying palm trees, Turner the placekicker said, "Yes, sir. We've come a long way from the Polo Grounds."

I have always believed that Namath's contention that his league's quarterbacks were better than the NFL's set the Super Bowl tone. Don Shula can deny it, but I think it put him and the Colts on the defensive. Every Super Bowl I've been to, there is a tone that pervades it, and it starts early in the week, sometimes even in the off-week. It could be something as simple as the Bengals' Forrest Gregg griping that he wasn't told his players would be interviewed just as he arrived in Detroit to face the 49ers in Super Bowl XVI. His complaining didn't stop. Or in that same week, when 49ers coach Bill Walsh put on a doorman's uniform and greeted his players when they arrived at their hotel. Two coaches, two attitudes—and two different reactions by the players.

Vivid, too, is the memory of tight-assed Dick Vermeil arriving with his Eagles to face the decidedly un–tight-assed Raiders in New Orleans for Super Bowl XV. The Eagles arrived wearing green jogging suits, all of them looking like kids attending parochial school in uniform. Vermeil also ordered his coaches to jog from place to place, as if they were West Point plebes. When I interviewed his quarterback guru, the 70-year-old Sid Gillman, it was while we both jogged.

"This crazy guy's going to kill me," said a panting Gillman.

The Raiders, meanwhile, got into all sorts of postmidnight scuffles in the French Quarter, and their wide receiver Cliff Branch missed the team flight. He also scored two touchdowns in the big game. When it was over and the victory tucked away, I asked Al Davis if he was going to discipline Branch.

"What the fuck's the difference?" suggested Al.

Shula's theme for the players facing the Jets was set early, in Baltimore before they left for the Orange Bowl: "Just remember," the coach told them, "that everything we've accomplished all season is riding on the outcome of this game." And this was to a team that had lost only once, that had shut out four opponents down the stretch: Shula had set his own tone, and perhaps he didn't realize it, but it had a negative ring.

At the week's major press conference in Miami, he allowed himself to get distracted by Namath's assessment of the NFL's quarter-backs. Shula had won a title with the aging Morrall replacing the aging and injured Unitas. No way could Joe Namath denigrate these two guys.

Shula was a live-by-the-rules guy. He was shocked when told that Namath hadn't been on hand for the biggest media day of the week. Joe claimed he overslept.

"Namath didn't show up for photo day?" the Colts coach repeated, astounded. "What the hell is Weeb doing?"

Then someone mentioned Morrall, asking Shula his reaction to Namath's comparison of Morrall and Lamonica. Suddenly, Shula found himself defending Morrall, the MVP of the NFL.

"I don't know how Namath can rap Earl," said Shula. It was apparent that Shula had read everything Joe was saying, for Joe had described how, in the AFL, the quarterbacks were more dangerous, how they took chances throwing the ball long—so their percentages weren't as high as those of the NFL quarterbacks, who tossed off ratty little passes with a high probability of success.

"Earl's number one in the NFL. He's thrown all those touchdown passes. He's thrown for a great percentage without using dinky flare passes. Anyone who doesn't give him the credit he deserves is wrong."

The veins in Shula's neck had thickened, and his square-jawed face suddenly betrayed his controlled anger.

"But I guess," the coach said, a rising edge in his voice, "Namath can say whatever the hell he wants."

Werblin loved it. His old Jets were coming into his backyard. He was in his oceanfront home on Golden Beach, perhaps the most exclusive spot in that part of South Florida. He was still rooting for the Jets, especially Joe, the star he had hitched the Jets' wagon to.

The price on the Jets was going up. It was 18 points now as Werblin, who played the horses heavily at his Monmouth Park, said, "I haven't bet on a football game in eight years. But I have to go for this price."

Walt Michaels had six brothers. One of them had been killed on Guadalcanal. Years after the Super Bowl, when Michaels would be taken to task by players or writers for his old-fashioned values, he would bristle, "Sure, I'm old-fashioned. I got my values from a father who went into the mines for 25 years. There was a brother who was killed in the war. If that's old-fashioned, I plead guilty."

He had another brother, Lou, who happened to be the place-kicker for the Colts. Lou was an old-fashioned kind of guy, too. He didn't like this longhair, this wiseacre, this Namath. His confrontation with Namath during the week has become a part of the Jets' Super Bowl legend. It has gotten embellished, as these things do, and why not? It is hardly common for the brother of the coach of one team to be playing on the opposing team—and then to confront the rival quarterback in a saloon, and almost come to blows.

What really happened has been pieced together from interviews with Namath and teammate Jim Hudson. Lou Michaels and Namath came across each other in a bar. All week leading to the Super Bowl, a bar, any bar, was a focal point. It was where teammates got together to bang glasses. And often, they would find their opponents drinking in the same place. This time, Michaels, a beefy 250-pounder who had been the Colts' placekicker for more than a decade, sought out Joe.

"Lou Michaels," he growled, introducing himself.

Joe knew all about Lou. Joe's older brother Frank had roomed with Lou at Kentucky.

"You're doing a lot of talking," Michaels told Joe.

"There's a lot to talk about," Namath retorted. "We're going to kick the hell out of your team."

"Haven't you heard of the word modesty, Joseph?" said Michaels, starting to burn.

Safety Jim Hudson was alongside Joe. Hudson didn't like the atmosphere that was now injected into the conversation. He suggested he and Namath sit down for dinner. But Michaels wouldn't leave Joe alone. Michaels and a teammate, Dan Sullivan, sat down uninvited with them.

"You still here?" said Namath.

"Damn right I'm still here," Michaels said. "I want to hear all you got to say."

"I'm going to pick you apart," Joe shot back.

"I never heard Johnny Unitas or Bobby Layne talk like that," said

Michaels, whose sensibilities were still in the Eisenhower Era, not in Bob Dylan's.

"Even if we're in trouble, we'll send in the master," Michaels continued, referring to Unitas.

"I hope you do," said a smiling Namath. "Because that'll mean the game is too far gone."

"Too far what!" snapped Michaels.

"Excuse me," said Namath. "I want to say hello to a few friends."

He got up and left, but Michaels was sizzling.

"Don't pay any attention to what Joe says," chirped up Hudson. "You've got to understand him."

Namath soon returned and Michaels continued his slow burn, asking questions that he knew would rile him, would be outrageous. Michaels was on a collision course with the future.

"Suppose we kick the hell out of your team?" wondered Michaels. "Just suppose we do that. What then, Namath?"

"I'll tell you what I'll do," he replied. "I'll sit in the middle of the field and I'll cry."

Joe had done it. He broke the ice—and broke everyone up. They all laughed.

When the check came, Joe grabbed it and paid with a $100 bill, one of many he had rolled up.

"You got a ride back to the hotel?" Namath asked.

"No, but we'll jump in a cab," said Michaels.

"Don't be silly. I'll drop you," said Namath.

When the two Colts got out of the car at the driveway of the Statler Hilton, they waved good-bye to Namath, thanking him for the ride.

"He's a helluva guy," said Lou Michaels.

.   .   .

The films. They didn't lie. And the Jets knew they had better be prepared by watching all those reels of this 15–1 monster, this Shula-led juggernaut, this collection from the NFL—the league that had won the first two Super Bowls by a combined score of 68–24, allowing Jimmy the Greek to cover the odds he had made each time.

Nine days before the game, the Jets were preparing to watch

their first films of the Colts. The Jets were not happy. Just before viewing their opponent, they held a private team meeting, mostly to complain about the fact that the team wouldn't pay for the wives' expenses. Some players were also upset after hearing a report that all they'd get for the AFL championship was a watch, not a ring. Some even contended that their AFL title share would be less than the $9,000 a man they had been promised.

The Jets, about to view their opponents in the biggest game of their lives, were worried about meal money for their spouses.

They voiced their complaints to Weeb, who tried to smooth things over and then said, "We've got a game to think about, and let's think about it."

Ewbank had set up two huge white screens at either end of a ballroom in the Galt Ocean Mile Hotel in Fort Lauderdale, where they stayed for 10 days leading to the Super Bowl. One side was for the offense, which would view the Colts defense, and the other end was for the Jets defense, to study Baltimore's offense.

These were near-legendary players the Jets were about to look at, and Ewbank needed to humanize these ferocious Colts. So he devised an interesting strategy. He compared each of them to players the Jets knew—players on other teams the Jets had faced and defeated that season.

He contemplated Bubba Smith, the massive defensive lineman whose Michigan State fans had chanted "Kill, Bubba, Kill!" when he was tearing after the enemy. This was Smith's second year in the pros.

"He's virtually a rookie," Ewbank told his players. "He hardly played a year ago. He doesn't have McDole's know-how."

Ron McDole was the Bills' defensive end, and a player the Jets respected for his consistent pass-rushing ability.

"And their rabbit, Billy Ray Smith, he's like Jim Hunt of the Patriots, and we've been able to handle Hunt."

He even minimized the impact, if not the talent, of tight end John Mackey.

"We can stop him. No tight end can win all by himself."

After scrutinizing the films for an hour, Namath looked up when the lights went on.

"Hell," he said, "they're not supermen."

.   .   .

Go to a Super Bowl as a member of the media today and you will be part of a choreographed environment worthy of a Rockettes' performance, or a military maneuver. Hotels swarm with uniformed and plainclothes police. Autograph seekers are rousted out of the lobby or kept behind a rope. Reporters can't even register at the team hotels (unless, and only with some teams, they are from the club's hometown).

If you're a member of the news media, and you're lucky, you can get through to a player's room by telephone, or you might talk to an athlete if he is willing to see you after hours. Essentially, though, the schedule is precise. We all receive a folder describing the routine: Interviews start on Sunday nights with both teams upon arrival, when the head coach and six players are available for a half-hour. The schedule is repeated Monday night.

Then there is the mammoth Media Day on Tuesday, an undertaking so huge it can be held only at the stadium because more than 3,000 members of the press are on hand. The place looks like a huge convention: A team's key players are given their own podiums to stand on and be interviewed, while others sit in the stands surrounded by notebooks, microphones, and cameras. This lasts an hour—and then breakfast, followed by the arrival of the other team and the same arrangement.

On Wednesday, media buses go in every direction. First they shuttle reporters to each team's hotel for a 1-hour-15-minute interview. Here the setting is more relaxed than at the stadium. Most players sit at huge round tables. To help you identify the players, their names are written on placards that sit on the table like a "Reserved" sign. There are also podiums for the quarterback and key performers.

Meanwhile, there is a simultaneous press conference in an adjacent room with the head coach and major players. From here, the press is driven to the opponent's hotel and the situation is repeated. On Thursday, everyone follows the same schedule.

Friday is the last chance to get your man. Each head coach arrives at the media headquarters for separate one-hour news conferences. They are followed by the commissioner's annual state of the NFL address, which often is a forum to make significant points about where the league is headed, or recent contributions, or how well it's doing. The commissioner has privately prepared with a sort of mock-conference in which an aide will go over likely questions.

When the Super Bowl is over Sunday night, reporters are led by guides down to the interview area. If the reporters are going by themselves, they follow painted arrows, color-coded, that lead them to the interviews. There, in separate sites in the bowels of the stadium, the head coach, the most valuable player, and key players speak on podiums.

Super Bowl III was nothing like this. If the New York writers wanted Joe, or any other Jet, they grabbed him and gabbed. Often, impromptu news conferences took place around the pool.

While guests at the Jets' hotel, the Galt Ocean Mile, often looked around for big, beefy people to gawk at, they might have missed another celebrity: Andre Kostelanetz, the internationally acclaimed conductor and official of the New York Philharmonic, was the guest of Jim Nicholas and his wife, Kiki. In the evenings, they'd all go to the bar and Kostelanetz would ask about the events of the day.

"I introduced him to Joe one night after practice," recalls Nicholas, "and he asked Joe, 'How did the rehearsal turn out?' Kostelanetz used to call practice rehearsal. Joe said, 'It went great. And wait till you see the actual performance.'"

.   .   .

One night, Weeb was in his room with his wife, Lucy. There was a knock on the door. Weeb opened it and there stood Johnny Unitas, his old quarterback. John brought along his wife, Dotty.

It could have been an awkward situation—Weeb's team about to face Unitas's team. Was Johnny U's right arm still ailing? Weeb wouldn't ask. "That wouldn't have been fair," he later explained.

They chatted, and Unitas spoke about his five children and how their mutual friends in Baltimore were doing. Then Weeb escorted the pair down the hall from his poolside room, but stopped just short of the lobby. How would it look to be seen with the opposing quarterback just before the Super Bowl?

So Weeb shook hands and watched as his old quarterback strolled on. Just then, Namath entered the lobby through the glass front door. Of course, they recognized each other, these two prized Ewbank possessions, and chatted for a while. Unitas, crew-cut, wore a gray suit and tie. The shaggy-haired Namath was in a mod turtleneck sweater under a blue blazer.

Back in high school, they used to call Namath "Joey U.," praising his talents as similar to Johnny U's.

Ewbank hadn't left yet. He still was standing off to the side as he regarded his two quarterbacks, the symbols of his two regimes. When they parted, Weeb turned and hobbled on his cane back to his room.

. . .

Three nights before Super Bowl III, Joe went to the Miami Touchdown Club's annual dinner to accept an award.

"I didn't plan on stirring up anything," he claims. "Hey, Weeb had told me to keep my big mouth shut. That week at poolside I had told a bunch of reporters that half a dozen AFL quarterbacks were better than Morrall. That drove Shula nuts. It didn't do Weeb any good either. Anyway, at the dinner I accepted an award, and then we got into a discussion of the game coming up. I said I was angry we were such underdogs. I was tired of answering questions about the big, bad Colts. I thought that it was ridiculous they were 18-point favorites, and I just said, in the middle of a long acceptance speech, 'You can be the greatest athlete in the world, but if you don't win those football games, it doesn't mean anything. And we're going to win Sunday, I'll guarantee you.' "

Namath kept talking, but Anderson of the *Times* knew he had three little words that would make his story for Saturday's paper. It was too late for Friday. No one remembers that Namath kept talking, drink in hand, after that "guarantee," that he said, "When we won the AFL championship, a lot of people thanked the wives. I'd like to thank all the single girls in New York, they deserve just as much credit. They're appreciated as much."

Finally, someone in the audience shouted, "Sit down!"

"Those words, 'I guarantee you,' were all I said, the only time I said it," recalls Namath now. "I didn't mean to sound like a wise

guy and I never thought that would turn into a somewhat historical statement, especially coming from me—you know, the brash
Broadway invader from Beaver Falls, Pennsylvania."

Of course, the guarantee has become part of that impossible-to-
recreate victory. It is one more aspect that helped turn the Jets'
greatest moment to a historical statement.

Suddenly, it was Saturday and the game was a day away.

Back in Beaver Falls, Namath's mother was very concerned.
Her television set had stopped working. She called Buzzy the
repairman.

"It's got to work tomorrow, Buzzy," she said.

"It will," he replied.

"It better," she said.

That night, Jeff Richardson, the backup offensive lineman, was
having dinner in a restaurant. He had been given a seat with his
back to Bubba Smith—his former Michigan State teammate.

Richardson decided to have some fun. He called over the hostess
and told her, "That big man, send him a drink on me. Anything he
wants—and as many as he wants."

The hostess informed Bubba, who turned to look at who his
benefactor was. He recognized his college buddy.

"No drinks for me," he told the hostess. "That man is not going
to get me drinking tonight. No sir, not tonight."

Then Smith turned to Richardson and said, sarcastically, with a
slight smile, "You're going to win tomorrow anyway. You have the
powerhouse. Your quarterback has guaranteed it."

Just before 11 o'clock at night, the Jets and officials and relatives
and friends and the news media gathered in the hotel ballroom.
Traditionally, the night before a game, the Jets had a late-night
snack. This time 200 people showed up for this informal offering.

Kostelanetz slid onto the seat behind a piano. Bake Turner, split
end and guitar player, signaled him to begin, and they played a
duet of "Malaguena"—Kostelanetz playing with one hand and con-
ducting with the other, to the delight of the players and friends.

"Hey, Bake," someone called out, "you really carried that piano
player."

The married players soon left for their rooms with their wives.
Weeb's philosophy on sex before a game was simple—better in

your own hotel, with someone you know, than prowling the city looking for love.

Namath listened to Weeb this night. He was ensconced in the Governor's Suite, and not alone. He had his Johnnie Walker Red— which his friend Joe Hirsch used to refer to as "rotgut whiskey"— and a friend.

Later, Joe was to explain the joys of sex the night before the big game.

"It relaxes you," he said.

Up in his room, Dave Herman was trying to get some sleep. His wife, Leah, started to cry.

"If you lose," she said, "all the blame will be on you."

For Weeb had decided on a daring strategy. In the AFL championship he had shifted Herman from right guard to right tackle because Weeb didn't trust rookie Sam Walton to handle the tough veteran, Ike Lassiter. Now, for the Super Bowl, Herman was staying put at that unfamiliar position, only this time he was taking on Bubba Smith.

"All this 'Kill, Bubba, Kill'—I don't want to be a widow. I'm so frightened," Leah Herman said.

As well she should have been. There were only about one-fourth the number of reporters and television talking heads that attend today's Super Bowl, but they made enough NFL noise to have everyone believe this was a colossal mismatch.

Sports Illustrated's famed pro football expert, Tex Maule, picked the Colts by 43–0. And a *Baltimore Sun* reporter, Cameron Snyder, predictably picked the Colts by 47–0.

But Ewbank's mantra overshadowed the expected barrage of negativism from the pro football Establishment. Early on, he had adopted as the Jets' season slogan "Poise and Execution." Whenever he felt it necessary, he reminded the players it was what they needed to do. He brought it up again on Sunday morning at their breakfast, four hours before game time.

They were tested in little ways even as they were driven to the game. One of Miami's many drawbridges was up, and their bus was stopped while players blamed John Free, as usual. But when the drawbridge operator saw the police cars and motorcycles and flashing lights, he quickly lowered the bridge, backing up the boat traffic.

At the Orange Bowl, the crush of fans threatened to keep the players from getting off the bus.

"Joe, better get off first or we'll never get to the game," Pete Lammons said.

Once inside the stadium, players distractedly leafed through the Super Bowl programs that had been left at their lockers. But some were printed not with the Jets' statistics but with the Raiders'—as if the wrong American Football League team had gotten to the Super Bowl.

Ramos explained that the printer prepared for both teams, but sent along the wrong programs.

"Damn," muttered Jim Hudson. "We get in the Super Bowl and the program's got the goddamn Raiders in it."

Meanwhile, Namath's backup, Babe Parilli, cautioned Dr. Nicholas to behave himself. Parilli didn't want another *Heidi* episode, with the good doctor berating the officials.

"Hey there, Coach Doc, stay loose," said Parilli. "No penalties on the sideline, Doc."

Meanwhile, Namath was having his knee ritualistically prepared for battle by trainer Jeff Snedeker. It was while sketching this scene of the stoic Namath, who stood on the taping table, his right leg bent, that leRoy Neiman was reminded of a matador. Snedeker taped the knee so that it could not be fully extended, then fastened an aluminum-and-black-rubber brace to it. Namath could not get down from the table by himself. Snedeker had to help him.

Weeb had reluctantly decided that Maynard, sore thigh and all, would start. Maynard insisted and Nicholas concurred. Weeb had prepared Bake Turner to start in Maynard's place.

"If it goes bad," Ewbank warned Maynard, "don't hide it."

"If it goes," replied Maynard, "you'll see it."

Minutes before kickoff, Weeb stood in the middle of the room. This was the time to leave his players with lingering thoughts to take onto the field. He found a kinship with them in that setting. This team, this coach, all these players either weren't good enough for the other league, or had been cut by the other team. This was the moment not merely for revenge for the New York Jets, but to stamp on each of them forever just who they were.

"Some of you men," Weeb began, "used to be with the Colts, but that team decided that you didn't have the skills to stay with them."

He was speaking to players such as Turner and Johnny Sample, and to Winston Hill, who had been drafted by the Colts but was turned loose before he ever had a chance to play in a game. And Weeb was also talking about himself. Although he never said "I," the players knew.

"Now, you're opposing that team," he continued. "You've proven to yourself you're capable. Now you've got an opportunity to prove it to that team."

Weeb even included Randy Rasmussen, the young guard from little Kearney State in Nebraska. Rasmussen had never played for the Colts, but he was an unknown.

"And you, Randy," said Weeb, "you've got a chance to prove that a player from a small college belongs in the Super Bowl."

Schmitt, the first player from Hofstra to make it to the big time, piped in, "You get $15,000 for proving it."

As a final reminder Ewbank cautioned, "No matter what develops out there, I expect you to maintain your poise and execution. That's what we worked on all season."

Following the prayer, Ewbank remembered something else:

"One more thing. When we win, don't pick me up and ruin my other hip. I'll walk."

The players went out to the Super Bowl field, laughing.

. . .

On the second drive of the game, Namath deployed Maynard for the first time.

Maynard had scored 10 touchdowns during the season. He had averaged 23 yards a catch. But now his thigh was troubling him, badly. It was too bad, for Namath believed that in watching the films he had spotted a key weakness in the Baltimore secondary: They didn't help one another out on deep passing patterns. Namath believed he could get the ball deep to Maynard, and Maynard believed he could get away from the Colts defenders.

Thus, Namath, on his own 35, called for Maynard to race down the right sideline. He needed to break beyond Jerry Logan, the Colts safety in their zone defense.

Maynard doesn't need the films these days to recollect that play.

"I beat the guy by six yards, and the ball was an inch too long."

It was off his fingertips.

On the sidelines, Ewbank second-guessed himself.

"Damn, if his leg's right, that's a touchdown," complained Weeb.

When the series ended, Maynard went to the sidelines and admitted to Nicholas that he had felt what he described as a "twinge." Essentially, Maynard wouldn't be much good the rest of the game on those deep patterns.

But the Colts didn't know that, thought Ewbank. After that near-miss, they had started to double up on Maynard. That allowed Sauer to perform one-on-one against Lenny Lyles. The only problem with that matchup was that Sauer lined up on the left side. Namath would have to throw across his body. Somehow he had jammed his thumb early in the game in such a way that it hurt like hell when he threw to his left. But the Colts didn't know that, either.

For the rest of the game, Namath threw toward Maynard only twice. One was a fly pattern in the second quarter when the Jets got to the Baltimore 32. Joe sent Maynard into the end zone, and again the pass was just a bit too long. "Off my fingertips," is the way Maynard still remembers it.

Thus, when you look at the statistics of Super Bowl III, you will find receptions by four Jets—but none by Maynard. One of the most dangerous receivers in history, a member of the Hall of Fame (and the only Jets player besides Namath in the Hall), did not catch a pass in their biggest game. And yet his effect was palpable.

Meanwhile, Curley Johnson had things on his mind. Curley was not only the punter, but he was employed on kickoffs. He knew Weeb was concerned about the Colts offense, so it was critical to keep them as far back from their goal line as possible on every drive. That meant his kickoffs had to be in the end zone and his punts had to be high and far.

The night before, Curley dreamed that his punts had gone straight up in the air and landed at his feet.

Curley may have been a cutup in the locker room, but he was

one nervous guy, all the time. His hands used to sweat when he was ready to punt, and he always feared that the snap would sail through his wet hands.

"Nobody recognizes something I did early in the Super Bowl," says Johnson. "I got off a kick from the end zone. In fact, I had to do it twice."

It was an important contribution. With the Jets leading by 7–0 (on Snell's four-yard run) in the second quarter, they were pinned back on their seven-yard line. On fourth down, Johnson had to punt from his own end zone. As he awaited the long snap, he noticed that his hands were bone-dry. He got off the kick.

It was hardly a boomer. But it sailed to the Jets 39. And then Johnson got the disheartening signal: The Jets were flagged for illegal procedure. He had to kick it again, from virtually the back line of the end zone.

"For the only time in my life I worried about the possibility of getting it blocked," he admits.

This time he boomed it to the Jets 46. It was returned only four yards. The defense held.

Good things were happening for the Jets, and uncharacteristically bad things were happening for the Colts. Baltimore players were starting to curse in the pileups, their frustration evident. One of their cornerbacks even complained to Sauer, "I was supposed to get help on that pass."

Actually, some of the things going on were, in sportswriters' jargon, "unbelievable."

Sample intercepted a pass at the two-yard line that was meant for Jerry Richardson. As Sample rose with the ball, he tapped it against Richardson's white helmet.

"This is what you're lookin' for," said Sample.

On another play, after Billy Ray Smith took a whack at Schmitt in a pileup, Schmitt snapped, "You do that again and you won't get up."

Amazingly, it was the Jets exhibiting the poise and execution, while the Colts, the NFL's best, were floundering. They had first-and-10 inside the Jets 20-yard line three times in the first half, and came away with nothing. In addition, Lou Michaels missed a field goal from 46 yards (to go along with the 27-yarder he put wide right), and Earl Morrall failed to spot a wide-open Jimmy Orr on the fleaflicker that ended the first half. In the regular season, Morrall had thrown the ball more than 300 times with only 17 interceptions—but he was picked off three times in just 14 passes in the first half alone. The Colts could easily have had a three-touchdown lead at halftime; instead, they were down 7–0 and were looking for answers.

To Baker at linebacker, the Jets defense was doing to the Colts just what the films suggested: "You start watching the films and you see they make the same kind of mistakes as offenses in our league. They had good players, but they had some weaknesses, too."

The Jets defense, as orchestrated by Michaels, actually was a forerunner of the famed Bears stack defense under Buddy Ryan. And Ryan learned much of that from Michaels, to whom he gave scant credit.

"We played a defense that was unconventional at the time," explains Baker. "We stacked our linebackers, and everybody on the Colts had to change their blocking. We did the things we did all year, but they never faced anything like that. I was the left outside linebacker, and most offenses are right-handed. So usually I'd be lined up on the tight end. But we pushed the defensive end to the inside shoulder of the tight end and I'd be behind him. They had to cross-block instead of the straight-ahead blocking, and that killed their momentum."

Shula made a key decision at halftime: He would give Morrall just one more series, and then, if the team didn't move, bring in Unitas.

Trouble was, the first drive of the second half ended in a fumble for the Colts, with Baker pouncing on the loose ball. Shula's plans were doubly disrupted. The Jets had the ball on the Colts 32—and Morrall had another series coming to him.

The Jets wound up with the first of Jim Turner's three field goals, took a 10–0 lead, and then the defense stiffened and Morrall was gone. Unitas came in, but by now the Jets were ahead by 13–0. Unitas was simply going to throw, and the Jets knew it.

Some of the Jets were astounded when they passed near Ewbank on the sidelines as he peered over at Unitas over the center. For Ewbank was coaching his old quarterback again.

"Come on, John, don't throw any interceptions," said Ewbank, forgetting himself.

The Jets defense had no flashbacks. It stacked the system against short passes, since Unitas was unable to throw long. By the time the third quarter ended, the Colts had been limited to only seven plays, for a net gain of 10 yards, in the period.

. . .

In what was to be the last period of Super Bowl III, Namath directed the team to the Colts' six. He stopped by the bench and told Weeb, "I'm not going to take any chances. I'm just going to get on the board. You agree with that?"

Weeb did, and another field goal followed a pair of smashes into the line and gave the Jets a 16–0 edge with 13:10 showing on the clock.

This was showtime for Sample, who carried on a crusade against the NFL. He had been cut by Baltimore, Pittsburgh, and Washington. He never let any of his teammates forget it. The first time he played against an NFL team after joining the Jets—in an exhibition facing the Eagles—he was ejected.

So now Ewbank was concerned about Sample going too far. On a collision near the Colts sideline, Sample was conked on the helmet by Tom Mitchell, who was on the bench. Sample yelled at Shula, "You tell your guys to cut that out. I'll get Mitchell the next time he comes out here!"

A few plays later, the sore-armed Unitas floated a pass toward Jimmy Orr. But it had no zip and Randy Beverly stepped in front of Orr to intercept it—the fourth Jets interception of the game. Sample, watching the play a few yards away, cheered, and in his enthusiasm swatted the helmet of Tom Matte of the Colts.

"It looks bad, buddy," he shouted at Matte, and trotted off toward the Jets bench.

Matte spun and raced toward Sample. The pair confronted each other, but the officials separated them.

"What did you do over at their bench?" Ewbank demanded of Sample.

"Nothing," Sample insisted. "I didn't do nothing."

"Okay, calm down now," said Weeb.

Meanwhile, the clock was ticking. Namath was using it wisely and Snell was pounding the Colts. The Jets got close enough for another Turner attempt, but he missed on a 42-yarder.

Only 6 minutes 34 seconds remained when Unitas got the ball back. He misfired on three straight passes, and was mired on his own 20. But on fourth down Unitas was magnificent again. He threaded a 17-yarder to Orr. Then, on a third-and-10, he hit Mackey for 11. He connected with Richardson for 21 and Orr again for 11.

The Colts got down to the goal line. The Jets held on one play from the two, and two from the one. But Jerry Hill finally plunged over from the one. The Colts had gotten onto the boards with 3:19 remaining. The score was Jets 16, Colts 7.

And then the Colts got their first break. Lou Michaels, as expected, squib-kicked the ball. Sauer, who had dropped a pass early in the game, mishandled the spinning kickoff. Tom Mitchell recovered for the Colts on the Jets 44.

Poise and execution. Larry Grantham told the defensive huddle, "Three minutes. That's $5,000 a minute."

Unitas knew that Grantham, the defensive signal-caller, would call for his teammates to play in a prevent alignment. And Grantham knew that Unitas would be passing every down.

He did. One of his passes brought Matte near the Jets bench. Players were tense, the game hung in the balance. Mike Martin, the son of one of the owners, hooted at Matte.

Even at this moment, Namath understood the social niceties.

"Don't do that," Namath told him. "If we're going to be champions, we have to act like champions. They didn't write what was in the papers. They're trying as hard as they can."

They were, of course, with Unitas directing them. If they could get a touchdown out of this drive, then recover the following kickoff—just as they already had—then they could win the championship with a field goal.

Unitas brought them to the 19, then missed on second and third downs. It was fourth-and-five and he looked for Orr. Grantham raced back into that area to help out Randy Beverly, leaped—and tipped the pass away. Only 2:21 remained.

Almost all of it was chewed up as Snell carried six straight times.

By the time the Colts got the ball back after a Johnson punt, only eight seconds remained. The Jets were world champions. The world was theirs.

When it ended and the first hint of night enveloped the Orange Bowl, an eerie light played on the field. Joe raised his finger skyward, shaking it. If you look at the film of that now, you might even think Joe was admonishing the naughty world for not believing that the Jets could win the Super Bowl.

.   .   .

Under the stands, Phil Iselin was scurrying to the locker room. He had repeatedly asked his friends in the final quarter whether the Jets could hold the lead. They assured him his team could.

He was surrounded by milling fans now and his nervousness hadn't abated. For he hadn't seen the final minutes in his rush to get into position to reach the locker room.

"Is it over?" he asked. Then he asked another question:

"Who won?"

Dave Herman was one of the first Jets into the locker room. His anxiety was ended. Finally, he babbled.

"Bubba! I guess I showed Bubba, I guess I did. I guess I showed big Bubba. . . ."

When Ewbank let in the news media, Namath immediately was surrounded.

"I only want to talk to the New York writers," he said. "They're the only ones who thought we could win."

Nearby, Sample opened his wallet and took out a tattered, two-year-old newspaper clipping. He unfolded it, showing the headline: "KC Not in Class with NFL Best—Lombardi."

Someone told Namath he had won the game's most valuable player award, which came with a Dodge Charger.

"Is that the one I have to give back after a year?" he asked.

Later that night the Jets were in the throes of a party at their hotel. The Colts owner, Carroll Rosenbloom, who lived not far from Werblin on Golden Beach, had his party, too. He had planned it and he was having it, having invited, among others, Senator Edward Kennedy, Vice-President Spiro Agnew, and Commissioner Pete Rozelle.

Rosenbloom, who was to drown in the surf in front of his home years later after a nighttime swim, was in the doldrums.

Kennedy tried to cheer him up. Ted Kennedy and Carroll Rosenbloom went for a swim.

Over at the Jets gala, 400 people showed up. Did any of them really understand what had been accomplished, that this was already a part of a historic happening? That whenever anyone talked about great football moments—make that great sports moments—they would have to mention Super Bowl III?

Iselin introduced Namath to the crowd.

"There's a whole lot of people changing their minds about us now," Joe said. He wasn't gloating. He was serious. "We beat Baltimore in every phase of the game. If there ever was a world champion, this is it."

When he got back to his room, Namath was amused to see a funereal bouquet of flowers that Lou Michaels had sent him as a joke before the game.

The next morning, still high from the great victory, the Jets took off for New York. Oh, one thing they had forgotten in the excitement: They left the Super Bowl trophy behind the front desk in their hotel.

6

Breakdown

Joe was a stubborn sort of guy, although he probably believes that it wasn't hardheadedness that created many of his problems with authority. He thought he was just being true to himself.

He uttered what was to be his most famous quotation—his Super Bowl guarantee—as a defiant anthem for the underdog because of his honesty, and he followed his most glorious moment in sports with his lowest point because of that same sense of integrity.

"I had become a restaurant owner not too long before then," he says. "The place was called Bachelors III. I was proud that I was 'clean.' When you own a restaurant in New York, and you're out among the people, a lot of shady operators come over to you. People had tried to sell me cocaine and other drugs, but I turned them down. The word got out quickly that I didn't mess around. That's why I was so shocked one night after a dinner in New York, where I was sitting with Phil Iselin.

"Phil and I went into a back room where we were joined by the head of NFL security, a former FBI agent. He told me there were 'unsavory' people at the restaurant. According to law-enforcement people who had wiretapped the phones at Bachelors III, it was a hangout for mob characters.

"And I had to get out in 24 hours. Just like that.

"I didn't think I was bigger than the system. It's just that, dammit, it wasn't right. They wouldn't give and I wouldn't give. So I quit. I was 25 years old, with a Super Bowl ring, and I was out of football."

It was less than five months after the Super Bowl. The Jets' moment—Joe's moment—was suddenly forgotten, perhaps even a bit tarnished. Training camp was scheduled to start within a month, and instead of the Jets followers and players becoming excited about the defense of their title, a cloud hovered.

This pattern of a great fall following a great victory or moment would shadow the club throughout its history. Joe's was merely the most noted.

"I went for a walk in Central Park," recalls Joe. "I sat down and saw a place filled with people playing with their children, or walking arm-in-arm, or playing with their puppies. At that moment, I thought to myself, 'What do these people care about football and my problem? There's so many other things that are more important to them.' I thought Commissioner Pete Rozelle was wrong, but I decided to return to the Jets. It taught me a lesson: that life wasn't fair. Before that moment, if something happened that I didn't like, I said, bull, I won't stand for it, and I did what I thought I should do. Now, I compromised. I was really sad about it. I was a little boy who had to do something he felt wasn't fair."

But the Jets' Super Bowl victory was part of a continuum of football life, and like all great moments in sports, it was too quickly ended. The business of getting on with the future took over, and the harsh realities of sports as the 1970s approached—money, stadiums, fandom, television, unions—conspired to change the Jets.

Just days after the great victory, Ewbank's chief defensive lieutenant, Clive Rush, left to become head coach of the Boston Patriots. He was followed soon by George Sauer, Sr., the Jets' head talent scout, who took over as the Pats' general manager.

Namath's retirement lasted six weeks, starting in early June.

Many of the Super Bowl Jets reflected on their moment in the Miami sun almost 30 years later when they came together for a reunion at Weeb Ewbank Hall, an enclave on the grounds of Hofstra University in Hempstead, Long Island. Rather than being "in their ruin," as were Dylan Thomas's "Boys of Summer," these Jets were an upbeat group of guys hardly wishing for what was once upon a time. But they didn't like what had happened to the franchise in the years since.

"We were the forgotten few," said Randy Beverly, the cornerback who intercepted Super Bowl passes thrown by Morrall and Unitas. "People don't remember us. They remember the win."

To linebacker Ralph Baker, who also is a former Jets coach, "Some of the older players were alienated when the team changed the logo back in the '70s. Changing the logo was a slap. I don't know if that was the intention of management then. But now," he said on the eve of the 1996 season that was to end with a 1–15 record and yet another housecleaning, "it's one big happy family again." For a while, at any rate.

That family began its disintegration right after the Super Bowl. Why, the players actually wanted more money. So here was this untenable situation: Ewbank the coach on the one hand stroking his guys, telling them how much better they were than the Colts, pumping them up with their success; and then, suddenly, after their victory, Ewbank the general manager denying them what they considered their due.

"It seemed that we tried to make too many changes too quickly and Weeb let a lot of guys go," suggests Baker now. "Probably a key in hindsight is that he never re-signed Bob Talamini. Then, when we played the Chiefs the following year in the '69 playoffs, Rasmussen got hurt and we didn't have a competent backup. We got down to the one-yard line and we couldn't get in. KC had a tremendously big line and linebackers."

The Jets had finished first again in 1969, posted a 10–4 record. In the fourth quarter of the playoff game against the Chiefs, trailing by 6–3, they had three cracks at the goal line. A Namath bootleg failed. So did two other rushes. Turner kicked a field goal to tie the score.

But two plays later, Len Dawson led the Chiefs into the end zone, first connecting with Otis Taylor on a 61-yard pass play, and then the final 19 yards to Gloster Richardson. It was the only touch-down of the game.

The Chiefs went on to defeat the Raiders in the last AFL title game ever played, and then smashed the Vikings in capturing Super Bowl IV. And the Jets went on to the failed 1970s, and beyond.

By the time the seventies began, Curley Johnson was also gone. "He was the most spirited leader of the team," suggests Baker. Another cut-up, Rocky Rochester, was dropped as well. John Sample's days had ended, as had those of Billy Baird and Bake Turner.

"Weeb," says Baker now, "would die in this era if he had to handle money."

Baker reflected on Talamini's departure—"I think it was over a thousand dollars." Curley, in fact, recalls now, "If I knew that's all it was, I would have come up with the money myself."

The team unraveled over money, it seemed. Money and fighting over money seemed to obsess everyone, especially when some players were turned down after asking for minimal increases.

"The standing joke," said Baker, "was that Weeb would tell us, 'Don't tell the other guy who plays the same position as you what you're making.' And we'd say, 'Don't worry, Weeb, we're as embarrassed about it as you are.' "

His players still refer to Weeb with affection and respect. But you also get the feeling they blame him for the decline and fall of the Jets.

"When you get rid of veteran ballplayers and replace them with rookies, the level goes down," contends Maynard. "Nobody outran me for 15 years."

Inevitably, players think about their own dismissal when they analyze a club's problems. It is no different for Maynard; he feels even today he could have continued catching Joe's passes. Then again, Maynard is unhappy with any coach who ever cut him. He still remembers the Giants' Allie Sherman with disdain.

"Here's something people don't know," Maynard says with pride. "I was the only guy who played for the Titans, Jets, and Giants."

Money, and age, broke up that Super Bowl team, said Beverly.

"I got $12,500 for the 1968 season," he recalled. He earned

$25,000 for the Super Bowl victory. "I had the two interceptions that game. I asked Weeb about a raise for the next season. I said, 'I'd like a $1,500 increase,' and he said, 'You're pricing yourself out of the league.'"

Herman, who handled Bubba Smith so well in the Super Bowl, allowing him only once within whispering distance of Namath, said he had been at a card-signing show recently and people started to ask him about the old days.

"Jets fans haven't forgotten," said Herman. "They want to re-member."

There just wasn't time for the Jets to capitalize on Super Bowl III, although there was one last, fine moment: their victory over the Giants. It may have been only a summer exhibition game, but to both teams and to New York's fans, it was Super Bowl IV.

Back then, many of the teams' players were living in Manhattan. Players regularly came across one another in P.J. Clarke's or other midtown bars, but they had never met on the field.

That was to change seven months after Super Bowl III. A funny thing began to evolve: The game took on an aura beyond anything either team could have imagined. The Giants had been only a 7–7 team the year before, but many of them considered the Jets' victory a fluke.

Ewbank had inadvertently given the Jets-Giants confrontation a significance beyond its real value when he said the game was for "the braggin' rights in New York."

"We were the Super Bowl champions," Rasmussen recalls, "but it seemed like it wasn't official until we beat the Giants."

Years later, Ewbank admitted, "When we went to the Super Bowl, we felt we could win. But this one I wasn't sure about."

The game took on incredible meaning and tension to Sherman, the Giants' coach. He was reeling. The Giants had become medio-cre, they had dropped their opening exhibition game to the Pack-ers, and he approached this game as if his future depended on it.

Weeb, meanwhile, employed one of his little psychological tricks: He named the Jets' three original Titans—Maynard, Grantham, and Mathis—as cocaptains.

The game was staged not in New York or New Jersey, but at the Yale Bowl in New Haven, Connecticut. Even an assistant football coach from West Point, Bill Parcells, drove to the game. He was rooting for the Jets.

It was a game in which the Jets were driven into a frenzy when a rookie named Mike Battle returned a punt 86 yards for a touchdown, hurdling the Giants' Dave Lewis directly in front of the Jets' bench. Namath went on to complete 14 of 16 passes for three touchdowns. The Jets clobbered the Giants.

Within a few weeks, Sherman was fired and the long ruin of the Giants was underway. The Jets? Wasn't everything coming up roses, as Wismer had suggested years before?

Yet Jets fans lost sight of their heroes at the one moment they should have been the most visible team in sports. For in that summer of 1969, the Mets made it to the World Series, capping their own Impossible Dream story—and at the same time keeping the Jets out of Shea Stadium and away from their hometown fans for almost half the football season. That's right, after winning the Super Bowl, the Jets couldn't even bring the celebration home. They played their first five games on the road in 1969.

Although they did not play their first home game until October 20, the Jets won their division in a final gasp of glory. But they bowed to the Super Bowl–bound Chiefs in their final AFL playoff game.

Weeb was about to preside over a steep decline—to 4–10 in 1970, followed by 6–8, 7–7, then 4–10. In fact, the Jets were not to post another winning record until 1981.

Bad things began to happen to them early as the 1970s dawned. There was a three-week, NFL-wide training camp strike. Then they opened up the decade as costars of the first *Monday Night Football* game on ABC, but bowed to the Browns.

More excitement came when they faced the Colts for the first time since Super Bowl III. But Joe fractured his right wrist and the Jets lost 29–22 to fall to 1–4. We think of Joe as being fragile and missing time, but he had not missed a regular-season game because of injury in his first five years. Now he was to be sidelined for the remaining nine games.

Okay, injuries happen. But Joe would be coming back in 1971, wouldn't he? First, 1971 would put Jets fans on a roller-coaster. The all-pro receiver, George Sauer, suddenly announced his retirement in April, aborting a five-year career. In June, Verlon Biggs, the defensive-line anchor, became the first Jet to exercise his option—indeed, one of the first players in league history—after he failed to get the raise he wanted. He left to sign with the Redskins, who yielded a pair of draft choices.

Yet, in this seeming gloom, Joe was coming back. And the Jets had this crushing rookie runner, John Riggins from Kansas, who could step right in for the faltering Snell.

All was right with the world as the Jets opened their preseason against the Detroit Lions. Of course, the game was played in another of those neutral sites the league always found for the Jets: Tampa, Florida. The Jets were famous for opening new territories, or for testing the expansionist waters, for the league. It came about because of the Mets' refusal to give over Shea during the summer, when the Mets played and the grass grew and Mrs. Charles Shipman Payson didn't want her lovely garden trampled by men in cleats—even though Shea was owned by the people of New York.

Thus, over the years, the Jets played exhibitions in Abilene, Texas; Mobile, Alabama; Greenville, South Carolina; Lowell, Massachusetts; New Brunswick, New Jersey; Kingston, Pennsylvania; Norfolk, Virginia; Allentown, Pennsylvania; Winston-Salem, North Carolina; Montreal; Memphis; Phoenix; and even Yankee Stadium.

Joe was frisky at Tampa—too much so. On the field for the first time in 10 months, he attempted to make a tackle when Detroit recovered a fumble. He seriously injured his left knee. Nicholas operated as soon as they got back to New York.

Namath didn't play again until November 28, missing 19 straight games going back to the 1970 season. He returned in the second quarter against San Francisco, and he was magical. He tossed for 358 yards and three touchdowns, but the Jets lost by three points.

Through some upbeat moments there remained a troubling undercurrent on the squad, however. The Jets had become just another team, albeit with football's most famous quarterback.

The venality of the game was symbolized by an exchange between Weeb and one of his best players, defensive end Gerry Philbin, the undersized performer who gave it everything he had.

A year after the Super Bowl, Philbin had injured a shoulder so

badly that when he wasn't playing he walked around with a har-
ness. A one-time all-star, he played hurt and his effectiveness
dropped. Philbin went in for his annual contract talk with Ewbank,
who told him, "You haven't had an all-star year." Philbin replied,
"I've been playing hurt and all I want is a token raise."

Weeb regarded him and said, "We're not in the business of
charity."

When Philbin tearfully related that story to teammates and
friends, they were hit with the realization that what everything
came down to, despite the Super Bowl, depite the mantra of togetherness, was money. Of course, deep down everyone must have
known this. But on the Jets the adventure had seemed something
more—a cause, perhaps. Okay, it was a fun cause and it was great
to be able to laugh in the face of the Establishment and the odds-
makers. But Weeb's negotiations also showed the difficulty he
faced attempting to cajole and teach and be benevolent and strict
—and then demeaning his players when it came to contract time.

Years later, Philbin's great friend and backer, Bill Mazer the
broadcaster, was walking down the street in Manhattan when he
spotted Weeb taking a stroll with Iselin. Weeb had been smarting
over Mazer's telling the story of how Philbin had been treated. But
on this day, Weeb went over to Mazer and said, "I made a mistake."

It wasn't the only one. As the Jets declined in the early 1970s,
Weeb was pressed into sharing his duties. He had to make a choice,
one or the other, coach or general manager.

So early in 1973, he made a startling announcement: He was
going to step down as coach after the 1973 season—and his son-in-
law Charley Winner, who had been the Cardinals' head coach and
now was a Jets assistant, would replace him. Meanwhile, Weeb
would stay on as general manager through Charley's first season
of 1974, and then retire.

It was tricky business: the father-in-law in the front office, theoretically in charge of his son-in-law the head coach. It couldn't
work, and ultimately it didn't.

. . .

Weeb Ewbank was 90 years old when I got his attention one day
to reminisce. It was almost 30 years after the Super Bowl. He

was home in Oxford, Ohio, about to celebrate his 71st wedding anniversary with Lucy.

Weeb still rarely talks of the drama inherent in what he was part of. If there is a shock of recognition that his team was to be the transition between two eras of football—indeed, all team sports—he doesn't let on. His life in football was merely a series of good breaks or bad breaks, obstacles to overcome, an interesting cast of characters to sit in with.

He is credited with using psychology on his Super Bowl Jets—talking to them of how they had been abandoned by the NFL and giving them a reason to whip the big, bad Colts and their big, bad league. Perhaps he did. He doesn't quite remember doing that. Or maybe, when he went to school just after World War I, they didn't talk much about psychology. Maybe it was just old-fashioned smarts.

"I did talk to them about where they had been," he concedes. "But I did a similar thing with the Colts in '58. We had a theme with Baltimore: Learn, Study, and Be Known. I wanted them to think of being on a high level, and the Giants were a great team back then. But we had seven Hall of Famers on the Colts team that played the Giants. Still, we had to replace them eventually, and that was my thinking with the Jets after we won the Super Bowl.

"The Jets were thinking they could be the team of the '70s. But they were almost unheard of after that. We had injuries in '69 and couldn't make adjustments in the playoffs."

Still, what went wrong with the Jets after Super Bowl III? No mystery to Weeb.

"It goes in cycles," he said. "And sometimes you can't replace guys. It was easier for us before agents came in and money became so important. On both the '68 Jets and '58 and '59 Colts—those players would have played for nothing. And what we had over other teams was teamwork."

Certainly, Weeb must have observed the phenomenon of losing that infected the Jets in the post–Super Bowl years—how his successors posted records of 141–209–2, leading to Parcells's coronation in 1997. In the 24 years from Weeb to Bill there were nine head coaches, including two interim leaders.

Weeb won't talk about the Jets losing.

"When I don't see the games or the practices, I can't criticize," he explains. "I thought Coslet was a mighty fine coach. I never dwelled on what happened to the Jets. I figured if they wanted me to, they would have asked me. I never said why or where. But I know the first thing they did wrong was when they changed the color of the helmet, and I know that was wrong. I still see Leon and Norma Hess when they go to Indianapolis. That's about as far as I'll go to see the Jets. I'm scared to death of flying."

Weeb is reminded that his players called him a tightwad, that he refused Beverly's request, and others'.

"I know some of them thought so, but I think they realized I never tried to get someone for less than they were worth. But it was worse to overpay."

And what about bringing in his son-in-law to succeed him?

"Here's what I said to Phil Iselin: 'Here's a man you should talk to.' See, Charley played for me at Washington University in St. Louis. When it came to putting my staff together in Baltimore, Blanton Collier said to me, 'Aren't you going to take Charley?' and I said, 'Gee, he's my son-in-law.'

"Well, I wasn't good to him. I sent him out scouting during Christmas. I left no reason for people to think I favored him."

If all Weeb did was say to Iselin, "Here's a man you should talk to," then even that halting suggestion must have made quite an impact. Iselin did not even interview anyone else for the Jets head-coaching job.

The team by then was merely a Super Bowl memory as so many players drifted away.

"What we tried to do was keep them from getting too old," Weeb explained. "That's what happened with the Colts. It's why we let Curley go. On the Colts there was Marchetti, Donovan, Pellington. Shula milked them for a few years. You know, I told Curley once that I let him go too soon, and he was 33 years old."

Still, Weeb's legacy is that he brought pro football championships to two cities and in two different leagues. He knows the numbers and he is proudly defiant in reciting them.

"It makes me sick to my stomach when they take me off the list of who won more than one Super Bowl. Why, in '58 and '59 we were the Super Bowl teams, only they didn't call it the Super Bowl then."

And did he have a favorite between the Jets and Colts?

"I guess," he said, "I love 'em all."

.   .   .

Weeb's last year also started with an eviction. Once again, the Mets had made it to the World Series, so this time the Jets played their first *six* games away from home. By the time they returned to Shea it was almost November and they were 2–4. They won only two more games that year.

The Ewbank era ended after 11 seasons with a negative distinction: O. J. Simpson came into Shea Stadium on the final day of the 1973 campaign needing 197 yards to become the first player to amass 2,000 yards in a season. No one ever goes into a game figuring on churning out 200 yards, and fans can't anticipate such a game. But pro football turned its eyes to Shea that wintry day.

What should have been a football farewell to Weeb instead became a celebration of O. J. Simpson. And it was Weeb who was in his ruin.

Before that last game, Weeb reflected on his career and perhaps was a bit defensive about how it was winding up. Too bad. It had been great.

"My coaching career has been much different from other people's," he recalled. "My first job in high school was in a situation where all the seniors had graduated and I had to start over. Then I took a college that was amateur at Washington University of St. Louis. One of my assistants said they wouldn't even give a kid the time of day there. Yet in two years we won 14 games and lost four.

"When I went to Baltimore it was an abominable situation, and when I came to the Jets it was even worse. But I managed to win three championships in 20 years, which I think is a pretty good average when you consider teams like the Steelers and the 49ers have never won one."

Hmmm. If Weeb could have looked down the road the next 20 years, he would have seen that the Jets were destined to win zero championships, while the Steelers and 49ers were to capture eight between them. They became models of how to build teams, of the value of—indeed, the need for—a strong man at the top, while the Jets went through a succession of erratic bumblings with no philosophical strongman.

Still, how would Weeb know that then? How could anyone have realized that the Jets' days without a strong, competent leader to furnish direction were over?

"Without mentioning names," Weeb continued in his monologue, "there are some people who have much better records overall, but they inherited their teams. They never had to put a team together and that, I think, is the most difficult problem.

"I think I've been successful at building teams for three reasons: I've been able to recognize talent and see the potential in a young guy; I've had the patience to stick with players; and I've been able to place them in positions where they do the team the most good. This season was very disappointing to me because I sincerely felt we had a good team. Naturally, I would've liked to go out a winner. I wanted to leave our owners and our great fans with a reasonable opportunity to have a good team, which I think we have. There will be no necessity to make any wholesale changes."

His grip on the past was more secure than his hold on the future.

When the game was over Ewbank was tearful. He had seen his career come to an end with thousands of people cheering on Simpson, who ran roughshod over a defense orchestrated by Weeb's son-in-law.

Simpson, on a snowy afternoon, had got his record, and even the Jets congratulated him when he got out of the pile after his final carry had carried him to the milestone.

How could America know that over the next few years Ewbank's image would slowly be forgotten, while Simpson would become a nationwide icon? In victory, Simpson was beaming but hardly showoffy. At the postgame news conference he brought along the other 10 members of the offense. O.J. wowed the largest news audience he had had to that time by thanking each member of the offense individually. He was described as "thoughtful" and "gracious."

"I may not always look it," the smooth Simpson said, "but I'm aggressive."

Meanwhile, the Jets held their own ceremony honoring Ewbank. Of course, they didn't know it, but they were also paying homage to the last of a Jets era.

First, Winston Hill, the affable plush-toy-sized tackle, led the team in the traditional prayer. Kneeling, and with a hefty arm around the roly-poly coach, Winnie said, "Thanks, Lord, for our rich relationship with Weeb. We want to thank you for Weeb."

Then Dave Herman gave him a gold watch.

Weeb started to thank the players as they formed a semicircle around him. But he began to cry. So did the players.

"It's a great game, it's a great life," the 66-year-old said. "I let you down. Don't let things like this get you down."

The next day Vice-President Weeb began the task of finding a place for the Jets to practice. He also suggested that the city should enclose Shea Stadium and put down artificial turf.

"Then," he said, "we'd have a stadium."

He was an administrator for his final year, when his presence began to evoke immediate Jets failures rather than his rich record of success. He had bowed out of football with a regular-season record of 130–129–7. With the Jets, it was 71–77–6 over 11 years, in only two of which the Jets made the playoffs. When his name came up for nomination to the Pro Football Hall of Fame in Canton, some voters dismissed him on that mediocre career winning record. One game over .500.

Then again, one game was all the Jets ever needed to become a legend in their time.

7

Jet Lag

Now Charley Winner was in charge, and on his first day running the training camp in 1974 he had one veteran, thanks to a players' strike. Over the next 15 years, labor unrest was to be a theme that haunted and hurt the Jets whenever a strike or crisis with management loomed.

I believe that these situations became more contentious on the Jets than with most clubs because of the same problem that would infuse the team for almost 30 years after the Super Bowl: no strongman at the helm to halt a slide. There was no one the players could feel would be there no matter how badly things went. No anchor.

As Boomer Esiason would analyze that long losing slope, "You have to look at Steinberg, Gutman, and Hess," he said of the men who were general manager, president, and owner during his three Jets years, 1993–95.

Charley had joined the team after a stormy tenure with the St. Louis Cardinals, where there was a revolt of black players who claimed they had been discriminated against. Winner, a good guy who couldn't control his coaching staff, suffered as the target of those charges.

Charley was a small man—probably the smallest in the entire organization, on or off the field—but he had a huge appetite for food. It went back to his time as a German prisoner of war.

"I vowed I'd never go hungry again," he explained to me one night over pasta. Have dinner with Charley, and you'd find people staring at you as he launched into a plate of spaghetti like a dive bomber.

More than 50 years after World War II, I asked Charley about that experience. He claims today that it didn't affect him psychologically or physically, but that it made him appreciate "what we have in this country." It is quite a story:

"We were on our 17th mission, flying over Hamburg. I was a radio operator and gunner on a B-17. You flew in a formation of 12 planes and the first one is supposed to show us where to drop the bombs, but he never did. So we had to circle back, and we were the last plane over the target. By the time we got there the flak was heavy because they were going at us the whole time. We got hit right near the cockpit. It killed the pilot.

"I had to bail out and landed in some guy's garden outside of Hamburg. I saw a bunch of young women running toward me and I thought they were greeting me. But they were running to grab the parachute fabric. And then the ground troops with their rifles came.

"They put us in a truck and took us to a small jail. The people from the town were throwing stones at us and spit at us. They had been told that American pilots were guys that had been in prisons and that they had been let out so they could bomb Germany. They called us 'Luftgangsters.' "

Charley was in a stalag along with 10,000 other British and American flyers, almost all of whom had been shot down.

"I always said if I got out of that prison camp I would never waste any food. You know how it is when guys in the service get together, they talk about girls. But after a week in a prisoner of war camp you talk about what you're going to eat when you get out. We used to create some fantastic meals in our mind. We'd start with the appetizers and go around the room and each of us would talk about what we'd have for the next course."

Six weeks after being captured, he was liberated by the Russians. Nothing much seemed to bother him after that.

. . .

Charley's Jets started out 1–7 in his first season, and they had the Giants coming up. Namath, still audacious, suggested the Jets could win their final six games to finish at .500. They did, and that simple fact may have helped mess up the Jets for the rest of the 1970s.

But first there was that victory over the Giants, Joe's last hurrah.

Joe's season had been miserable to that point: 17 interceptions in the eight games. The Jets had lost six straight. He always did toss his share, but now with the team breaking down, with his pass-blocking collapsed, Namath was exposed every play. He was 31 years old and he was going nowhere with a lost team.

This time he came out firing and completed his first seven passes. Then in the fourth quarter, with the Jets down by seven points, Joe went into the huddle with the Jets on the Giants' three-yard line. He called a handoff to Boozer for a running play off right tackle. That's not what Joe had in the back of his mind, though.

He took the snap and saw that Giants linebacker Brad Van Pelt was running to the inside. Joe decided to keep the ball.

"I didn't tell Boozer," Joe said. "I didn't tell anybody. The fake always works better that way."

Boozer meanwhile thought that Namath had fumbled. He didn't know where Joe was.

Joe was circling to his left in a stiff-kneed hobble. He wobbled untouched into the end zone. Just as he was about to cross it, two Giants zeroed in on him. But he put up his right hand as if ordering them, "Don't touch me." And they didn't. People (the Raiders don't qualify) never gratuitously tackled Joe Namath. They understood what he meant to the game and they understood his bad knees.

So the Jets tied the game and then produced the first overtime victory in NFL regular-season play. The Jets were rolling.

Unfortunately, they won all their remaining games.

After finishing the 1974 season at 7–7, Winner and the brain trust figured that 1975 was going to be their year. Why, all they needed was a pass-rusher. So the Jets unwisely traded their number-one draft pick in 1975 to the New Orleans Saints and acquired Billy Newsome, himself a former number-one draft choice. Lately, he had been an unhappy Saint.

It was the first time in Jets' history they traded away their first-round pick. Then with their second-round selection they chose one of college football's glamour players, Anthony Davis, the Southern California running back.

The eve of that fateful draft day, marking the decline of the Jets' front office, was punctuated by the team's discovery that three veteran defensive players had signed contracts with the World Football League months earlier. The Jets were shocked to learn that Mark Lomas and Ed Galigher, the starting ends whom the team hoped to sign, had actually planned to quit. So did Bill Ferguson, a backup linebacker.

The revelations about Galigher and Lomas probably played a part in the Jets' stunning decision to trade away their top pick for Newsome, although Winner denied it.

"You don't know what a rookie might be able to do," Winner reasoned, "but you know Newsome can step in and be a starter for a long time."

The Jets also mortgaged part of their future, trading fourth-, sixth-, and seventh-round picks for players who never made a difference.

Newsome lasted two seasons. The last time I ever heard his name mentioned was in a newspaper story I picked up. It had a Denver dateline and it said that Billy Newsome had menaced his wife with a loaded revolver.

Davis, meanwhile, never played a game for the Jets. Although he had broken O.J.'s rushing records at USC, he claimed he wasn't sure if he wanted to play baseball or football, or soccer, and even if it was to be football, maybe he was better off in Canada. They were offering him more money there.

Ultimately, he signed with the Southern California Sun of the

World Football League. It folded. In 1976 he went to the Toronto Argonauts of the Canadian League, but he broke his leg. In 1977 he switched to the Tampa Bay Bucs and his former USC coach, John McKay. The next year he went to the Houston Oilers and then the Rams.

Then Davis quit football. He tried films. He played minor roles for four years, then suddenly surfaced again at the age of 30 with the Los Angeles Express of the United States Football League in 1983.

"It's still in my blood to play football," he said.

This was the type of personnel the Jets under Charley thought could produce a winning franchise. Everyone on the team was suffering from delusions in the wake of that season-ending six-game winning streak, the acquisition of the monster pass-rusher Newsome, the drafting of Davis.

So when the 1975 exhibition season started, the idea was to play the veterans and get a sense of winning under their belt. It, too, was a flawed strategy, and it taught me something very simple about preseason play: The team that wants to win will win. All you have to do is leave in your veterans when the opposition takes a look at its rookies.

Thus, the Jets roared through the 1975 preseason by winning four of five games, three against playoff teams.

This was my first daily experience covering a football team, yet I wondered about something. The other team always seemed to score on the first drive—Fran Tarkenton leading the Vikings, Jim Hart of the Cardinals, the Redskins' Billy Kilmer. They ran over the Jets' first-string defense.

And then, when these experienced veterans sat on the bench in the second quarter or after halftime, the Jets' regulars were still in there. The Jets were fooling themselves and their public by winning in August.

I remember Helen Dillon getting on the plane after one of these victories and beaming, in that infectious, enthusiastic way, "Boy, we really look good, don't we?" I agreed.

But Larry Fox of the *Daily News,* whom old-fashioned journalists would describe as a "veteran scribe," cautioned me, "Don't get excited. It's just a preseason game." Odd, I thought, that here was a neutral putting it in perspective, and yet one of the owners didn't get it. If an owner doesn't get it, then the team is in trouble.

Of course, a great reason for optimism was a healthy Joe. He flirted with the World Football League, but instead signed again with the Jets for what was described as a contract making him one of the wealthiest athletes in the world—$450,000 a year. When I asked Iselin about it, he put his arms around me and whispered, "Jerry, he makes more money than I do." And Phil was so happy about it, he was cooing.

Joe's signing created excitement that summer among the players, who anticipated that for the first time since the Super Bowl days Joe might be able to put back-to-back injury-free seasons together.

"It's so good to have the massa back on the plantation," the diminutive receiver Eddie Bell said.

On Joe's first day of practice, Ken Shipp, the offensive coordinator, was hardly enthusiastic, even though Namath had brought in three pages of notes to show him. Shipp was one of those old-fashioned types who believed a player should be in camp on opening day.

But others celebrated his return. Hill hadn't practiced because of a foot injury, but as one of Namath's prime protectors, he felt he should hobble out to his tackle spot. And David Knight, a receiver from an unlikely university—the small, elite William & Mary—brought his longhaired sensitivity to the job in reflecting on Namath.

"Catching a pass from Joe," he told me, "is like listening to a Rolling Stones concert."

No wonder coaches couldn't understood David. He was just too human.

The only exhibition game the Jets lost was filled with irony. It came against the Giants, who were mired in their 15-year decline. The Jets were in position to win at the end. Pat Leahy, a field-goal kicker who had come up the year before when the incumbent, the British-born Bobby Howfield (known as "the Limey"), was injured, had a chip-shot for the winner. The man who snapped the ball was Joe Fields, a rookie the Jets had taken on the 14th round.

Of all the players the Jets drafted in 1975, Fields was the only one to make it into the 1980s. In fact, if you want a reason for the Jets' slumber of the seventies, take a look at the 1974 draft as well; no one from that draft made it into the 1980s either. That year's number-one pick was the world's largest cream puff, Carl Barzilauskas, defensive tackle.

Thus, two straight drafts generated a total of one long-term starter. When the Jets ended the decade, rather than have a core of players in their fifth and sixth seasons, they had mostly younger players. It took years—the rest of the 1970s, in fact—for the Jets to live down 1974 and 1975.

Fields had played for Widener College outside Philadelphia. Originally it was known as Penn Military Colleges. Whatever its name, it had sent only one player of note to the big-time, Billy (White Shoes) Johnson.

Fields was a kid in a dreamworld. But he had this knack of snapping a football on a swift and true spiral, able to maneuver the ball between his legs so that the laces wound up in the holder's hands facing forward. Kickers never want to see the laces.

On the biggest snap of his young professional life, Fields, the rookie center, tossed the ball high. It sailed over the head of the holder, Greg Gantt. The Jets lost.

The next morning, I knocked on the door of Fields's dorm room. I figured he was a goner, that he knew he had just blown his chance.

He said, "Come on in." He lay comfortably on his bed, arms folded behind his head, and spoke easily about the snap.

"You're here because you think I'm going to get fired, right?" he said to me.

If he was nervous about that possibility, he didn't let on. Instead, he just talked easily about the poor snap, about how he had rushed it, twirling it before he was really ready. He seemed unconcerned about his future, although to me and a few other colleagues there it was almost as if he had committed the ultimate act of incompetence, blowing a play against the Giants.

Years later, Fields told me, "I couldn't understand what you guys were so excited about."

Despite the gaffe, the Jets won their next two preseason games and were going to end the exhibition season against the Patriots. And then a week after that was opening day up in Buffalo. The 4–1 preseason Jets were on a roll.

But the Jets never played that final preseason game. It was scheduled against the Patriots in New Haven, where the Jets' fortunes had turned for the better the previous year.

Instead, on Saturday night, the Patriots, all excited about so-called "freedom" issues and led by their player rep, the pint-sized receiver Randy Vataha, voted to strike because there was no contract between the union and the NFL. Vataha was described as having been "a radical at Stanford" by the Rams' loud-mouthed owner, Carroll Rosenbloom.

The strike action at first confused the Jets. And then it split them. Loud-mouthed players, many of little talent but airing their grievances, began to call for a Jets strike, too. By the time the Jets returned to New York on Monday, ostensibly to begin preparing for the start of the 1975 season, the team was in turmoil.

In a confusion-filled locker room where, one player said, "It took an hour to explain what we were voting about," the Jets voted to strike. They became the second team to go out.

Ostensibly, it was to show support for the Patriots, but really it was about the haves and the have-nots. Namath was against the strike. So was the enigmatic John Riggins.

To be fair, John was an enigma only if you didn't listen. He laid everything out. John had an exterior soul.

He was the most fluid big runner I had ever seen. But that was no secret. Everyone knew just how good he was, how he generated 769 yards as a rookie, and followed that up with 944 more the next season.

Over those two years he earned a total of $87,000 while carrying the ball 387 times. Namath was earning a quarter of a million dollars a year.

When Riggins's second season ended, Weeb sent him a bonus check. It was for $1,500.

"It would have been more if you got 1,000 yards," Weeb wrote.

The note and the money radicalized the radical-leaning Riggins. He was never quite the same after that—either on the field, or internally.

Soon, he held out. He opted to remain home in Centralia, Kansas, where the 499 other residents noticed he was doing funny things to his hair. He shaved most of his head and sported a Mohawk. He was not coming back to the Jets, he claimed.

Eventually, he realized what football was all about at a certain level: "I was a great admirer of Weeb as a coach," he explained later. "As a general manager, Weeb and I never saw eye to eye." That 1,000-yard figure, he understood, "looks better in print. From that point on, I took a more businesslike approach to the game."

The Mohawk was merely one of many dome-toppers. Once, he showed up bald. And then there was the time he grew an Afro with his naturally curly hair. Sometimes he'd show up in blue denim overalls, looking like the world's biggest hayseed at six-three and 240 pounds.

"I wanted to show everyone I was the boss. Of what? Of my own destiny, I guess. I always wanted a Mohawk as a kid and my parents wouldn't let me have one. Suddenly, I realized I wasn't a kid any longer. Or, maybe, I was more of a kid."

Now, in 1975, he looked at himself as the Jets' best player. Everyone was talking about Joe and his gaudy contract. Riggins was earning $63,000. He decided that summer he would never play another year for the Jets.

Everyone seemed to know that except management. I'd watch practice and note how he separated himself from the team. After a play, he'd find a little bit of space, plunk down his helmet, and sit on top of it, as if watching the world from his private dome. Then he'd stir himself back up, take the handoff, churn out his yardage by toppling defenders like matchsticks, and return to sit on his helmet.

Meanwhile, strike talk heated up over the summer. The Jets' player rep, Richard Neal, handed his teammates misinformation about the state of negotiations. Players took a hard line. They shouted about issues and they hollered that management was unfair in talks to the union, even though no one there had been at any contract talks.

Despite the "strike," the offensive line and linebackers sat with their coaches in meetings. Some strike. Most players went home.

The wide receivers convened at one of the players' houses to discuss plays.

Meanwhile, Namath loosened up by throwing to his receivers on the practice field while some of the linemen played touch football.

The man running the Jets on a daily basis had been general manager for six months. He was Al Ward, who had been an assistant to Tex Schramm on the Cowboys but had never run an operation like this. Some operation. Al was a pleasant man with a courtly manner whose brief term was a disaster.

He tried to open talks with Riggins, who always put him off. "We'll talk later," was the line. Or Riggins would tell him to wait to see what kind of season he had.

Al also had the unpleasant job of kicking the Jets off the practice grounds since they were on strike.

Imagine a factory where the employees say they're not coming in to work, but they show up to use the gym, shower, hold meetings, bring in food, go home. That's what was happening in the surreal atmosphere of the Jets' camp. No one was really mad at Jets management. The players thought they were making a statement against the NFL's high-handed negotiating committee.

Kicked out of the camp they really wanted to be in, on Tuesday the Jets went to a public park to work out—Eisenhower Park, a few minutes away. Everyone was there except Namath and Boozer. Joe stayed away because there was a clause in his contract that said if he got hurt in a nonteam activity, he would not be paid for his absence.

Everything conspired against the Jets. Their opening-day opponent—if the game was ever to be played—was Buffalo. And the Bills refused to strike. They were blithely practicing for the Jets, who were running around unsupervised at a public park without their quarterback.

Finally, on Thursday, three days before the opening game, the strike was settled. The Jets came back, but to an acrimonious and confused locker room. Whatever they had felt for one another in the wake of the six-game winning streak that put the exclamation point on their previous season, they were now a bunch of disorganized performers.

Even one of the Bills saw this. "The Jets are a little bit divided and we're pretty much united," suggested linebacker John Skor-upan.

The Jets were creamed by 42–14. So much for the six-game winning streak carryover from 1974, so much for all those presea-son victories, so much for draft-day dealings, so much for the franchise. That was the beginning of the end for a nice guy, Charley Winner.

This was the start of my tenure covering the New York Jets football team.

"You know, I thought with the winning streak in 1974, I thought we could do pretty well next season," says Charley, affable as ever, more than two decades later. "And we did well in the exhibition season. But then there was the strike and some things were said that hurt the team's togetherness later on. I don't think we ever came back from that. I can remember some of the meetings among the players, and they never felt close after that, and I believe that hurt our football team."

Charley couldn't put the Jets together by the force of will because that wasn't his style. It was, believe it or not, almost out of his hands.

"I couldn't force the players to play. There was nothing managers or owners could do about it," he claims today. "The major thing in a situation like that was to stick together, but some ugly things were said. It was hard to get back on the same page when it started to unravel."

Charley's finale for the Jets occurred at Baltimore later that sea-son. His Jets were smashed by 52–19, their sixth straight loss. During the game, Jets teammates fought on the sidelines, a symbol of the team's descent into chaos. One of the players involved was Galigher, whom Charley had lobbied to keep.

Now, from the safety and comfort of retirement in Fort Myers, Florida, Charley Winner understands his Jets days were doomed.

Was he worried about replacing his father-in-law?

"Yes, I was," he admits. "The day of the press conference I was almost ready to decline the job. There was a little gathering before the press conference. Frank Gifford was there, and he said to Weeb, 'Well, Weeb, it's all in the family, isn't it?'

"And I thought, 'Do I want to get into this?' I thought I'd have two strikes against me with the New York media. In retrospect, I think I shouldn't have taken the job after Weeb—for the family relationships, and Weeb's relationship with the press. And so many in the press favored Walt Michaels. I can remember when I got fired, Dick Young wrote, 'It's a shame that Charley Winner got fired because Weeb Ewbank was his father-in-law.' "

Charley actually had a substantial background. And almost through no fault of his own—unless you think he acted badly in bad situations—he lost two head-coaching jobs that had started with promise.

"I spent 12 years in Baltimore," he recalls. "Most of them were with Weeb, then with Shula. The funny thing about Don, he played for me at Baltimore and I always figured if I became a head coach, I'd hire him as an assistant. I always liked how well he knew the game. And then he wound up hiring me."

From there, Charley got the Cardinals' head-coaching job, a post that lasted five years.

"I have," he says, "the second-best winning record with the Cardinals—35–30–5."

But the easygoing Winner missed seeing something very dramatic and important. There was an undercurrent of racism on the Cardinals' coaching staff.

"We had some players from the South. And one assistant coach, he couldn't get it through his head that things had been changing. I wasn't really aware of it or I would have done something about it. The coaches didn't grow with the times, and treated some players differently and said some things. As head coach I suffered the brunt."

Yet he also had established an outstanding relationship with Ernie McMillan, whose son Erik was to wind up playing for the Jets, as well as Johnny Roland, who later coached the running backs under Bruce Coslet and Pete Carroll.

"In fact, I'm surprised that they don't mention Johnny Roland when they talk about head-coaching material these days," says Charley.

It almost came full circle for him. After being fired by the Cardinals he had two years with George Allen's Redskins, and then the Colts offered him the head-coaching post starting with the 1973 season.

"I talked to the Jets, though, and Phil Iselin convinced me to take the job under Weeb. I'd be assistant coach on the Jets for one season and then take over."

There were still five games remaining in Charley's second season when he was fired. The club was a disaster, and when Phil Iselin let him go he said it was not only for the good of the team, "but for the good of Charley Winner, too."

Still, Winner, who turned down every chance to quit before he finally was dismissed, claims now, "I feel I didn't have the chance to complete the Jets job—I think chiefly because I followed the wrong man. If he wasn't my father-in-law I would have stayed there."

For Charley Winner, former prisoner of war, his last victory as a head coach was memorable. It occurred at Shea Stadium in the third game of 1975, and it was attended by Emperor Hirohito of Japan.

The Secret Service asked Frank Ramos when the best time would be for the emperor to make his appearance. Ramos explained that the crowds would be heavy and potentially unmanageable before game time. Better to come late in the first quarter, or early in the second.

So long after the crowd had settled in, Emperor Hirohito appeared. There wasn't much fanfare as he made his way to his seats. But just as he appeared through an entranceway, Jerome Barkum of the Jets caught a touchdown pass. The crowd erupted in a spontaneous roar and leaped to its feet.

The emperor looked around at all these cheering Americans and was very grateful. He smiled and waved and continued to his seat amidst a greeting befitting a conquering hero.

That was Winner's last shining moment as a coach.

Charley's football career continued for almost 20 years, though. Paul Brown tapped him for assistant-coaching duties in Cincinnati, and from there Shula called on him again, this time in Miami. He stayed 11 years, before retiring. His job was to assess and sign pro talent. With the Jets, that was a theory; with the Dolphins, it was a reality.

So, Charley, what do you think happened to the Jets over the years?

As he regarded the question, I thought he had lost touch with reality for a while. He paused at least five seconds. Then he gathered his thoughts:

"The main thing, I think, is that after Walt Michaels they really didn't have anybody running the organization who knew pro football. I don't think they had anybody that really knew what to do. My feeling is that to have a strong NFL team the head coach has to have the responsibility in selecting the players and who's going to play and to have something to say about everything to do with football. Ultimately, it comes down to the head coach. Who's going to get fired? The head coach. That's why he needs to have the power to make decisions. I think that's probably why Dan Reeves left the Giants. You've got to have that ultimate control. Don Shula had it wherever he went.

"Anyway, I still follow the Jets because I have a certain pride. I'd like to see the Jets win."

Under interim coach Ken Shipp, the Jets floundered through the remainder of 1975. Only one goal remained in that season's finale at Shea against the Cowboys: could Riggins get his 1,000 yards, becoming the first Jet to reach that figure?

He struggled mightily behind an ineffective line. Namath gave him the ball more than 20 times and all Riggins could get was 46 yards. But he pushed, or rather inched, his way above 1,000. And on his final run, when he stood with 1,005 yards, Ramos called down to the field from the press box to tell Shipp that Riggins had his 1,000. They took Riggins out of the game. The way the Jets were playing, he could have gone backward and slipped under 1,000 again.

Of course, Riggins soon quit the Jets. A lapse in the contract between management and labor had allowed a number of players' options to be open with no compensation to their original team.

He joined the Redskins and became a Hall of Fame player, setting a season record for touchdowns, turning in star performances in the Super Bowl.

First, he played four seasons under George Allen and Jack Pardee, then sat out a year when the Skins wouldn't renegotiate. "I'm bored, I'm broke, and I'm back," he announced in 1981 when he returned to Washington to play for Joe Gibbs. His great years were just starting.

But when his career ended, and his drinking filled his playing void, he bought a trailer, moved it to his Virginia property on the banks of the Potomac, and tried to think about life. He thought about an acting career as well, but he was never to equal his most famous public moment off the field. It came at the National Press Club dinner in Washington when, sloshed, he looked across the table and told Supreme Court Justice Sandra Day O'Connor, "Lighten up, Sandy baby."

He sent her a dozen roses the next day.

.   .   .

John Riggins's final Jets season began the string of Jets disasters. Their 3–11 record in 1975 was matched a year later, and again a year after that. There would be times when it seemed the worst was over, but just when they seemed to get it right, they didn't. Their erratic behavior was symbolized by 1983 (a 7–9 record after going to the conference championship game in 1982), by 1989 (4–12 after sporting a respectable 8–7–1 record), by 1992 (4–12, after getting into the playoffs the previous season), and 1996's 1–15, equaling history's worst 16-game season, after committing $70 million in long-term contracts in the greatest offseason financial splurge in league history.

The Jets didn't just do badly for merely a month or so. They did badly decade after decade.

8

Lou

First, you must suspend belief when you consider Lou Holtz's tenure with the Jets.

Hard to believe, isn't it, that the man who became one of the legendary coaches of Notre Dame was a New York joke in his fling at trying to coach a pro team? The Jets will do that to the best of them. We know what it does to the worst of them.

Lou created more excitement and aggravation than anyone I've been around all these years.

But he was wonderful for a reporter, and I'm still grateful for the thousands of words I wrote about his screwball tenure. The losses —and they outnumbered the victories by better than three to one —were beside the point.

Before latching on to Holtz, general manager Al Ward did a courting dance with Ara Parseghian, who was the first acknowledged case of coaching burnout when he left Notre Dame in 1975. But Ward insisted that whoever the coach would be to replace Charley Winner in 1976, he would not have the final say in all personnel matters; Parseghian, who was contemplating a return to coaching, wanted that control. So did Joe Paterno of Penn State.

To many New Yorkers, Lou Holtz the coach was then the second-most-famous Lou Holtz. For those of a certain age, the name Lou Holtz conjured up a Borscht Belt and vaudeville comic of the 1930s. That Lou Holtz did Jewish dialect jokes with a character he called Sam Lapidus, and was a fixture on the Rudy Vallee radio show.

Indeed, earlier in the day when the Jets made the announcement, Phil Iselin was invited to dinner by Mervyn LeRoy, the movie producer.

"I can't. We're naming a new coach today," Iselin told him.

"Who is it?" asked LeRoy.

"Lou Holtz," replied Iselin.

"But, Phil, Lou Holtz is 80 years old," said LeRoy.

In the spirit of the moment, I called the radio and television personality and king of showbiz trivia, Joe Franklin, to ask him if he ever heard of Lou Holtz the comedian.

"I have a record of his made in 1924," Franklin replied proudly. "It's called, 'When It's Night-Time in Italy, It's Wednesday Over Here.' "

Coach Holtz was an angst-filled 39-year-old who seemed always to be worrying about whether he was doing the right thing. He was stringbean-thin, and his ash-blond hair flopped down one side of his head, giving him the appearance of a perpetually confused teenager. Why, he never even dated until he was a sophomore in college. And the girl he took out then wore a huge ring on a chain around her neck.

"What is that?" he asked.

"Oh, it belongs to a Marine I know," she replied, sending him deeper into his shell.

His coaching record at North Carolina State was very good. He was the first coach there since 1919 to have a winning career record, and he had inherited teams that had failed to win more than three games and converted them to winners, bringing them to bowl games each season.

On his first night in New York, he woke up at one o'clock in the morning. It had suddenly occurred to Lou Holtz how he should approach his job as the new coach of the Jets.

"What in the hell is wrong with me?" he said. "I don't have to change. Maybe the reason so many college coaches failed in the pros is that they didn't do what they did in college. McDonald's doesn't change the menu, and it's successful. Lou Holtz will not change!"

So he had decided on a strategy, and it was to prove fatal: He was going to bring a college coach's sensibility to the pros.

I had a corny idea for a story. Here was this country boy, and I was going to take him for a walking tour of Manhattan and record his comments. First, he gave me a copy of his book of inspirational sayings, called *The Grass Is Always Greener*.

"To Gerald Eskenazi," he wrote, "who I hope to be worthy of one day."

How could you not like this guy? He had won me over.

The Jets business office then was in midtown. This was definitely different from the West Virginia town he was born in, or the East Liverpool, Ohio, hamlet where he was raised.

At 5:00 P.M., on the corner of Madison Avenue and 55th Street, he asked, "Where do all the people come from?"

He stared up at the spires of the Fifth Avenue Presbyterian Church ("I feel like a hick gawking like this"). He quipped that in Raleigh at 5:00 P.M., if he stopped for a red light he'd create a traffic jam.

"But there's excitement in New York," he suggested. "Why do you think that is? What is there about this place?"

Lou might have liked to play the rube for a city-slicker newspaperman, but he was also a wily guy who played things for effect.

What would his first practice be like? we all wondered. The Jets had drafted quarterback Richard Todd from Alabama with their first pick. They still had Namath, on his last legs, but Lou was going to teach Joe a thing or two.

In his office, Lou suddenly darted from behind his desk and bent over an imaginary center in the middle of the room.

"We'll have a moving pocket. Instead of Joe Namath dropping straight back, we'll make a half-roll. He'll go back at an angle. If he can't do that, he needs Medicaid."

At his first summer-camp practice, the players got the Lou Holtz shtick in all its glory.

Todd brought the other rookies into the huddle and, with the traditional hand-clap, they broke.

"No! No! No!" screamed Holtz. He flung his clipboard 15 yards downfield as players scattered. "That's not the way you break a huddle."

So it began.

Lou had hired back Walt Michaels to run his defense and coach the linebackers. Walt had quit two years earlier over Winner becoming head coach. Even though Walt was an assistant, he wasn't crazy about some of Holtz's college ideas.

Michaels especially thought Holtz was wrong in trying to run the veer offense, in which the quarterback often keeps the ball. It might work in college, Michaels believed, but not in the pros against those big marauding defensive linemen. Moreover, Michaels was determined to prove the point: No way, he said, is any kid quarterback going to make my defense look bad, even in practice.

One of Holtz's intriguing ideas had been the drafting of the Buckey Boys—twins Dave and Don, who had played for him at North Carolina State. Dave was the quarterback, undersized at five feet eleven inches and 167 pounds. Don was a six-foot-tall receiver.

"The veer?" Michaels said with a sneer. In the first week of practice, Walt sent one of his linebackers after Dave Buckey. The hit ended Buckey's pro career, and ended Holtz's infatuation with the veer as a viable vehicle for the pros.

Holtz's tenure lighted up the sky like an accidental explosion in a fireworks factory. He wanted to do everything himself. He was going to make Joe Namath a mobile quarterback. He was going to make Richard Todd the quarterback of the future. He was going to run Michaels's defense.

Lou slept on a cot in his office. Why didn't he go home at night? "I don't understand why you have to sleep in the office, or come in after a game and have the film crew develop all those pictures at five in the morning," I told him. "The president of IBM doesn't work as many hours as you do."

"Yeah, but he's got more assistants than I do," Holtz replied.

His hand was everyplace. He lined up his players by size for the national anthem. He spoke at Kiwanis Clubs and performed magic tricks. At a luncheon in neighboring Suffolk County, he told the guests, "I know you have a lot of questions about me and the Jets, so go ahead. Don't be afraid. There are no stupid questions."

The first man raised his hand.

"Coach, what are you going to do about a pass rush?"

"That's a stupid question," Holtz replied.

Despite his quips, despite the control he tried to exercise over every aspect of Jet life, he never was comfortable in his new surroundings.

"I hate the cold," he said one spring day when the temperature was in the low 70s and he was bundled in a warmup jacket.

There was also the ambience of the area. Lou came from a leafy college town where, I imagine, he had a white clapboard house and the azaleas bloomed. Lou and his wife picked out a house on Long Island's tony North Shore, in a village on the water. But since his life was proscribed by football, he was rarely there. Instead, he spent his off-hours at the Hofstra dorms. These were concrete high-rises with a view of the Meadowbrook Parkway and Hempstead Turnpike. His room was painted a drab, almost military gray and green and had no pictures on the wall.

One twilight, he put his head back on the cot in his tacky dormitory room.

"So this," he said, looking up at the Hofstra ceiling, "is the big leagues."

It was worse when he was outside. His Jets lost their opening exhibition game by a point to the Cardinals in St. Louis. Still, for the first time in Jets history, they were about to play an exhibition game in New York. That's right—since their creation in 1960, they never had a preseason game at home.

They were the most famous gypsies in football, and Abilene or Sacramento fans would pay good money to see an ex–Super Bowl team perform.

This year, though, the Jets pressured New York City to let them in. They still were barred from Shea, but they got into Yankee

Stadium, where they were scheduled to play the Giants in their second exhibition game. Yankee Stadium, which had been re-vamped as a baseball-only field, now had to be reconfigured to accommodate football. The end line of one end zone nearly touched the left-field stands. But it was a field, and the Jets were going to be in New York for the first time in preseason play.

A hurricane killed that idea. The game was washed out. But so many tickets were sold, and this was, after all, a Jets-Giants affair, that it was rescheduled for the following Wednesday. The only trouble with that idea was that the Jets also had a game Friday night against the Raiders.

No problem, said Holtz. We'll play two. The Jets lost both. The Raiders trounced them by 41–17 after the Jets lost by two to the Giants. But at least no one crashed into the left-field stands.

Now Holtz was 0–3 as a head coach in the big leagues, although the record didn't count. Still, the day after the trouncing by the Raiders, I was sitting with Holtz, who was becoming introspec-tive and troubled. He was surrounded by negativism, getting criti-cized in the press, and the public was wondering whether the Jets had made the right choice. He had a road game in Houston coming up. This was in the days of the six-game exhibition sched-ule, which was like playing half a season before the season even started. They spent a lot of energy on games that didn't count in the standings.

Suddenly, Holtz blurted out, "If I knew that coaching in the pros was going to be like this, I never would have taken the job."

My pencil didn't move. I knew from past experience in these confessional situations that if I started to take notes, the speaker would realize what he had said and take it back. I simply nodded, and the conversation moved on.

What a story: The head coach of the Jets, who hadn't even been through a regular-season game yet, was sorry he had taken the job. I could see page-one headlines. But after a few minutes, Holtz came out of his funk and he said, "Please don't write that." I didn't. I simply held it for a few decades.

Later that week, I passed Holtz's office and saw him with pen and paper.

"I'm writing a Jets fight song," he explained. "When we win, we'll sing it."

The song was ready at Houston. The Jets behind Namath were leading the Oilers in the closing minutes, and Lou felt comfortable putting in the rookie Todd to mop up. Joe came to the sidelines and took off his knee braces.

Joe never went on the field without wearing those protective devices. They were as much a part of his uniform as a protective cup. The man with football's most famous knees was fragile, after all.

Greg Buttle was a rookie linebacker on the sidelines. He still remembers the moments that followed.

"I was a few feet away from Joe on the sidelines," recalls Buttle. "Lou was upset because Richard Todd, who was mopping up for Joe, had fumbled two snaps near the goal line. Joe had already taken off his knee braces, had unstrapped his shoulder pads, and Lou yells, 'Joe, get in there! Todd's going to cost us the game.' "

Namath went in without his braces, a foolhardy act.

"Joe came in with a huge smile on his face and I think he had Skoal in his mouth," recalls Richard. Namath said to the Oilers, "Fellas, I'm just going to go down on one knee. Let's not get any-body hurt."

After the victory, Holtz whipped out sheets of papers and distrib-uted them to the players.

"I've written a fight song," he said. "We're going to sing it after every Jets victory."

The piece, sung to the tune of "The Caissons Go Rolling Along," started: "Win the game, fight like men, we're together win or lose, New York Jets go rolling along."

The players were reluctant to sing, but Namath started and the others chimed in.

"I remember me and Mr. Hess holding the paper with the words to the song," recalls Namath, "and the two of us were singing."

Outside the locker room, we waited for the doors to open. In-stead, we heard singing. When we asked Lou about it, he couldn't understand what was so surprising, and why did we have that tone of derision in our questions?

I got a copy of the entire song a few days later and thought it would make a funny sort of story for us—the paper of record printing the Jets fight song. So I typed it up and handed it to one of the editors. Since we were always printing complete texts such as long-lost Mozart sonatas or Supreme Court rulings, why not this?

The fight song was handed back to me with the explanation, "The editors on the City Desk don't think the song's good enough to print."

Lou's Jets lost their last two exhibition games by a total of 66 points. With the season opener a few days away, with the Jets playing their usual first four games on the road, things looked bleak. Ward and Holtz felt the Jets needed a few more players. Perhaps they could get some off the waiver wire.

This was the list of players that other teams were dropping. Sometimes, a pearl would appear. These players had made it to the final cut, so they had some talent.

Ward put in claims for nine players, thinking he might get a couple from that lot but certainly not all, since other teams could also choose them. But hardly anyone wanted the players that Ward chose. Instead, he wound up with seven—and by league rules he was forced to take them all. Thus, Holtz had to cut seven of his own players off the team—about one-sixth of the total club—four days before the opening game.

Strangers made up much of the cast of the Jets as they lost those four opening road games, failing to score a touchdown in three.

The Jets won three games under Holtz before he quit with one game remaining. Two of the victories came over the Bills, who won only two games themselves all year. And the other victory came against the hapless first-year Tampa Bay Bucs, who lost every game they played. In other words, Lou Holtz's only three professional victories came over teams with a combined record of 2–26. The Jets scored one-fifth of their season's points in that victory over Tampa Bay.

As the season dragged on, there were reports that Lou already was talking to the University of Arkansas for next season. If so, he had to get out of the Jets soon, because there were college recruiting commitments in December. So, after the club suffered a 37–16 drubbing by the Redskins, Holtz quit. There was one game remaining.

A few weeks earlier I had invited him to my house for a season-ending party. The day he quit he called me and said, "I won't be coming over Friday night. I think you'll understand."

I should have seen it coming. A few days after Lou had become head coach, he had asked his secretary, Elsie, to get Namath on the phone.

"He doesn't give us his phone number," she explained. "You have to get it from his agent."

By leaving, Lou missed Joe's last game as a Jet.

.   .   .

I remember asking the genial Mike Holovak, who replaced Holtz as head coach for that finale, whether Joe would start or if he would go with the rookie Todd.

"This may be the only time in my life I get a chance to start Joe Namath at quarterback," replied Holovak.

I had known Joe only two years when he left. I didn't meet him until 1975, when he was already an icon and was long past the adolescence of his 20s, in which he became a national figure. He was also past the symbolism of youthful revolt. I suspect he probably was voting Republican by the time I started covering the Jets in his decline.

I cherish our casual meeting at an airport one day more than 20 years later, when we spoke for 30 minutes about what it was like in that moment when he knew the stadium's eyes were on him and the place was rocking.

"Sure I was aware of the noise," he said. "And I appreciated it."

"Joe looked prettier than anyone throwing the ball," Todd, his successor, once explained to me. "Some people can wear a suit better than other people."

Joe was one athlete who not only appreciated what it meant to be famous in a way that other people pinned their dreams on, but could express it.

When we said good-bye, he told me to call him at his place in Florida and maybe we'd play some golf. Then he wrote down three names on his business card: Tatiana, Jessica, Olivia. "My wife and daughters," he explained, "so if they answer you'll know who they are."

His consideration was one more surprise I discovered about Joe as the years go by.

One of the first things I noticed about Joe and the Jets in 1975 during my early days on the beat was the dynamics of the locker room.

First, if you thought of it as a human body, then as you walked in there was Joe at the head. Next to him were the receivers, then the running backs, then the offensive linemen. On the other side of the room were the defensive linemen at the top, with the room narrowing to the linebackers and defensive backfield.

Joe's locker was a no-man's-land. You didn't hang around there. It wasn't that Joe gave off vibes that said "stay away," or he wasn't friendly; it's just that he was a legend on a team of losers. It was top-heavy with his status.

And when you think about it, how could you not be intimidated by his presence?

Greatness was past. He had played on only two playoff Jets teams, and they came consecutively in 1968 and 1969.

His last game in New York as a Jet was an eerie affair. Joe's skills had eroded. I had written a long story about how the swirling Shea winds—the open end faces onto Flushing Bay—were playing havoc with his spirals. I called a meteorologist, who explained how the wind came in and, at different elevations, caused various weather effects. If you looked at those little yellow ribbons fastened to the tops of the uprights, you'd see them blowing in four different directions. Oh, the *Times* loved that scientific aspect, gussying up my story with diagrams of vortexes and currents and meteorological data and charts. The paper of record, indeed.

Some of my colleagues felt I was allowing Namath a cop-out. "He never complained about the winds in the 1960s," griped the *Post*'s curmudgeon, Paul Zimmerman.

Before Namath's final game, Zimmerman, who, like Larry Fox of the *News,* wasn't allowed to ask questions of Joe, wrote a column describing the quarterback as a "million-dollar statue." In other words, Joe stood back there and got sacked.

You'd think after all those years, all that fame and acclaim, that one column wouldn't upset Joe. He had stopped talking to Larry and Paul after misreading headlines over their stories and then blaming the two for writing them. For all the sophisticated veneer he and other long-time players may acquire, they still have a sneaking suspicion that we really write the headlines, too.

Joe's last game ended on a muddy field, in front of a few hundred remaining fans who chanted, "We want Joe!" Below them, the Bengals were running out the clock in a 42–3 trouncing as the 1976 season ended. It was one of the worst days of football in Jets history.

Everyone knew this was it for Joe. He stared only at the floor in the post-mortem at his locker.

How would he sum this all up? I wondered. How did he see his wonderful career? How would he feel ending it this way?

"How could he call me a statue?" Joe asked of nobody in particular.

.   .   .

Five years after he left the Jets I saw him again. It was at Jones Beach on Long Island, where he was playing in *Damn Yankees.* Joe had become something of a performer, doing summer stock. His last season in pro football had been in Los Angeles, where he was sacked repeatedly, then replaced by Pat Haden. His knees still bothered him. He was to suffer increasingly after his glory years, undergoing more surgery that ultimately kept him out of games. Now, as a part-time hoofer, he had to have both knees drained. Eventually, they were replaced by metal.

Broadway Joe. How out of place he used to seem in Hempstead at the end. Oh, he wore cut-down shorts and T-shirts and went sockless in his sneakers. He went drinking in Bill's, across Hempstead Turnpike. He had a place for the winter in Garden City. Just like every other player, he lived on the Island in season. But he was never really like any other player. You looked at him then and you just felt he was being polite. His heart was not in being a Jet, and certainly not in living on Long Island.

Now, five years later, it was showtime. The orchestra played "You Gotta Have Heart" and "Whatever Lola Wants, Lola Gets," and the overture was over and it was time for Joe Namath to light up the room again.

Eddie Bracken, the comedic actor from the 1940s, played the Devil, who transforms an aging baseball fan—who sells his soul to help the Washington Senators defeat the Yankees—into young Joe Hardy. The older man goes through a door; the person who will return through that door will be Joe Hardy.

Suddenly, Namath appeared. Joe Hardy lived. He smiled. They applauded him madly. He strode out to center stage. You remembered that something about him hadn't changed—that awful posture. "Roundshouldered" was the way sportswriters described it. His head was tucked practically below his shoulders.

He sang a little, he danced a little, he acted a lot. Once, he even got to kiss the girl. And when he did, someone yelled out from high in the back, "Touchdown!"

Namath's head bobbed up and down, laughing during the kiss. But he didn't ad-lib. He stuck to the script. He didn't acknowledge the crowd. No index finger raised to show we're number one. He played his part well.

The applause was spontaneous and loud at the end. The theater was virtually empty when his longtime factotum, Hoot Owl Hicks, appeared on stage to collect the many Namath friends for the backstage ritual. Hoot Owl had been with Joe since his freshman year at Alabama, when Hicks was the student manager of the football team.

"Come on back," Hicks told this theatergoer. I was accompanied by my wife, Rosalind, our eight-year-old, Michael, and my mother-in-law.

"Wait here," Hoot Owl said. "Joe's taking a shower." We waited a few minutes and finally Hicks poked his face through the door and said, "Come on in." It was a fair-sized dressing room. There were a few empty bags of pretzels and potato chips, two apples, and a can of beer. Namath was still in the shower.

But he quickly emerged. His hair was blow-dried—in the old locker-room days it was towel-dried and tousled. He wore a robe, just like a stage actor between changes in his dressing room. He had a drink in hand—not much difference there—and the old smile. He recognized me and he even remembered my son, Michael, who had the same name as one of his nephews. Joe had never met my wife, though, and went over, extended his hand, and said in that Beaver Falls, Alabama, drawl, "Nice to meet you."

Then he went to the couch where her mother was sitting and took her hand, too, and smiled. He chatted with everyone. He spoke of his summer place in Massapequa, Long Island, and his boat. It was suburban chitchat, and he did it comfortably.

Hoot Owl apologized for not having anything around to eat or drink, but he gave Michael an apple. The women beamed. Joe really did have a way of blocking out everyone else and concentrating on you, especially if you were a woman. Joe Namath in his dressing room was more relaxed and happier than Joe Namath in his locker room.

Finally, I thought as I left, Broadway Joe was truly happy on Long Island.

.   .   .

Many years later, I discussed writing his autobiography with him. He was very receptive.

I figured, naturally, that he would be willing to discuss his bachelor days in the book. Joe was as famous for being famous as for being a heck of a dramatic quarterback, who had this crazy belief that no matter what the score, he could bring his team back with his right arm.

But then Joe reflected on his wife and his two young girls. Joe, who had married at the age of 40, wanted his wife and daughters with him wherever he traveled. He hated the road now. America's most famous sports bachelor had become its great homebody.

"I want my daughters to read the book," he said, "and I don't want to put anything in there that they shouldn't be reading."

To write about Joe and not mention running around would be

like doing a biography of Muhammad Ali and forgetting he was once Cassius Clay. And so we never collaborated on a book.

When I told him some time later that I was writing this book, he was eager to talk about how his life had evolved, about how he was a person now defined by his wife and family.

"I followed the Jets more closely the last 15 years or so," he said. It was almost as if he could look at his team again once he got married and had a different life. "There was a time after I stopped playing football that I lost interest. It's easy to look back and say what we should have done, what a team should have done. You just can't do that."

Ask Joe about his businesses now and he talks of being busy with the Classic Sports Network, which shows old (that is to say, from his time) film and game clips and talks with past heroes. He is also working with a CBS online service. He doesn't sing and dance anymore.

"I gave up show business. The main reason was family. It's one thing for a bachelor to do it."

And what about his girls? Do they know about the football?

"They've learned it's a bit different background. I guess my wife explained to them a bit about my past."

His life might be dramatically different from Beaver Falls, but in the way he tells it, it doesn't sound all that changed. "I'm still excited and want to grow. Maybe now I don't want as much as I used to. I never had a new car. Now I give myself more time to analyze things. I have been monitoring myself for a long time. I don't know if it started with the injuries, but it's always been part of my mind. I've always been a dreamer. At night as a kid I dreamt and had lofty goals. I used to think as a youngster it was silly to waste time dreaming, until I was told it was all right to dream."

And his current dream?

"I'm looking forward to having a good weekend in L.A., and then getting home."

He is consumed with the simple life, a startling turnaround for a man who was consumed with stretching his life.

The first time I saw him in person, I wasn't prepared for the concentration of noise and energy that attended Joe's first pass of the game. The instant he started to backpedal, in that little pit-pat, almost awkward style, everyone in the stadium stood, and in the press box you felt the vibration of noise.

"Heck, I was aware of that, people standing," he said. "It's a great feeling. I miss it now."

So do the Jets.

9

It Only Hurts When
You Laugh

There are no accidents, said Freud. Or perhaps the Jets' team trainer.

For a team defined as much by Joe Namath's knees as by the glories triggered by his arm, it is not surprising that so many Jets stories revolve around injuries. What is surprising is how many of those injuries have stemmed from circumstances that were, to put it mildly, a little weird.

The accidental injury became a part of the Jets' losing lore in the years I chronicled them. One that always resonated was the pop made by Bobby Jackson's hamstring when he was engaged in the ritualistic, and quite ordinary, pregame stretch.

It came at a time when there was a tantalizing (as usual) upturn in Jets fortunes. In 1984, Joe Walton's second season as head coach, the club seemed en route to resuming the victory stretch that had marked Walt Michaels's last two years.

The season started brightly with a 3–1 mark and the erratic Patriots looming. It was a Jets home game and hopes were high.

This was their first year in Giants Stadium and almost 70,000 people were on hand.

The team warmed up on the field and then went into the locker room to regroup for the opening kickoff. On the green carpet in front of his locker, cornerback Bobby Jackson was lying on his back raising his left leg to stretch the hamstring muscle.

Jackson was a tightly muscled, tense sort of guy, who also had an odd indentation in one of his biceps.

"I used to hitch rides on garbage trucks when I was a kid back home," he once explained. "One day I fell off." Hence, the hole in his muscle.

Now he was limbering up to face the Patriots' young quarterback Tony Eason. He began to raise his right leg to stretch.

"POP!" was the noise teammates around the locker room heard.

"All of a sudden, I heard a loud crackling noise," he was to recall. "I knew it was my hamstring."

Yes, incredibly, Jackson popped his hamstring warming up to prevent a hamstring injury. Just as the team prayer was about to begin.

Teammates heard Jackson groan with pain as he rolled over on the carpet. Soon he was in the trainer's room, a lump high on the back of his right leg.

If Jackson was tightly muscled, Walton was tightly wound. Someone came into his office and told him what had happened, while outside in the locker room, the chatter of Jackson's teammates turned to nervous whispers. The ambience of the room had suddenly changed dramatically.

Up in the press box we heard the announcement: "In pregame stretching in the locker room, Bobby Jackson pulled a hamstring. He's out of the game."

At first, the writers looked at one another not quite comprehending what Bill Shannon, the PA announcer, had just said. And then, as is the wont of writers in press boxes everywhere, there was snickering and the hints of "I told you so," or "What else is new?" or whatever the snide remark of the day is among sports' Fourth Estate.

Jackson once had been the team's defensive captain. Walton

knew how important he was to the club's psyche as well as performance. The coach immediately addressed the team.

"Forget about it," he said. "Don't let it affect you."

Of course, it depressed the hell out of them. A player named
Davlin Mullen replaced him, only to be benched late in the game
for a rookie, Russell Carter. Eason, meanwhile, had his best game
as a pro with three touchdowns in a 28-for-42 passing performance
that amassed 354 yards.

Walton was furious with his defense, blaming everybody for not
tackling. Of course, there was another problem besides Jackson's:
linebacker Lance Mehl was taken out with an ankle injury.

Later, Jackson walked around with a cane. Did anyone ever hear
of a player being hurt in the locker room before a game? Never.
But Jackson had decided to do the stretching exercises there because he had felt "sluggish" during the warmup.

"If I'd a hurt it in the game . . . but in the locker room . . ." said
Jackson.

The Jets went on to a 7–9 season.

Four years earlier, Richard Todd also had a bizarre happening
before a game against the Patriots.

Richard was—and I'm going to use a word not associated with
pro football—sweet. He just was a pleasant guy with no anger
toward anyone. And he married a girl named Lulu.

Here's the kind of guy Richard was:

He invited me one offseason to visit him in Mobile, Alabama. I
flew in, checked into a nearby hotel, and set off to visit him and
his family for dinner. This was a few years before he got married.

I didn't know what to buy him, so I stopped off to get some wine.
When I went inside the store, I noticed it was also a pharmacy and a
five-and-ten. In Alabama, you could buy wine in that kind of place.

The wines were in a glassed-in refrigerator. I never heard of any
of the wines the store had, so I picked out something that, if memory serves, was called "White French Wine," or maybe it was
"French White Wine."

When I got to his house, Richard answered the door. I walked in
and handed him the bottle of wine and he immediately called out
with excitement, "Daddy—Jerry brought us some wine!"

Well, everyone made a fuss over it. There was his mom (a professor of nursing), his dad (a professor of education at the University of South Alabama, or USA), his brother and sister-in-law, and his maiden aunt, Miz Duckworth.

The buffet spread was out of a party scene in *Gone With the Wind:* macaroni and cheese and collard greens and fried chicken and black-eyed peas and some other down-home dishes.

Then Dad—Carl Todd—had to open the wine.

"Uh, Richard, do you know where a corkscrew is?" asked Mr. Todd.

They started going through the drawers. Carl Todd wasn't going to start the meal without opening the wine his guest had brought. But no corkscrew.

Richard then found a metal nail and began to pound it into the cork. Then he put a screwdriver to it and tried valiantly to get the cork up, or down, while all I could think of was the headline, "Jets' Quarterback Tears Open Thumb on Wine Brought by Reporter."

After a few minutes of screwing around, Richard couldn't get the cork to budge.

"C'mon, Jerry," said Richard cheerfully. "We'll go out and buy a corkscrew."

So we left everyone at the dinner table and hopped into Richard's van. He put on his International Harvester cap at a jaunty angle and we went downtown. No corkscrew after repeated stops.

We went back to his house, where I suggested that maybe we could just push the cork in and strain the wine out. This sat well with father and son. Richard got himself a hammer and banged on the nail in the cork until he knocked it in.

Finally, Carl Todd poured the wine, which came out with bits of cork floating.

"Jerry," pronounced the elder Todd after a sip, "I 'spect this is the best bottle of wine I ever had."

How wonderfully gracious he was. Later I was to appreciate him even more when I found out he was a devout Baptist who had never had wine before.

I tell this story so that others can appreciate the disarming kind of guy Richard Todd was, and how unlike his predecessor, Broadway Joe. Yet those of us in the press always tried to make the comparison—two guys from the University of Alabama, both quarterbacks. But very different.

So I was not totally surprised to see Richard's face in an aw-shucks attitude one afternoon when I said "hi."

"You're not going to believe this," he said, "but I think I broke the other toe, too."

First, we backtrack. Poor Richard's almanac of bruises started on Thursday night at the Long Island home he shared with running back Scott Dierking.

"I got up to get a Coke out of the refrigerator," Todd explained. "I was alone in the house and it was dark. I was wearing only socks, and I hit a chair with my foot and went 'Aaargh!' I heard a pop. So after I heard the pop, I took a beer instead."

He had broken the little toe on his left foot. It was bad enough the Jets had started the season 0–4. Now their quarterback had a broken little toe—the first of two damaged little digits, as it turned out.

Still, he practiced the next day when trainer Bob Reese taped the toe to the adjoining one and put a protective, hard plastic shield over Todd's left shoe.

Todd worked out easily and showed no signs of the injury. But then he backpedaled on a play-action pass—faking a handoff and passing instead. Just then Stan Waldemore, a 250-pound offensive lineman whose responsibilities included protecting Todd, instead stepped on Todd's unprotected little toe, the right one.

It was one of those impossible-to-recreate combination of circumstances. Waldemore was playing left guard because Randy Rasmussen, who had played 144 straight games, had been hurt in practice a day earlier.

The injury to the right little toe actually was more serious. As a right-handed passer, Todd had to plant on his right foot. But he wanted to play against the Patriots on Sunday—had to play, in fact. The backup was Pat Ryan, one of a handful of number-two quarterbacks in the league who had never started a game. And the Jets had never lost their opening five games. Richard figured the Jets couldn't do without him.

As Todd limped out of the trainer's room, Reese, who was developing a whistling-past-the-graveyard sense of humor, said to him, "Hey, Richard, which foot you limping off of?"

Ever polite, Richard replied, "I'm not limping because of one. I'm limping because of two."

"So," I asked Reese, "you really think Richard can play Sunday?"

"Sure," the trainer replied. "Unless he drops a refrigerator on it tonight."

He might as well have, as the Jets of 1980, who had seemed poised to enter a new era of good feeling following consecutive .500 seasons under Walt Michaels, instead fell to 0–5. Todd was sacked five times on his battered toes.

Yet Michaels was not above seeing the irony in Todd's injury. As he contemplated Waldemore having stepped on Richard's foot, the coach said, "It was toe-wrestling." Then he quickly added, lest he be quoted in the newspaper, "No, I'm just kidding."

Walt was an educated man. He majored in psychology and he had taken enough science courses so that he understood physics. But he didn't want to come off sounding foolish. Once, he quipped about a statistic involving football, "Statistics are like loose women —you can do anything you want with them."

Unfortunately for Walt, the quotation made the newspaper the next day when Al Harvin, the fellow covering for me on my day off, saw fit to print it. Afterward, when Walt said something outrageous, he would quickly add, "But don't print that, Al."

Walt's joke about toe-wrestling was a reference to still another freakish Jet injury that had repercussions all through the 1980s.

In 1979, Walt had conducted a shoot-out for the starting quarterback job between Richard Todd and Matt Robinson. Robinson, with his flare for throwing deep to Wesley Walker, emerged as the winner as the 1979 season opener approached. Three days before the first regular-season game, against the Browns, Robinson went out and stayed out. As part of the boys-will-be-boys thing, Matt had challenged the redoubtable Joe Klecko to a wrist-wrestling competition. Klecko took it easy on him and exerted no pressure. Then Robinson went back to his room and challenged teammate Bobby Jones, an unheralded wide receiver who had been pumping gas not too many years before he made it as a Jets walk-on. Jones, who never attended college, was said to come from Texaco Tech.

Robinson and Jones began roughhousing. And at one point Robinson's grip slipped and Jones accidentally twisted the quarterback's right thumb.

"Matt came in on a Friday morning and told me, 'I sprained my thumb,' and I asked him how," recalls former trainer Reese. "And he said he was about to go into his room from the hallway when a teammate suddenly opened the door and banged his thumb. I said, 'Matt, you're staying at the Holiday Inn and the doors open inward.' And he admitted it didn't happen that way but didn't tell me just what did happen. But he got real upset and said, 'Look, Walt really doesn't want me, but I'm getting the quarterback job and he'll try to get rid of me if he has a good reason.' "

So Reese made a deal with Robinson. "I told him, 'I'll tape you up today and won't say anything unless they ask me.' The funny thing is, neither Walt nor John Idzik noticed it." Idzik was the quarterbacks coach, who liked to call his boys "Galumpkies," which they took as some sort of Polish curse.

Anyway, the way Reese remembers it, Robinson's thumb was fine that day, but it swelled up on Saturday, the day before the season's opener. Robinson had to tell Michaels about the injury. He changed his story slightly; this time he said that he was inside the room when the door opened in on his thumb. But however it happened, the Jets hierarchy was seething.

"When they found out about it on Saturday, that not only got Walt angry, but Jim Kensil was furious because of the rule you have to report injuries," says Reese.

Kensil, the president of the Jets, had been Pete Rozelle's number-one aide at the NFL and had presided over much of the impact that the league had in the 1960s and 1970s, when it established itself as the smoothest operation in the world of sports. One of the league's tenets was to report injuries, which started because the league understood that everyone in America bet on football, and if injuries were announced there would be little suspicion that teams and players were hiding information from the bettors. Now, as president of the Jets, Kensil was passionate about the league rules.

Reese didn't want to know what really happened, and Michaels and Kensil apparently accepted Robinson's revised story.

That night, says Reese, "We used compression for the swelling. I also applied a cream that the trainer for the New York Cosmos [the soccer team] had picked up in Germany. It was supposed to help the swelling. Matt saw Walt the next day and showed him that the swelling went down."

So Matt Robinson started. "And we're winning the game in the last minutes and he comes over and hugs me and says, 'It feels great. Take the damn tape off.' The game is ending and Brian Sipe throws the ball and it bounces off Donald Dykes's helmet and the Browns catch the ball, then Gastineau got a roughing-the-passer penalty and they tie the game."

Suddenly, the Jets were in overtime, but Robinson's thumb began to swell with the tape off. Reese worked feverishly to retape it, but the damage had been done. Still, in sudden-death play with Robinson at quarterback, Walker broke free over the middle. He was in the clear. Robinson put his hand around the ball—and, unable to grip it properly, unloaded a pass that floated like a wounded duck. It was intercepted. The Browns returned the ball close enough to set up a field goal. They won.

Michaels was beside himself. He still didn't know what had really happened. Someone told him about Klecko's involvement with Robinson in the bar, and that steamed Walt against Joe. But mostly, Walt was furious with Robinson for hiding the injury.

"You work, you plan all week, and then the kid hides an injury from you," said Walt.

"I thought I was gone," recalls Reese. He wasn't, but Matt was.

Matt Robinson never threw a pass again for the Jets. Walt had a great memory and harbored a grudge better than almost anyone in football. Richard Todd was his quarterback again.

That particular injury also had a tremendous negative impact on the Jets in the 1980s. Its ripple effect was palpable. Michaels didn't want to look at Robinson anymore. There were repeated instances in 1979 when Todd was injured, but Richard played and played; no way was Walt going to employ Matt.

Because of their 8–8 record in 1979, the Jets had the 12th pick of the draft the next year. They wanted a speed-burner. "You can't coach speed," Walt liked to say. He already had his bookend tackles in Marvin Powell and Chris Ward. He had one great receiver in

Walker, and now he fantasized what life would be like with another speedster at receiver.

The Jets had their eye on Johnny (Lam) Jones, a world-class sprinter from Texas who had decided to put on a football uniform. It was a mistake on both their parts.

The Jets, who had not made a player-for-player trade in the 1970s, made a beaut this time. They packaged Robinson and traded him to Denver for the Broncos' first- and second-round picks. Then the Jets made a deal with the 49ers, who were bad back then. The 49ers owned the second overall pick of the draft. The Jets gave up two draft picks so they could get into that second slot. With it, they chose Jones.

It was another glaring error. He was fast, all right, but his major problem as receiver was that he couldn't catch the ball. He was a very nervous kid as well. They worked with him diligently, especially a receivers coach named Pete McCulley, whose spiritual adviser was the Reverend Norman Vincent Peale, celebrated author of *The Power of Positive Thinking*.

"Look it in!" McCulley used to tell the slippery-handed Jones.

Finally, Jones hit on a unique idea. He discovered that if he leaped just when the ball was coming in, it somehow made it easier to catch. However, most balls that were thrown to him were not over his head. Still, he leaped. So here was this odd scene: He'd be standing out in the flat alone, the ball would come in chest high—and he'd leap for it. Oh, he caught it all right, but by the time he came down with it, defenders were all over him. That leap completely negated his speed because he had to land on his feet before he could start running.

Jones's career started, in a sense, with a freak accident to Robinson. But Jones's career ended because of a freak accident to himself, caused by the frustration he carried with him as being the highest-drafted player the Jets had ever chosen to that time. The dream of a speed tandem, of Wesley Walker and Jones, never was to be. In fact, Jones was such a nervous player that Walt wouldn't even start him. He'd allow a sure-handed, slow-footed Derrick Gaffney to start the game and then when Jones calmed down on the sidelines, he'd come in.

One training camp I asked Jones to give me a few minutes for an interview. He seemed reluctant, but finally said okay. We sat in my car and I was thinking of an ice-breaking way to begin. The focus of my story was to be on the failed expectations of Lam Jones. Before I could even say anything, he said to me, "Why do you want to interview me? I've never done anything."

Precisely, Johnny.

Jones's career ended because of an uncharacteristic display of anger.

In an exhibition game he darted over the middle and was free. The ball came at him straight and true, and he dropped it. It took a funny bounce and came right back up toward him. In his frustration, he swatted it away. He didn't hit it just right, though; instead of hitting it with his palm, he struck the ball with a finger—tearing a tendon.

The Matt Robinson saga, which began with wrist-wrestling with Bobby Jones, ended in a sense with another Jones and another silly accident.

The Jets had been given a total of four draft picks in the first two rounds in 1980—a pair of firsts and a pair of seconds. And five years later they had nothing to show for it.

Robinson, meanwhile, never made it as the Broncos' starter. By his second year there, Dan Reeves, the new coach, opted for 38-year-old Craig Morton. Still, Robinson was optimistic. When I spoke to him back then he said, "There's a long-range opportunity for me here."

How could he know that Reeves would draft a quarterback named John Elway two years later?

No, Jets quarterbacks are not immune from injuries. *Au contraire*, they find novel ways to hurt themselves.

If no one had ever heard of a player injuring himself as Bobby Jackson had done in the pregame warmup back in 1984, then it was just as unusual for Neil O'Donnell to tear his calf muscle while dropping back to pass during some pregame tossing 12 years later.

O'Donnell's injury again was as much a symbolic as an actual disaster: He was the showpiece of an offseason buying splurge that marked the Jets as the greatest acquisitors in NFL history. They committed almost $70 million in long-term contracts to the club in 1996 following their franchise-worst season of 1995. That year they were 3–13. Hess, the still-wealthy, still-generous owner, vowed to give head coach Rich Kotite whatever he needed.

What Rich needed was a quarterback who was young, healthy, and winning instead of the problematic Boomer Esiason. Boomer was a wonderful competitor and understood the game, its nuances, its drama, better than anyone in the organization. But he was angered with his surroundings, the attitude, the organization. And while he insisted there was nothing wrong with his arm, in his last year with the Jets he threw only one completion that actually traveled 30 yards in the air.

Now Boomer was gone from the Jets, and O'Donnell, a losing Super Bowl quarterback only a few months earlier with the Steelers, was leading the club. O'Donnell's $25 million, five-year deal was the fourth most lucrative in league history. It made perfect sense for the Jets. As President Steve Gutman explained, "It's one of the few times a team will ever have a chance to get a quality quarterback in his prime, and all it will cost is money."

O'Donnell spearheaded an offseason buying spree of free agents that was offense-friendly: a pair of bookend tackles in the experienced Jumbo Elliott and David Williams. The canny, expert receiver Jeff Graham. They added the league's overall number-one draft choice, wide receiver Keyshawn Johnson of Southern California. All for the greater glory of O'Donnell. By season's end, every one of them was to suffer injuries that kept them out of games.

The ever-affable Kotite was friendly with one of the Nassau County cops assigned to the area. Both liked cigars. Rich liked to say, "Me and Mr. Hess are the only ones allowed to smoke in the building." In the policeman, Kotite found a fellow cigar aficionado. The coach gave the cop an expensive cigar.

"I'm going to keep it and smoke it when you get your first victory," the cop said.

By October 6, the ruin of the entire offseason revision was complete. By then, the cop had told Richie, "I'm going to smoke this cigar before it gets ruined," and did.

This was not a series of injuries so much as a string of cosmic collisions, a bumping up against history, a karmic contretemps. Someone on the Jets wasn't praying right.

First to go were the tackles. Before training camp even began.

First to go was Jumbo, so called because he is very big, although very affable. Near his New Jersey home the night before the start of summer camp, he decided to limber up. So he went to the local high-school track and started to sprint. Pop went the hamstring.

The next morning, Williams—who had achieved more fame with his role in "Babygate," missing a game with the Oilers because his wife was having a baby, than as a player—also tried getting the kinks out before putting on the pads for the first time. Pop—an apt word, in his case—went his hamstring.

But as training camp was starting, O'Donnell did not have his prime protectors.

Before the season was a few weeks old, it was obvious that the offense was unable to mesh. There was Keyshawn Johnson's missed summer camp because of his inability to come to terms with the Jets, while his lawyer, Jerome Stanley, dropped hints of racism, fueling the negotiating. There had been the tackles' absence for much of the summer.

Still, the injured began to heal, and so did Johnson's ego once he became a starter. They couldn't win, though. In Game 5 at Washington, Graham was leveled with a knee injury. That took away O'Donnell's most experienced receiver as the Jets fell to 0–5.

Later that week in practice, Keyshawn was lost for a month when he was whacked in the knee accidentally by a teammate's helmet. And then O'Donnell went down in Game 6 when he was blitzed and fell on his right shoulder, separating it. In that same game, another major offseason pickup, wide receiver Webster Slaughter, was lost for a month.

With their 0–6 start, they set a Jets record for futility from the beginning of a season. Although the 1996 campaign was essentially lost, they figured O'Donnell would be back for the final few games and perhaps the club could build on something for the next season.

O'Donnell had become distant during his injury, baffled by what had become of him and his team. He had never seen such negative attitudes, he confessed to me, had never been around players who seemed to care little and who anticipated the dropping of the next shoe—which, of course, always dropped.

Still, the competitor in O'Donnell helped brighten his days as December approached and he was getting set to return. In between, Frank Reich had replaced him.

Since Reich was a Jets quarterback now, and his glory days as the most famous backup in football to the Bills' Jim Kelly a receding memory, it figured that he would suffer some stupid injury, too.

In one of the games he started for the sidelined O'Donnell, Reich swallowed a tooth. He was crunched on the game's final drive just as he completed a fourth-down pass to Johnson. The hit broke one of Reich's teeth. They never found it, of course, but they did stitch up his jaw so that he could play the following week.

Finally, O'Donnell was set to return. By now, the Jets were 1–11 and facing the Oilers. A few days earlier, following a loss to the Bills, Kotite had told Hess that he would step down after the season, but the team wouldn't make that announcement just yet.

O'Donnell missed six starts with his torn shoulder. His return was on a gloomy December day, a Sunday in which the Jets were attempting to achieve their first December victory since 1993. It was drizzling and the stands were virtually deserted. This was not a late-arriving crowd. It was a nonarriving crowd. In fact, the Jets set an NFL record—indeed, a professional sports record—that day when 55,985 people who had bought tickets instead stayed away.

The quarterback was backpedaling over the painted area of the grass. Suddenly, he stopped short.

"Someone's thrown a baseball at me!" he thought as he felt a searing pain in his right calf.

No, he had done it himself. Somehow, he pulled a muscle. Kotite looked up to see O'Donnell being helped off the field by two assistants. Jumbo Elliott could not believe what he was seeing. A few seconds earlier, there had been a healthy O'Donnell.

"It was," Jumbo said later, "a little strange, without a doubt."

The prior injury had separated O'Donnell's shoulder; this one separated him from the team. Players were surprised as the season wound down that he wasn't even on the sidelines.

"Where is he? Why isn't he here?" wondered one veteran.

Then again, if you were the quarterback of the Jets of 1996, would you have wanted to be seen with them?

Say this for O'Donnell—at least he suffered his odd injury on the field. Joe Namath's final knee problem happened on water skis.

There is a misconception about Joe—that he missed a lot of action. Actually, he played less than half the schedule in 1970, 1971, and 1973, but in his other nine Jets years he was available the entire season. In that span, he had four knee operations (two on each), a fractured bone in his right wrist, and a separated right shoulder.

And then he went water-skiing in the Bahamas.

It happened in 1976 off the Berry Islands, which he used to visit in the offseason on cruises from Florida in his yacht. His left hamstring tore when the tow-rope broke just as he was coming out of the water with his legs taut against the skis.

Joe's "hammy," as players like to call the muscle, rolled up like a windowshade. At first it was taped when he worked out, then he wore a pad, and finally an elastic sleeve to help hold the muscle in place. It stuck out as big as a grapefruit. He never talked about it, but it severely limited his mobility his last three years—even more than his celebrated surgical knees did.

How ironic that Broadway Joe's career on Broadway was shortened not by his gimpy knees scarred in battle, but by something so mundane as watersport.

Probably the funniest Jets injury—or at least the one that was most embarrasing to the medical staff—was Joe Klecko's broken leg—you know, where the bone protruded through the uniform. What's so funny about that?

Klecko was the great Jets warrior. He was good enough to go to the Pro Bowl at three different positions on the defensive line—nose guard, end, and tackle. This particular night he was performing in Seattle, site of so many odd Jets moments. It was on a Monday night, to boot.

As usual, Joe was making a tackle. But someone piled on him. The play ended and Joe was moaning in pain. The stadium was roaring with delight. Trainer Bob Reese was busy with another player and Pepper Burruss, his assistant, marched out and poked around. Pepper felt what he believed to be bone protruding through the uniform.

"Compound fracture," he announced somberly, relaying the information to Reese. As usual, Jets PR director Frank Ramos, high in the press box, was in instant communication with Reese on the sidelines. This was a Monday night game, remember, and America and Howard Cosell had to be told instantly. Frank heard about the compound fracture, a truly frightening injury, and relayed the information to the TV truck. Howard somberly intoned the news on the air.

After they hauled Klecko off in the meat wagon, though, someone discovered that it wasn't bone that was protruding. Klecko's shin guard had slipped. In the anxiety of the moment, Burruss had fingered the protective plastic and identified it as bone.

Realizing this was seen all over America, that the announcement had gone out about Klecko's injury, and concerned about looking foolish, Reese had a ready response.

"Pepper," he said, "you better break Joe's leg quick."

Cosell was not amused when he heard that Klecko was going to play the second half. "Frankie Ramos just told me that Joe Klecko will return, that his leg wasn't broken," he announced. In the press box, we were stunned.

"Miracle recovery," someone suggested.

Howard took everything personally. Rather than rejoice in the fact Klecko was not hurt, Howard's feelings were hurt and he let everyone know it.

Another body part played a role in the Kingdome, which was Walt's personal hall of horrors. Or, rather, an emission from a particular unmentionable body part.

It was 1979, and the season was slipping away from the Jets, who had been 5–5. Now, though, they had lost two straight games and were performing against a team that always gave them fits—trick plays, special-team gimmicks, even a loss in his first start to David Krieg, the quarterback from Milton College, which was defunct by the time he made it to the big leagues.

Chuck Ramsey had been my favorite punter. He had his little magic tricks, such as the ability to flip a coin behind him, let it drop on his shoe, kick it up in the air over his shoulder, and have it land in his shirt pocket. Sometimes he would bring his "mongoose" into the locker room, a furry little creature that he used to keep hidden in a box. You could see the tail, though, and Chuck would say, "Get closer and take a peek, but not too close," and suddenly he'd release a spring and the thing would fly in the air, scaring the heck out of some rookie. The mongoose was just a piece of fur.

But whatever mischief Ramsey liked to inflict on others, he never bargained for what befell him this night in Seattle. He was victimized twice in this particular game—once he mishandled a bad snap and once he had a punt blocked which the Seahawks converted into a touchdown.

After the game, the Jets' most decisive loss of the season, I saw Ramsey standing in the middle of the locker room, looking lost and tearful.

"Why are you crying, Chuck?" I asked.

"How would you feel," he replied, "if the head coach singled you out in front of the entire team and said, 'I can fart farther than you can kick'?"

Whoa! Fart? When I heard that I was about to break into laughter, but he was so serious that I held it in, so to speak. The other reporters who gathered round sort of looked at their feet or up at the ceiling.

Okay, so Chuck said it. Now, how do I write about that for *The New York Times*?

This called for an editorial conference among my colleagues.

Steve Serby of the *New York Post*, the most raucous tabloid in New York, if not the country, called his desk. They told him to substitute the word "bleep." I'm not sure I even gave my paper an option. I wrote that Michaels had said, "I can spit farther than you can kick." I put the word "spit" in brackets to indicate that I was changing the real word, but some copy editor saw fit to remove the brackets.

Only *Newsday* did the F-thing.

We have a good-taste policy at the *Times*, but the next day I was told that we were not to alter quotations. Instead, we were to write the actual quotation and then have a higher-up determine whether it could be used.

But *Newsday* wasn't through with it yet. In *Newsday*'s Wednesday paper, the quotation was altered to "bleep" or something like that. It prompted *Newsday*'s media critic to write a lengthy column about what Ramsey really said, and how the New York papers reported it. It was a somber lesson in journalism, replete with "farts."

Ramsey's lousy punt, and Michaels's remark on farting, had a shelf life that would not dissipate.

But at least only Chuck's feelings were hurt, unlike so many more serious injuries that have afflicted his teammates over the decades.

10

Walt and Revival

If you count the interim coaches who replaced Winner and Holtz, Walt Michaels was the Jets' fifth head coach in 18 months when he took over in 1977. In retrospect, Holtz had begun the process of returning to respectability by bringing along players such as Buttle and Todd, who were drafted by Mike Holovak. Holtz got rid of some players whom Buttle now describes as "criminal types." And who knows? Perhaps Holtz might even have gotten good at the pro game. Certainly, he flirted with the idea of a return 20 years later in 1996, telling friends there was unfinished business in his life.

While Holtz was fun for the string of stories he created in his tumultuous tenure, Walt was more interesting to be around. Often, he furrowed his brow in contemplating some dark event. Then he'd forget about it and joke about a foolish play. He had a framed picture of his Polish-born father, wearing his coal-miner's outfit, staring down at him. Under the painting, the artist wrote, "Glad he made the boat." There was no situation in football, or life, for which Walt Michaels failed to find a Polish aphorism.

Did a player complain about bad weather hindering him? Walt had a story:

"It reminds me of the Polish sea captain," Walt reminisced. " 'Don't tell me if the sea is stormy. Did you bring the ship in?' "

He was Ward's choice to replace Holtz, "really, more of an election," said Ward. Walt had been with the Super Bowl Jets, the memory of which was fading fast on these terrible Jets teams.

Walt coached the Jets for six years and understood how to build a base. But he was a very erratic man despite his solid grounding in the game, his clever handling of players, his old-fashioned values.

Team president Jim Kensil, who replaced Ward, stuck with Walt through an often-troubled and turbulent first four seasons, in which marks of 3–11 and 4–12 were sandwiched around two 8–8 records. And then Kensil spearheaded the move to drop him just days after the Jets' finest moment since the Super Bowl, when they went to the American Conference championship following the 1982 season.

By then, the impact of 1977's draft, the greatest in the post-Ewbank era, also was dwindling. Players and the team and coaches were running out of time. Every club must maintain a nucleus of good performers who also have experience. When a team suddenly loses its identity, when this core breaks up too quickly or isn't replaced—well, look at the collapse of Yankee baseball in the 1960s, of Giants football of the same time, of the Namath Jets just a few years later.

In sports, new players must understand where they are, what their team is, and what is expected of them. Who can tell them if the defining players have been cut or have withered away, and the coach doesn't have the history to make them pay attention?

The 1977 draft produced seven starters. It was also Michaels's first as head coach. But typical Jets luck—it also was the last Jets draft run by Mike Holovak. Mike was nearing the age of 60 when he conducted that last draft. He didn't do another for the Jets because they had passed him over for head coach in favor of Michaels, so Holovak quit.

Holovak's departure and what happened after he left is eerily similar to the Jets' fortunes following the defection of George

Sauer, Sr. The club suffered because the personnel people who followed weren't as good and the drafts were abominable.

The year before Holovak left, he had mopped up for Holtz, coaching the final game of the season. As that quirky 1976 campaign ended, I speculated about who might be the Jets' next head coach. I didn't mention Holovak's name.

I was surprised, though, the next day when Holovak chided me for leaving his name out as a potential successor. I had no idea he was interested in becoming head coach, but in any event I knew that he wasn't being considered for the post. Mike had been an All-America running back at Boston College in pre–World War II days, went on to a successful stint coaching the Patriots, and had been one of the respected football men. He was also one of the most pleasant guys to be around. And he was one of the first joggers I had ever seen.

Once, I asked him why he ran and what he got out of it, and he explained that he started to jog following the death of a daughter. "It took my mind off things," he said.

When the Jets passed him over, though, he told them he was quitting. Stay, they asked him, for the draft. So his final act with the Jets almost helped the franchise to an era of dominance. Almost.

Marvin Powell was the first player the Jets drafted back in 1977. Holovak had hoped to make a draft-day trade to get Tony Dorsett, but that didn't work out. Still, Michaels was pleased. The coach understood how to build a team, and he knew he needed strength at offensive tackle. You couldn't run, and you couldn't protect your passer, without an offensive line.

Powell spoke unashamedly of becoming America's first black president. Marvin was the son of a career Army man, had traveled extensively, had starred at Southern California. If you introduced Marvin to your wife, he'd "Yes, Ma'am" and "No, Ma'am" her to death. He knew which way the Jets' winds blew. He was also an upstanding Republican.

To prepare himself for a career in politics he used to practice speeches at home, walking around the rooms saying, "Ladies and gentlemen, thank you very much."

The brain trust of the New York Titans risks split trousers and acrophobia for a photo op in April 1960. The "quarterback" is head coach Sammy Baugh; team owner Harry Wismer is third from the right, flanked by (from left) assistant coaches Steve Sabo, John Steber, John Dell Isola, Dick Todd, and Hugh Taylor.

(AP/Wide World Photos)

Don Maynard—the only man to play for the New York Giants, Titans, and Jets—poses in his Titans uniform (readily recognizable by the T on his white socks) in 1960.

(AP/Wide World Photos)

A beaming Sonny Werblin stands as coach Weeb Ewbank watches Alabama quarterback Joe Namath sign his astounding $427,000 contract on January 2, 1965—or reenact the signing, anyway.

(AP/Wide World Photos)

One of the other two quarterbacks taken by the Jets in the same draft as Namath was Heisman Trophy winner John Huarte, who threw 48 passes in his pro career, none as a Jet.

(AP/Wide World Photos)

Dr. James Nicholas, nationally renowned orthopedist and an integral part of the Jets scene, with his former patient, halfback Emerson Boozer.

(Courtesy of Dr. James Nicholas)

Fullback Matt Snell teamed with Boozer to give the Jets two punishing runners with surprising speed; he scored the only Jets touchdown in Super Bowl III.

(Barton Silverman)

Owner Phil Iselin celebrates with Weeb at the Jets' 1968 Thanksgiving dinner when word came that the Houston Oilers had lost, clinching first place for the Jets.

(Barton Silverman)

Defensive end Gerry Philbin stretches, while ubiquitous sideline presence leRoy Neiman sketches.

(Courtesy of leRoy Neiman)

On the sidelines
during Super Bowl
week: Namath, Weeb,
and, visible in the
background between
them in glasses,
assistant coach
Buddy Ryan.

(Barton Silverman)

LeRoy Neiman's
pregame sketch of Joe
Namath being taped,
"like dressing the
matador."

(Courtesy of leRoy Neiman)

Split end George Sauer, son of the Jets' player personnel director, grabs a Namath pass ahead of Lenny Lyles in Super Bowl III. Sauer caught eight passes that day, as the Colts chose to double-cover the faster deep threat, Don Maynard.

(AP/Wide World Photos)

Defensive mainstay Verlon Biggs (86) sits with Rocky Rochester during a 1968 game.

(Barton Silverman)

Namath in characteristically understated attire by the bench in 1970,
when he was sidelined with a wrist fracture.

(Barton Silverman)

Kicker Jim Turner
points out a problem
with the grass
to Weeb in 1970.

(Barton Silverman)

Guard Dave Herman (63)
with reserve tight end
Wayne Stewart (89).

(Barton Silverman)

Defensive tackle
John Elliott sacks
Bills quarterback
Dennis Shaw
in 1970.

(Barton Silverman)

Mike Battle (40), who hurtled his way into Jets fans' hearts in the 1969 exhibition game against the Giants, goes high against the Colts in the 1970 season.

(Barton Silverman)

Lou Holtz—at the time, the less famous of the two Lou Holtzes—with a rare smile during his abbreviated tenure with the Jets.

(AP/Wide World Photos)

Walt Michaels leaves the field after the infuriating 14–0 loss to Miami in the 1983 AFC Championship Game, not knowing he has coached his last NFL game.

(AP/Wide World Photos)

Quarterback Richard Todd (right) indicates the location of his injury—a broken collarbone—to his friend and backup (and nearly his replacement) Matt Robinson. Robinson's deception about an injury of his own cost him Walt Michaels's confidence and his starting job.

(AP/Wide World Photos)

Punter Chuck Ramsey has a kick blocked in Seattle in the game that led to a memorable Michaels moment.

(AP/Wide World Photos)

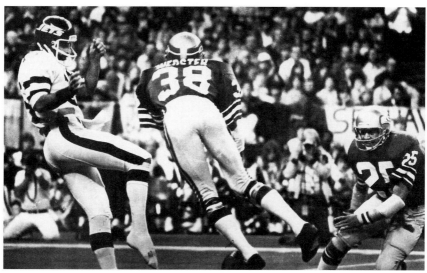

As a defensive line, you're nothing without a nickname. The Jets knew they'd arrived when these four became known as the New York Sack Exchange. From left: Joe Klecko, Marty Lyons, Abdul Salaam, and Mark Gastineau.

(Courtesy of the New York Stock Exchange)

Richard Todd gets hit by the
Dolphins' Kim Bokamper
during the 1983 AFC
Championship Game.

(Courtesy of Gerald Eskenazi)

Muddied, but not unbowed:
Marty Lyons on the sidelines
in the quagmire of the
Orange Bowl during the
closing moments of the AFC
Championship Game.

(Courtesy of Gerald Eskenazi)

Trainer Bob Reese
helps Al Toon off the
field after Toon
suffered one of the
many concussions
that led to his 1992
retirement.

(Courtesy of Bob Reese)

Coach Joe Walton
scratches his head—
as so many Jets
coaches have—while
watching his team
fumble on their own
one-yard line during
the 1989 season.

(AP/Wide World Photos)

In this image taken from the television transmission, defensive end Dennis Byrd collides head-on with teammate Scott Mersereau in a 1992 game against the Chiefs. The care taken of Byrd in the immediate aftermath of the collision probably prevented his paralysis from being permanent.

(Courtesy of NBC Sports)

Coach Bruce Coslet and general manager Dick Steinberg stand with Dr. Mark Kirchner during a news conference concerning Dennis Byrd's condition.

(AP/Wide World Photos)

Why are these men smiling? Because neither is clairvoyant. Owner
Leon Hess, declaring that he wants results *now*, stepped in to hire
Rich Kotite—then riding a personal seven-game losing streak—to be
the Jets coach in 1995. Kotite's two Jets teams went 4–28, including a
1–15 season in 1996 that followed a $70 million spending spree for
free-agent and rookie talent.

(AP/Wide World Photos)

Wide receiver Keyshawn Johnson just gets the damn ball in a 1997 game against the Bears.

(AP/Wide World Photos)

A leader at last: coach and designated savior Bill Parcells stands with Mo Lewis (57), Adrian Murrell (29), and Wayne Chrebet (80) as the Jets unveil their new-old look for 1998—a return to the logo from their glory days, however brief.

(Courtesy of the Official All-Star Cafe)

Marvin believed in fate, that his destiny was greatness. "Events just follow me," he used to say.

Often he meditated at his locker while around him players were screaming or beseeching or throwing up. With the Jets, he became the best tackle in football.

There was much that was contradictory about him. He liked to describe himself as a "laissez-faire capitalist." Yet in 1982 he accepted the Jets' pleas that he become their player rep. Even though he had once told the head of the Players Association that players should take a cut in pay if the team doesn't make money, he felt that by becoming a voice in the union he could bring in some capitalist sanity.

Marvin had everything mapped out. He would:

• Receive his law degree by the time he was 31.
• Make the Hall of Fame after retirement.
• Go into the Marine Corps as a military lawyer.

"I used to go around saying, in the seventh and eighth grade, 'I'm going to be All-America in high school. I'm going to be All-America in college. I'm going to be all-pro.' And their taunting made me more determined. I heard the same taunting when I said I want to become president. People told me, 'Marvin, you're a black man in America. Marvin, you've got a white wife. Marvin, you can't be president.' "

He did in fact become a lawyer. He did not make a serious run for the Hall of Fame, although he performed in the Pro Bowl, but as far as becoming president . . . well, would the fact he was a Jet be held against him?

Wesley Walker was Holovak's second pick of that draft. And if it seems odd that such an outstanding playmaker wouldn't have been plucked in the first round, it was because he'd had knee surgery that could have affected his speed. And, oh yes, he had another problem that could have made it difficult for him to catch the ball: He was legally blind in one eye.

"He also had a bowed knee," recalls Dr. Nicholas. "And Marvin Powell had a torn cruciate ligament. He played with a brace his whole career. We rated both of them P2 in health, but we drafted them."

Wesley used to memorize eye charts so that no one knew there was a problem with his eye. The Jets caught him cheating after they drafted him, but by then it was too late. Still, Michaels was philosophical about his pick. How bad could Wesley's eyesight be, the practical coach remarked, if he had caught all those passes in college? It was a good thing for the Jets that Michaels understood this. In Walker's first three seasons he led the NFL in yards per catch, averaging a gaudy 21.1, 24.4, and 24.7.

Farther down the draft, Holovak took a running back, the useful Scott Dierking, who was to lead the team in rushing one season. Joe Klecko came on the sixth round. It would be four more years before he would become the leader of the group known as the Sack Exchange.

Kevin Long, another running back who had one productive season in which he was the Jets' top rusher, was the team's third choice of the seventh round. Then came Dan Alexander, an offensive lineman from Louisiana State known as "Gator," and finally, on the ninth round, quarterback Matt Robinson. Seven players who would start at various times, including the bulwark of the offensive and defensive lines and a Pro Bowl receiver.

Alexander liked to hunt in the Louisiana bayous. Once, on an expedition with Dierking, he warned him, "The green eyes are the frogs. The red eyes are the gators. Don't reach for the red eyes. They'll take your arm."

That was his clipped way of speaking. He also had a no-nonsense style of playing right guard. Because he said little, everyone just assumed he was a country boy from Louisiana.

Actually, he was from Houston, where he made his home. His father was a stockbroker. Dan had a degree in law enforcement. He liked to believe that when his football career was over, he would join the Federal Bureau of Investigation.

But as a Jet, his closest brush with the criminal-justice system came in the locker room in 1981. That was when Todd, emerging as a key player, got into a famous fight involving journalistic ethics. Todd decided to settle it by choking a reporter.

It swirled around the *Post*'s Steve Serby, who infuriated management and Michaels and some players with his penchant for digging up dirt. The thing is, even though Steve's comments and quotations often were outrageous, they also were accurate. Even Kensil privately acknowledged that Serby was extremely accurate in getting his quotations down. Sometimes he would go off the deep end, and at these times his machine-gun approach missed the mark. He had embarked on a Get Michaels campaign years before, and he wasted little time and few chances to zing the very zingable, suspicious coach.

Serby also had been close to Robinson and favored him over Todd. Once Steve fixated on something, his fingers wouldn't let go—as if he were gripping his dilapidated typewriter, which always looked as if it had just survived a crash-landing in the Peruvian jungles. When computers came in, his electronic machines didn't fare much better; he was always giving them a whack to get them started. Steve was famous for blacking out press boxes when he'd insert a plug from his faulty computer into an electrical outlet.

Earlier in the season, Steve had written a column that contended that the Jets could never win a Super Bowl with Todd at the helm.

Steve, along with Ed Ingles of CBS radio (who was doing the play-by-play), was in Todd's doghouse. They both decided this particular day to patch things up by seeing Todd at his locker. Instead, it escalated into an expletive-laced verbal exchange between Serby and Todd. Finally, frustrated after several "Get lost's" and worse from the quarterback, Serby told Todd, "Well, that's not very mature of you."

"So now you're telling me how to act," said a suddenly seething Todd.

"There was a pause," recalls Serby, "and I sensed the whole thing unfold and danger was imminent. I stopped and remember clutching my reporter's notebook. And he grabbed my throat with his right hand and he knocked me into Bobby Jones's locker. I must have been out for a few seconds and I woke up and saw Gastineau —and how would you like to wake up to see him?—hovering over me and saying, 'You'd better get to a hospital. It looks as if you broke your nose.' "

That wasn't hard for Todd to do. He was six-two and weighed

205 pounds, while the man he sacked was six inches shorter and 50 pounds lighter.

At the moment Richard hit Steve, the locker room was half-empty. Most of the players had gone onto the field for the start of practice. Writers were allowed into the locker room before practice began, and I was standing at one end talking to Powell. Alexander was next to me when we heard the commotion, looked up, and saw Steve sagging.

Powell reacted in his typical political fashion when he saw what happened.

"Uh-oh," he said, "now we're really gonna get it."

Alexander had his own spin on it.

"Did you see Serby push Richard?" asked Alexander, the law-enforcement wannabe. "At least, that's what I'm gonna say if anybody asks me what happened."

Serby was taken to a hospital. While he waited for treatment, someone there gave him a Band-Aid for his nose, which was bleeding but not broken. Meanwhile, I asked Kensil for comment. Todd refused to talk about what happened, but he did discuss it with Kensil.

Kensil's response surprised me, although it shouldn't have, given his feelings toward the reporter:

"Richard told me he told Serby to leave at least three times," Kensil said. "We certainly don't condone pushing on or off the field, despite long-term provocation."

Essentially, Kensil had sidestepped Todd's responsibility and put the blame squarely on Serby, the victim. The incident actually provoked a wider debate than the locker room. It became a national discourse on how much a player is supposed to take from a reporter—as if walking away from him wasn't an option.

Meanwhile, the *Post* gloried in Serby's tumble. It couldn't have happened to a better paper. The *Post* exalts the outrageous, and if it happens to their own man—why, it's just perfect. First, their lawyer threatened criminal-assault charges against Todd. Then the lawyer had a word or two for Kensil:

"If Mr. Kensil regards the printed word as provocation, then Mr. Kensil is living in the wrong country."

That night I waited at the Jets' complex for Serby to return to get his car. He came back from the hospital sporting a Band-Aid over his nose, and shaken. But what was delicious about that moment in the parking lot—the scene of so many of Steve's secret interviews with players who did not want to be seen speaking to him in the locker room—was his reaction to my questions.

"No comment," said Serby.

The next day's *Post* had a back-page headline that screamed, "Todd Assaults Our Man," and showed a photo of Steve with his Band-Aid.

The following day the locker room resembled a crime scene, but out of a "Naked Gun" movie. Someone had taken adhesive tape and formed the outline of a body on the floor in front of Todd's locker. Then several of the players walked in—wearing Band-Aids over their noses.

"If that happened today, Kensil would not have been able to take the stand he did," contends Serby. "But a couple of days later my tires were slashed in my parking lot in Bayside, Queens. It was a terrifying period for me. Then of course Todd had the game of his life in Baltimore a few days later."

Watching that game from home—the *Post* told him to lie low for a while and avoid Jets contact—was like getting smashed twice for Serby.

"The Jets were winning big and so there wasn't much to talk about in the game. So in the second half I'm watching Bob Trumpy and Bob Costas debating whether Todd had a right to do that, to knock me into the locker." Trumpy, the former hard-nosed tight end player, was "pro" Richard shoving Serby.

Well, the *Post* did in fact file criminal charges and the cops interviewed Serby, as did NFL security. But the Nassau County district attorney, Denis Dillon, who once fired an assistant for possessing marijuana, declined to make an issue of the charges. "I think he ruled I was not hurt badly enough," says Serby. However, the league did fine Todd.

"Later on in the year we shook hands," Serby recalls.

.   .   .

The Serby–Todd set-to was another incident that showed just how fragile the Jets were as a team. Suspicion was everywhere, especially when Serby continually quoted an anti-Michaels source he described with sinister glee as "Deep Jet." Serby used to quote Deep Jet about the inner workings of the team: Some statements were on the mark, while others simply had no basis in fact. It all made for paranoia.

The players took everything to heart since they lacked the big, bad player who could unite them. There was no Reggie White for them, and when things went wrong, there was no leader who could help right the team. In time, Klecko and Fields would serve that function, but just as they once had led the team with their courage and action, they also split the team in later years between young and old because of their decision to cross the picket line during the 1982 strike.

Meanwhile, the locker room contretemps helped harden the re-solve of management to keep the news media at bay. The Jets had always been known for their openness. It began with Weeb. I used to sit next to Namath when he was being taped in the trainer's room before practice. Reporters could stand behind the huddle in practice: We just had to make sure to get out of the way when Joe took the snap. It wouldn't do to have him run into you.

But year by year, as failure piled on failure, new restrictions came into place. The time for interviews in the locker room was cut back. Reporters were shuttled to the sidelines. They couldn't fly with the team any longer. Increasingly, an air of suspicion hov-ered over reporters. And it wasn't much better among the players, who mistrusted management more than management mistrusted the press.

Kensil's firm hand on the team was as much a function of his conservative philosophy as his understanding of football. On the Jets, you never criticized management. Ever. The day after you did, you were gone. Jim, a former newspaperman, had his own view of the First Amendment:

"Freedom of speech," he once told me, "doesn't give you carte blanche to knock your employer."

Kensil made that pronouncement in 1979 after cutting a line-backer named Bob Martin, who had criticized Michaels. When I quoted Kensil on his freedom of speech philosophy in a story, one of the players, Clark Gaines, asked me, "What does this mean?" as he pointed to the words "carte blanche."

Gaines was to learn. He was part of a procession of players who became the Jets' union representatives but in short order found themselves kicked off the team. Looked at coolly and dispassionately, it was not their union jobs that cost them their playing jobs. Every team must have a union rep—and Kensil himself tried to explain to players who were reluctant to take the post that the Jets needed someone who could make their teammates understand the issues. "I want them to know what's going on," he insisted. It is also true, though, that since most player reps are older, their future is limited. They are expendable.

Logic, though, doesn't go very far with football players. They react on emotion, and the Jets seemed to be more emotional than most. Martin's outburst, and subsequent swift dismissal, set a tone for the team that persisted for a decade: The front office hates the players. At least, that's what they thought.

The next year, Shafer Suggs, a defensive back, angered because the club would not activate him following his recovery from a rib injury, described the team as "a lost cause." Suggs soon was an ex-Jet.

Incidents like these followed quickly on the controversy swirling around the Jets and the union. First, player rep Burgess Owens was traded. Then Gaines, who had taken Owens's place, was waived following his recovery from injury. Gaines was an outspoken, passionate union advocate who had the respect of players. When he left the team, the scar was permanent.

Meanwhile, a rift developed on the Jets between those who blindly followed the union and those who never believed in a strike. The most outspoken antiunion man on the premises was Greg Buttle. So guess who became the next Jets union rep? It was Buttle.

This was a guy who would loudly criticize any player who dared knock Michaels. When Buttle learned that some players had given off-the-record comments to Serby, Buttle shouted loud enough for anyone in the locker room to hear, "Any player who's a man should not hide behind anonymity."

He had a 1950s sensibility in the 1980s. His father was an FBI agent. His sister was an FBI agent. Greg was already investing in businesses on Long Island. He joined the union not because he saw himself leading a march of workers toward a new dawn, but because he didn't trust anyone else to take the job.

Ultimately, Buttle quit before the 1982 season because of what he called players' paranoia and endless worrying. Not only did Buttle quit, so did his assistants, Klecko and Schroy.

"There's too much bullshit," said Schroy.

The Jets were thrown into turmoil in the summer of '82 when they met to decide who would replace Buttle. No one wanted the job. As the exhibition season was about to begin, the Jets were the only team in the NFL without a union representative.

The union even sent two officials from headquarters in Washington to calm the players' fears before they voted. The head of the union, Ed Garvey, a man who would have been more at home in the 1930s, had once even suggested that the Jets traded Owens because he had been on the league's committee studying race relations.

Now the Jets were forced to vote. And the man they chose was —and this should be hard to believe, but then again, this was the logic-defying Jets—Marvin Powell,the self-styled "Churchillian conservative" who just a few days earlier had said he was not interested in the post. Walker was voted his alternate.

Powell, like Buttle, claimed he had taken the job because he wanted to make sure the players got the right information. This future president of the United States wound up suing the Jets years later when he charged they traded him because he had been elected president of the union.

Of course, in time Marvin was sent away and Johnny Lynn, a defensive back, took his place. Within a year, Lynn was told he had failed the Jets' physical. Retire, the club told him. That angered him. In the next strike year of 1987, more confusion and problems: When the players met in minicamp before the season to vote for another player rep, Lynn stood up to tell the players that, like Powell, he would begin grievance proceedings against the Jets, charging them with discrimination based on union activity.

That's all the players had to hear. Now no one wanted the job. Freeman McNeil, their fine runner who had a live-and-let-live philosophy, had publicly announced he would cross a picket line if there were a strike. When the Jets met to figure out what to do, he walked out of the meeting before the vote. He wanted no part of a union.

Despite the appearance of Gaines, who had become an official of the union in Washington following his retirement, players didn't want the rep's job. Some were asked point-blank to accept it and they said no.

The Jets were so skittish about committing themselves that they sought safety in numbers. They formed a "council" of six players. Most were untouchable by management. From this group, certainly, someone would step forward: quarterback Ken O'Brien; wide receiver Al Toon; tight end Mickey Shuler; strong safety Lester Lyles; offensive tackle Reggie McElroy; wide receiver Kurt Sohn. The first five were all starters.

No one from the council stood up. So, said Sohn, "I'll do it if there's no objection."

He was the number-three receiver behind the two stars, Toon and Walker. It was highly unusual for a backup player to be a team's union leader. But he got the post in a Jets version of the old Army slapstick routine—the one in which the sergeant asks for a volunteer to step forward, and everyone else takes a step backward except some sad sack who is left all by himself.

And what about McNeil, who vowed he would never strike?

He gave his name to the landmark case that brought free agency to the NFL in 1993. For when the union sued the league demanding free agency, the lead name on its suit was Freeman McNeil. Forevermore, when players leave one club for another for their million-dollar bonuses, McNeil—the man who once said, "What do I have to strike about? I made a deal with the Jets and they're upholding their part of the bargain"—should be thanked.

Bizarre? Yes. But also dangerous, as the festering paranoia kept the Jets from developing the cohesiveness that marks a successful football team.

. . .

For Richard Todd, there is no mystery about the lean years that followed his time with the Jets. The reasons are similar to those expressed by his teammates and even generations of Jets players he never performed with.

"It's been management all the time," Todd says. "They got a number-one pick for me when they traded me. And they took Ron Faurot and then cut him the next year. Or they took Lam Jones. He couldn't catch the ball."

Richard makes an admission:

"I never wanted to play quarterback. In school, I always wanted to be a receiver. But they lined us up in high school to see who could throw the farthest."

Thus, when he arrived in New York in 1976 to succeed Joe Namath, it wasn't as if he was a lifelong quarterback. He was never bothered by the pressure of replacing Joe, he contends:

"Joe and I were friends. I didn't sit there and try to be Joe, just like someone can't come in and be Marino."

At first, being drafted by the Jets, and being reunited with Namath, whom he had come to know from visits to his alma mater, Alabama, was thrilling. He didn't realize the decay and ruin that the Jets were in.

"I came in as a rookie thinking everything was going to be great. But coming to the Jets was taking a step backward."

Of course, Richard wasn't used to getting booed. But waiting six seasons before having a winning campaign can be trying. Thus, he remains very aware of the New York fan and his schizophrenic nature.

"Was I aware that they would turn on you? Oh, yeah. I think I was one of the ones they turned on. I'll never forget the signs they would hold up. I'd have a good game and it'd be 'Todd is God,' and a bad game, 'Todd is a Clod.' I remember a game as a rookie. First they were cheering Namath, then they booed him. And when I went in they cheered me. Then they booed me.'

Eventually—actually it wasn't until his sixth year—"I developed as the team developed. We weren't very good and then we got better. We took on Walt's personality. We became tough like he was. We got nasty on the field. We wouldn't take crap."

Todd gives the defense credit for what the Jets ultimately became. Indeed, it is an enduring phenomenon of football, a game almost always dominated by talk of quarterbacks and running backs, that when the quarterback talks of playing on a winning team, invariably he will start with the defense.

The Jets knew what they had when Walt was made the coach in 1977. He knew defense. I remember watching him with his coal-miner's hands using a little compass to draw neat circles as he diagrammed plays on a piece of white paper, neatly and precisely. He may not have talked that way, and he didn't act that way. But he was smart and he knew what he wanted.

He was a man who gloried in the past, who confronted his players with threats of physical violence. Once, when the great Jim Brown knocked him down when they were scrimmaging on the Browns, Walt looked at him and said, with great surprise, "What's this?" as if some kid had come over and whacked him one. Walt wasn't to be messed with, although he respected those who did. Thus the affection he had for Buttle. It went back to the linebacker's rookie year of 1976, after Walt had gone into a tirade against the unit.

"Don't put me in the same bag with those guys!" Buttle shouted in the locker room.

"Sit down," growled Walt.

I asked Buttle what he did.

"I sat down," replied the linebacker.

Walt had trouble forgiving or forgetting. Yet he forged the Jets into a group that was noted for its heart.

He was a defensive-minded coach, very good at constructing formations to halt enemy offenses. He had scope, though. The first draft pick of his regime was an offensive lineman, right tackle Marvin Powell of Southern California. And in his second draft, in 1978, the Jets plucked Chris Ward of Ohio State. Walt was surrounding Todd with the necessary protection to get going. Indeed, in Walt's second season, with those bookend tackles, the Jets were 8–8 and provided him with a dilemma.

He didn't know who his quarterback would be for 1979. Matt Robinson had come out of nowhere during 1978 with his riverboat gambler's mustache and his flair for the long downfield pass to Wesley Walker. Robinson had replaced an injured Todd, and with the new quarterback the Jets discovered a deep-passing game. But now, in the summer of 1979, Michaels was in a quandary. There is the old football adage that you don't lose a job to injury. Since it's a sport in which everyone—truly, *everyone*—suffers from something, you couldn't keep the troops going if you took away their jobs because of an injury.

Yet Michaels felt he had to reward Robinson's often-spectacular throws during Todd's absence. Robinson had teamed with Walker, whose receiving average of 24.4 yards a catch was one of the highest in history. When Wesley went deep, Matt found him. So Walt decided on a quarterback shootout in the exhibition season. This was an exciting moment in Jets history, even though it divided the club. Attention was paid to the team. The quarterbacks, meanwhile, made a pact: They would not allow the shootout to affect their friendship. Richard, though, not as savvy or as sophisticated as Matt, often was badmouthed by Robinson, someone he considered his friend.

The battle for the job ended ignominiously with Robinson's wrist-wrestling injury and Todd's subsequent return to the starting job. An injury could not cost you a starting job, but hiding and lying about one sure could. Walt Michaels would not abide a player he couldn't trust, and Matt Robinson's days with the Jets were numbered, his last pass being the interception he'd thrown in overtime on opening day.

· · ·

There had been limited expectations in the few years before Walt took over, but after the 1979 season, when the team went 8–8, Walt's good buddy, Jimmy (the Greek) Snyder, did him no favor.

Snyder, who acquired an undeserved national reputation as a football expert because he was on television, actually blew the biggest prediction of his life, making the Colts 17-point favorites over the Jets in Super Bowl III. Jimmy, though, sailed along blithely, and some people, and reporters, listened to what he had to say.

After the Jets' second straight 8–8 season, Snyder predicted on national television they were going to the Super Bowl. Not quite. Instead, they lost their opening five games in 1980 and that was that for their season, as they finished 4–12. Later Snyder was to complain that he really didn't mean to make that prediction, "But we were running out of time and Brent Musburger asked me who I liked and I was rushed and I picked the Jets to win the American Conference title and go on to the Super Bowl."

Super Bowl? Midway through the 4–12 record of 1980, Townsend Martin, one of the owners, wanted Walt fired. But Hess, who also spoke for Helen Dillon, overruled him. Walt was staying.

"I have learned in my oil business that sometimes it's worse to make a change than to stay with what you've got," said Hess.

The hounds were baying at Michaels's heels even louder in 1981, when the Jets opened at 0–3. His Jets coaching record at that point was 23–42. Some ex-players were saying things about Michaels, and even one of his players, free safety Shafer Suggs, became the first active Jet to suggest that Walt must go. Walt traded Suggs and installed second-year player Darrol Ray in his spot. Ray became a star creating big plays.

Somehow, Michaels held the 1981 Jets together despite that terrible start. They were a nervous lot, some of them whispering off-the-record things to selected newspaper reporters, while others, such as Buttle, whom I once dubbed "Walt's son," were irate that these players were talking behind Walt's back.

There was one memorable point when I thought Walt wouldn't make it. They were blown out by Buffalo, 31–0, in their opening game, then lost, 31–30, to the Bengals.

That led to some of the more unusual moments in the history of jurisprudence and journalism, when a pressroom full of sportswriters debated ethics—ethics!—and the niceties of the First Amendment. I had my little role to play in this bizarre endeavor.

The morning after the Bengals loss we were jolted to life in the press room.

Walt appeared suddenly in the doorway. He was boiling.

"Bill Verigan, get in here!" he commanded the writer from the *Daily News,* a good reporter but a nervous sort of guy with a high-pitched voice.

Michaels was angry after having received a phone call from Emerson Boozer. Boozer read him a sentence in the article Verigan had written that day. To Boozer, it suggested that Michaels was giving up on the team. Boy, that was all Michaels, who couldn't abide a quitter, had to hear.

He brought the frightened Verigan into his office. Then Michaels pried off his Super Bowl ring and flung it onto his desk.

"You never got one of these, you cocksucker!" Walt screamed.

Michaels was shouting so loudly that Kensil, having heard him, went into the office and closed the door. Elsie Cohen, a grand-mother who was Walt's secretary, shuddered.

An hour later, Walt returned to the press room for his usual Monday followup interview. He was unshaven. He wore tinted glasses. His words were slurred and his sentences rambling. In other words, he looked and sounded drunk.

It was a brutal press conference. We were all over him. His coaching record showed almost twice as many losses as victories. His team had blown leads of 14–0 and 17–3 to a Bengals squad whose resilience and talent we hadn't guessed at. They went on to the Super Bowl that season.

But we continued to hammer Walt, who may have been ham-mered himself. We asked him what was wrong with his prepara-tion ("I don't fault myself for one thing in the game," he declared). We asked him what was wrong with the team's preparation; it had been hit with 14 penalties.

This was hardly a day he enjoyed listening to second-guessing. Normally, he was robust and voluble at these sessions. He might give one or two of us a sly dig about something we had written. His words, though, were coming with apparent difficulty and he spoke in what sounded like a stream of consciousness.

He concluded his press conference defiant still:

"We're on schedule as far as what I consider a championship, playoff caliber."

The words resonated after he left the room. We looked at one another and broke out laughing. Zero-and-two, he appears drunk, and the Jets are "a championship, playoff caliber"?

We had to write this stuff—the Verigan "cocksucker" thing, the slurred speech, the glazed look. The problem was, how to slip it into the newspapers.

Informally, I was appointed to preside over this gathering of newshounds as we discussed the ethics of our trade. Can you call a guy drunk because he looks and acts it? Would we write about Verigan? Newspapers love to write about anyone except other newspaper reporters.

I called our legal department. We always were big on legalities and checking, and at times like these, my adrenaline surged. Why, this was beyond sportswriting. The landmark First Amendment case, in which newspapers were granted virtual carte blanche to write about public figures, is called *The New York Times* v. *Sullivan*.

I spoke to a lawyer in our legal department. Her advice to me: If you point out the symptoms—that his speech was slurred, that he might have walked unsteadily, that he had a glazed look—then you were within legal guidelines for writing that he appeared to have been drinking.

I relayed this information to my colleagues. It seemed pretty safe for us to write that, at the very least, Walt was under the weather. The question now was going to be how we depicted this situation. I also suggested we get Kensil and tell him what we saw and what we might be writing. Fair play dictated we get comment from the president of the team whose coach seems to be unravelling.

"I see a man extremely tired," contended Kensil. "He's been watching films since five o'clock this morning. He's got no sleep. He looks at the films and he gets madder and madder."

No help there. Nor was any expected. Jim Kensil was the last man who would have been worried about another's drinking. It did not seem to be a negative value to him.

The locker room was edgy. I sidled over to one of the players and asked him if he thought Walt was acting funny that morning. I told him what I had observed.

"If you're asking me if I thought he was drunk," said the player, "I'll tell you this: You ask 25 guys here and they'll say no." Then he added, "But you got to write what you see."

That was confirmation enough for me.

I hedged my story. I didn't say Walt was drunk, but I did use "slurred" and "rambling," and mentioned his dark glasses.

We saw Walt again on Wednesday. He was upbeat and smiling in preparing to face the dangerous Steelers. Before he started talking, he looked in my direction and said, "Well, can you see my eyes now?"

He survived not only that assault but the following Sunday's onslaught by the Steelers, who crushed his team by 38–10. A huge number of columnists had made the trip to Pittsburgh, thinking they were about to preside over the demise of a coach. We all collared Kensil after that game and he continued to stick up for Walt, calling him once more "a good coach."

After that 0–3 start, more than half the players refused to come to the locker room the next day to talk to newsmen. Todd, the most approachable of Jets, stopped giving interviews. (This was about a month before his confrontation with Serby.)

Walt saved his mind games for his team before Game 4, when another loss might have simply destroyed the season. He cleared everyone except the players out of the locker room—the trainers, the assistant coaches, the equipment men, the team physicians.

"I'm going to leave it up to you," he said before his 0–3 squad faced the Oilers. "If you want to win this game, come out. If you don't want to win it, don't bother to come out."

The Jets produced a spectacular turnaround. They trounced the Oilers, with Todd having his best game in the pros.

"My coaches at Swoyersville High School in Pennsylvania used to do that once in a while," Walt remembered. "Sometimes you've got to do something, even if it's wrong."

After that 0–3 start they went 10–2–1. They lost only to the Seahawks, whom they faced twice. That 10–5–1 record was good enough to squeeze them into the playoffs for the first time since the 1969 season.

You could sense that the Jets, with their Sack Exchange, with Todd connecting with Wesley Walker, with rookie running back Freeman McNeil, the first-round draft pick out of UCLA, making his presence felt, were on the verge of a run that would take them into the mid-1980s. They won seven of their last eight games and faced the Bills in the playoffs.

It ended badly but dramatically. Indeed, Walt's guys almost pulled off the greatest comeback in postseason play after falling behind by 24–0. But in the closing seconds, trailing by 31–27, Todd looked for wideout Derrick Gaffney in the end zone. He was in front of the scoreboard flashing "WE CAN DO IT!" Todd never saw Scott Dierking all alone, calling for the ball, and he never saw the Bills' safety Bill Simpson cutting in front of Gaffney. Simpson intercepted the pass on the one-yard line to seal the Bills' victory.

The next day Walt had another of his strange moments, which started to come more frequently when the Jets were in extreme pressure situations.

He was supposed to address the players at a final meeting and then, of course, hold his closing press conference. Walt walked into the team meeting, said, "Happy New Year," and was gone.

Players looked at one another wondering if he was angry at them, wondering if he was still coach, wondering just what they could have done, this winning Jet team that, briefly, revived memories of another generation.

Walt never came in for the press conference. "He's exhausted," said Ramos. There never was a further explanation.

Big things were expected of the 1982 Jets, which was a surprise. For years, people had stopped expecting anything from this club. But now with Joe Walton solidified as the offensive coordinator, Todd playing with confidence, with Freeman McNeil at running back, with the defense having shed more than 100 points, and with four players going to the Pro Bowl for the first time since the merger of 1970, the Jets were on their way, weren't they? And at the helm was Walt, in all his humanity.

"Walt had always been a fiery guy. He took every loss personally," remembers Ralph Baker, who was one of Walt's Super Bowl linebackers and later his linebacker coach. "Sometimes we'd come into meetings and you didn't dare lift your head for fear you'd meet his eyes. And if he saw you looking at him he'd light into you."

The first time the Jets played the Cowboys was 1971. But Baker still shudders at Michaels's reaction:

"After the first quarter we were down, 28–0. At halftime he started screaming at us. He yelled, 'If any of you guys don't back up to the window when you get paid, I'll break his leg.' He was always threatening physically. Remember the *Heidi* game, how he tried to break down the officials' door? He'd work himself into a rage and you couldn't do or say a thing. You'd have to wait for him to calm down. Look at the Super Bowl—he had a brother on the other team and he never said a word to him the whole week."

There were two demons that chased Walt incessantly. One was clad in turquoise: Don Shula, coach of the Dolphins. The other wore black: Al Davis, who had the odd title of Raiders managing general partner, but whom Dave Anderson always described as the managing general genius.

In a way, Walt was right, for Shula and Davis both ultimately conspired to oust him as coach of the Jets, though neither man would understand his role.

Walt had a thing about them. It went beyond jealousy or respect or not trusting them. He believed they plotted against him, that they devised ways to torment him. He and Shula came from the same part of the country, had even been teammates on the 1952 Browns. Shula wasn't good enough to start on those great Browns teams, though Walt was. He knew Shula firsthand. As for the con- niving Davis, Walt's anger at him went back 20 years. Al Davis had fired Walt from his very first pro coaching job. When Davis was made the Raiders' head coach he cleaned out the 1962 staff that included Michaels, then a rookie assistant. There had been other incidents over the years that fueled Walt's anger and imagination, such as the time the Raiders refused to allow the Jets to practice in Oakland the day before a game because the field was wet and covered with a tarpaulin. Michaels told the security guard he was going to cut up the tarp with a knife. The guard relented.

Once, during a Jets practice on Long Island, a helicopter flew overhead.

"If you're watching, Al Davis . . ." screamed Walt, shaking his fist skyward. Walt saw me looking at him, bemused. "Just kidding. Don't print that, Al," he said.

With the 1982 opener against the Dolphins looming, Walt sud- denly had something to say about Shula, the man with a genius reputation of his own. While Walt's Jets were notorious for their huge number of penalties, Shula's Dolphins perennially were the league leaders in committing the fewest infractions. Walt was among the rival head coaches who believed that Shula's commanding position on the league's Competition Committee—which graded the officials—had something to do with it.

Now, though, Walt went into a tirade against football's Mr. Clean. There was something funny about the films the Dolphins sent to the Jets, claimed Walt.

All NFL teams are required to exchange game films of the last few contests. But the quality of the Dolphins' films, charged Walt, was the worst. You couldn't see their uniform numbers, and that meant you couldn't tell which players Shula was shuttling in and out for key situations. The film quality was washed out, as if deliberately overexposed.

"Ask Jimmy Pons about it," said Walt. We did. Pons was the Jets' film coordinator, a job he created after having carved out a career as a guitarist for one of the more famous bands in American rock —the Turtles, the group that brought you "Happy Together."

Jimmy confirmed Walt's complaint. So I called the Dolphins' own filmmaker, the guy who made copies of the game films to send to the Jets.

"There's no hanky-panky going on," he insisted.

Finally, I called Shula and relayed Michaels's charges. Shula's reply told me something about Shula.

"Boy, Walt really reached all the way back to Swoyersville for that one," said Shula.

How many other head coaches in the history of pro football knew that Walt Michaels was from Swoyersville, Pennsylvania? Michaels heard of Shula's remark, and filed it away.

The Dolphins throttled the Jets, who came back to win the following week. But the Jets' march to respectability was interrupted for two months by a players' strike.

Because of the nationwide impact that *The New York Times* has, and enjoys, Jim Kensil invited me to lunch one day to discuss a matter of utmost urgency.

We met at the Hofstra Club. Kensil, remember, was the straight arrow—play and live by the rules (although his interpretation of the First Amendment was somewhat offbeat), follow the best interests of the league and football, don't do anything that has even the appearance of impropriety.

What he proposed was that he would break the league rules.

The Management Council, the negotiating arm of the league's then-28 owners, had put in a gag rule when talks between the players and the owners had heated up. Any executive or coach who made any statement to the press regarding the talks would be fined $100,000.

Now Kensil not only was the Jets' president, he had been the long-time executive director of the NFL. If anyone symbolized the league and its rules besides Pete Rozelle, it was Kensil.

"I would like to be a management source for your stories," Kensil proposed. "There is so much misinformation out there and we need to get it right. The union is filling the newspapers with misinformation. It would take too much time for the Management Council to rebut everything the union says. But I can be a source for you and try to explain what's really going on."

There was, of course, no doubt in my mind that Kensil was speaking to me after receiving approval from the Management Council, or Rozelle, or both. The council had been created following the previous strike (the one that so devastated the Jets on the eve of what they expected to be their glorious 1975 season). It was formed, Wellington Mara once explained, so that owners didn't have to negotiate with their own players. He didn't want a barrier between the sides.

The council hired its own lawyers and negotiators, while the union had its representatives. It kept the lines clean and clear between players and owners. There was a buffer between them in negotiations. Nobody should take it personally.

Kensil proposed acting as my private Deep Throat.

"I will call you. If you're not in, I'll leave a message that 'Mr. Lewis' called. That's my middle name."

Of course I was intrigued. Secret messages. Unnamed highly placed sources. I was going to get something no one else in the writing business would have. I ran it by my sports editor, Joe Vecchione. He said it would be okay, but just be careful.

It was hardly a watershed, or Watergate, series of stories I wrote. I quoted the "source" just once, an innocuous quotation about the union's intransigence that I realized later was so self-serving and meaningless as to be worthless. I thanked "Mr. Lewis" for his offer and didn't bother using him anymore.

But perhaps I learned a useful lesson: The NFL, or the union for that matter, postured publicly in taking the high ground. Behind closed doors, or cloaked in anonymity, they might try anything.

Perhaps, I thought, the players on the Jets had good reason to be paranoid about management. Then again, if I were paying someone a few hundred thousand a year, maybe I wouldn't be happy if he said nasty things about me to a tabloid writer.

When the season resumed in late November, it was only Game 3. The Jets trounced the Colts by 37–0. Michaels was rewarded with a game ball. It wasn't for his game plan and it wasn't for the fact of victory. The players had given it to him for his humanity, the way he held the team together during the strike by not taking sides, by not making the players feel they had let him down by walking out.

Michaels was also battling a real personal emergency. His mother was dying of cancer back home. After each game he'd stay up until five in the morning to see the films, which had to be developed. He'd talk to the players, and then he'd drive to Pennsylvania, spend the night, and get back to the Jets the following day.

It turned out to be only a nine-game season, but the Jets posted a 6–3 record and were part of the Super Bowl tournament. For the second straight year, and for only the fourth time in their history, the Jets were a playoff team. McNeil led the league in rushing, Todd threw almost twice as many touchdowns as interceptions, and the so-called "golden blend" that Walt had envisioned when he took over—the four- and five-year veterans leading the team—had become reality.

Freeman had the second-biggest rushing day in playoff history with 202 yards as the Jets stormed through the first game by crushing the Bengals. Now came the Raiders, in their new home in Los Angeles.

Walt put up the barricades around the practice field. He used to suspect that when the Jets practiced at Shea Stadium in the old days, and they were going to face the Raiders, Davis had sent spies.

"Anybody could've gotten into Shea," Walt explained.

So he told the Hofstra security guard, a fellow we affectionately referred to as Harry the Cop, that no one got into the Jets complex in the days before the Raiders game. Harry was very good at enforcing these regulations, indeed, seemed to live for them.

Harry wore a Smokey the Bear hat as part of a storm trooper's brown outfit, and had a gruff manner if he didn't know you. You were guilty until you proved you were not a threat. Harry loved growling, "Lemme see some ID."

Walt, though, had a coterie of friends Harry routinely allowed to pass through the iron gate. There was a guy named Rocky, who used to wear a warmup jacket. There was Footsie, who ran a restaurant. There was Eddie-Oh, who furnished Walt with Chinese food.

Now, though, no one got in.

"I'm sorry," Harry told a friend at the Thursday practice, "but Walt doesn't want anybody here this week."

Marty Lyons could have used a security guard of his own in the locker room before the Raiders game. For this was the game of games up to then in Lyons's professional life, and he felt he had to bring his pregame ritual to a new level of spirituality and Animal House crassness. Marty tried to whip his team into a frenzy by going nuts himself.

These were the big, bad Raiders, and the Jets were the underdogs. He wanted them to turn tiger, not to fear the fiercest team any of them would ever meet. So Marty picked up a movie projector and held it over his head and was about to throw it through the window.

"No, don't do it—you'll get fined!" shouted tackle Marvin Powell.

Safety Kenny Schroy took it out of Lyons's hands. After all, breaking a table—which is something Lyons did routinely—was one thing, but smashing a projector, so important in film sessions, was football-related and would hurt the team.

"So I thought I'd break a piece of wood instead," says Lyons. What he didn't realize was that the Raiders had painted a window to look like a piece of wood. Why would they do that? Maybe it was part of an Al Davis scheme. Marty rammed that wood with his fist, and instead of merely breaking a panel, he heard glass shattering.

"When I pulled the arm out, the jagged edges of glass started to pierce it, and blood was going every which way. It was pretty bad. But they taped me up and I played."

The Jets, presumably for having practiced in private, perhaps psyched out of their mind by the sight of Marty's blood, were a finely tuned unit. They grabbed a 10–0 lead by halftime. They were serious but energized as they trooped into the locker room at the ancient Los Angeles Coliseum for their 15-minute rest before the third quarter.

As Michaels was striding through the hallway to meet with his players, a security guard had a message for him.

"Mr. Hess is on the phone," the guard said, pointing to a black wall phone inside a small storeroom nearby. "He wants to talk to you."

This was the first time Hess had ever telephoned Michaels during a game. Of all the clubowners, Hess was the least likely to phone his coach at halftime, or any other time. Michaels hurried over and picked up the phone.

"Tell Mark Gastineau he's crazy," said the voice. Michaels listened for about 30 seconds, and then realized this was not Leon Hess. But who was it? Michaels conjured up the answer.

"Al Davis, I'll choke you!" Michaels shouted into the phone.

Shaken, furious, Michaels hung up the phone.

Whether the Jets responded badly to Walt's new emotional state after halftime is impossible to determine. But they came out flat and the Raiders came out charging and produced a pair of quick touchdowns to take a 14–10 lead. Todd and Walker combined in the final period to position a touchdown run by Scott Dierking, and the Jets led by three points in the closing minutes. Then Lance Mehl intercepted Jim Plunkett and it seemed a sure thing that the Jets could run out the clock.

But McNeil, playing on the same field where he had starred so often for UCLA, fumbled, and the Raiders, with their threat of the bomb, were back in contention. Instead, Mehl produced his second clutch interception to hold them off.

The Jets were headed to the American Conference championship. I headed down to the locker room, expecting to see a jubilant Walt. Instead, he was carrying on about Al Davis.

Nearby, Leon Hess was sitting on an equipment trunk looking bemused at Walt's tirade. At that moment I thought: Hess is not going to forget this. At a time in Jets fortunes when Walt should have been excited about a victory, congratulating his players, talking of the excitement of going to the championship game, he started to obsess about Al Davis. Clearly, something was wrong here.

Since I had gotten to the locker room late, I asked Walt to repeat what he was talking about. He told his strange tale.

"I don't know if it was Al Davis who put the guy up to it or not," Michaels snapped. "But he didn't hurt us. He helped us. There are certain ways to play the game. He was the first to move a franchise without permission. What do you care if you win a game if you have no principles? The phone thing was a cheap L.A. trick," he insisted.

Just then, Gastineau walked by and asked what all the commotion was about.

"A man who said he was Leon Hess called Walt at halftime and said you were a jerk," I told Mark.

"Leon Hess said that?" the impressionable Gastineau responded.

I dashed over to the Raiders' locker room just as Davis was leaving and asked him about the call. Davis, the guy from Flatbush, Brooklyn, had an answer:

"Walt's out of his fucking mind," said Davis.

Back up in the press box, Phil Pepe of the *Daily News* got a phone call. It was from a bartender in Queens, New York. He had heard Walt's postgame comments on the radio.

"I made the phone call," said the bartender. "I bet on the Raiders and I wanted to rattle the Jets."

After the game, I took a redeye flight back to New York so I could see Walt the following day, Sunday. That was when the Dolphins and Chargers were going to meet in their playoff game, with the winner facing the Jets for the AFC championship. I wanted to be around Walt when he learned which team he was going to face.

There were no players around when I got to the training complex the next day. Walt was in his office. There were a few cans of beer on his desk. He had the television on. The Dolphins-Chargers game was about to start.

I told him that a bartender from Queens had admitted making the phantom phone call. Didn't that change his mind about Al Davis? Walt would not be swayed.

"How do you get on one of those little black phones that's for inside calls only?" Walt retorted. "That call was made from inside the stadium."

Just then, the cameras showed Shula prowling the sidelines.

"There's the fucking genius," said Walt, glaring at the TV screen.

.   .   .

Maybe Walt was on to something about Shula. Certainly, the Jets' closest shot at the Super Bowl since the Namath era was sabotaged. Was it an Act of God, or an Act of Shula?

In the days before the championship game at Miami, it rained hard and more was predicted. In an ironic note to this whole soggy mess, Al Ward, who left the Jets after Kensil was hired, had become assistant to the president of the AFC. In this position, Ward's major responsibility was to make sure the field for the championship game was in good condition.

Instead, Ward messed up the Jets in his newest capacity as surely as he had as their general manager. The Dolphins, who claimed they didn't own a tarpaulin—and anyway, the Orange Bowl was owned by the county, not by them—never covered the field. It was composed of a special grass mixture that was supposed to drain quickly, but it obviously didn't work right under the intense downpours.

When Kensil got to the stadium Sunday morning his usually florid face flushed even more. He was an even-tempered man who liked to run an even-tempered team, but he was having trouble choosing his words, complaining over and over, "It's inexcusable."

The field was a quagmire and was precisely the antidote the Dolphins needed to offset the Jets, football's best running team. Not only that, but the Jets had great defensive speed, too, with their pass rush. And Ward kept insisting that the experts had told him the field would drain properly.

Well, the rest is history, failed Jets history. McNeil, who had produced rushing performances of better than 200 and 100 yards in two previous playoff games, was held to 46 in 17 carries. Todd described his own game as "my worst as a professional." He was intercepted five times, including three by A. J. Duhe, who ran one back for a touchdown. Walker, double-teamed, caught one pass for no gain. The Jets were shut out, 14–0.

Jets management to this day blames Shula. Ask around the front office and they can recite the league rules on tarpaulins. But the players look at it differently, especially Todd.

"I wish we had a dry field, first of all. But you look at the game film. You've got to give Shula credit—they beat us three times that year. We couldn't put them off guard. Look, I threw five interceptions. But people didn't look at David Woodley's stats. He threw three interceptions. The score was tight. We didn't try something else. We didn't put Wesley in motion. We had to do something to help him and didn't adjust. I definitely think we were outcoached on that one."

They couldn't know it at this moment, but none of them would ever come this close again—indeed, no Jet team would the rest of the decade, even stretching deep into the 1990s.

"You go to the playoffs twice in a row and you think, 'Boy, this is great. We're going to do this every year,' " recalls Mike Kensil, who was the club's traveling secretary and ultimately became the director of operations.

Actually, one player saw that this sort of magical chance doesn't happen often. The Jets had played only a nine-game season, had entered a postseason tournament that was different from other playoff setups, had won two games as an underdog—and nearly made it to the Super Bowl.

Fields, the captain, understood.

"There will never be another 1982 New York Jets football team, and the 1982 Jets didn't do it," he said. "Next year it will be a different team. There'll be some different players. This exact team will never have the same chance."

How right he was. He neglected to add that there'd be different coaches, too.

Walt Michaels refused to cry publicly about the field after the defeat, although he certainly alluded to it.

Joe Walton, meanwhile, was up for three head-coaching jobs. He planned to go for interviews immediately. Thus, Todd tried to sneak out of the locker room before the press cornered him. But we collared him and he was very polite in talking about the failed offense that had accumulated just 139 net yards, the worst in the 23 years of the AFL/AFC title game. He never criticized Joe Walton. Neither did Walt Michaels. There never was any evidence that Walton was sniffing around for Walt's job, and Walt was content to allow Joe to run the offense. Walt was good that way: He hired you, he respected you, and he expected you to do your job.

Late that day, the Jets were preparing to take their charter back to New York. McCulley and other assistants had asked Walt in advance if they could bring their wives back with them. Walt didn't want spouses on the flight, didn't believe in it. But it troubled him to have to tell that to his assistants. So Jim Kensil told him, "Don't worry about it, Walt, I'll tell the assistants it's my idea."

But before the flight took off, Ramos learned that his wife, Jackie, a flight attendant for TWA, could not get back to New York that night because her flight was canceled. And Donna Janoff, who worked for the Jets and who was to marry running back Mike Augustyniak, was on that same canceled flight. Both were permitted to return on the charter.

When everyone loaded onto the Jets' flight, some of the assistant coaches saw Jackie and Donna and complained to Walt. He was hardly in a good mood, in fact was in a very foul mood. He began to complain and berate Jim Kensil for favoritism in allowing those two women aboard while banning the coaches' wives.

Kensil's son, Mike, stood up and said, "Now, Walt, you know that's not true." Michaels stood up, stared at young Kensil, and headed for him. Mike Kensil got out of the first-class section quickly and made for the back of the plane.

Walt sat down again and contemplated Shula this time.

"If he says anything about my hometown again," said Michaels, "I'll kill him."

There was another passenger on that flight who was taking it in: John Hess, the son of the owner and a man of substance in his own right. John had no interest in running the Jets, and eventually he replaced Leon as the head of Amerada Hess. But in those few hours, John Hess was surprised at the depth of Michaels's irrational behavior.

When the team arrived back at New York's LaGuardia Airport, Walt insisted that the airport shuttle bus, which goes to the parking lot, take him to the Jets' camp at Hofstra. Michaels shoved the bus driver, who eventually talked him into taking another bus.

Walt's anger did not abate. The next morning there to was to be the traditional end-of-season meeting with his players—the one at which he had issued a terse comment the previous season—and his final press conference.

Instead, Walt prowled the halls. "They broke every rule in the book," he repeated to no one in particular. Some people there said he had spent the night awake and angry, in pain from a neck injury dating to his playing days, taking painkillers to ease the hurt.

The locker room emptied a few minutes before the scheduled 11:00 A.M. meeting as the players hustled to the huge conference room to be on time. Michaels was the kind of guy who always consulted his pocket watch, as if he were a train engineer. He did not excuse lateness.

But when the players showed up for their meeting, they were greeted instead by Jim Kensil. He told them Walt would not be coming. Then Walton addressed them instead.

Since those of us in the press room didn't have Walt to sum up the game, and the season—or the era, as it turned out—we called on Walton. He was, as usual, available and gracious. He also was not yet the head coach.

It was still Walt's job, but in the next few days he started to drop hints to his assistants that he was going to be fired. Still, there was another job to do: The Jets' coaching staff had been chosen to go to the Pro Bowl in Hawaii. The game is staged a week after the Super Bowl.

When he returned, he met at a motel on Long Island with Kensil and Leon Hess and the Jets' medical staff. There was also a physician there who specialized in substance abuse, although that was not a term widely used then.

Hess and other members of the Jets' hierarchy had been concerned all season long about Walt's behavior. Indeed, once during a practice that season, Michaels had fallen, apparently for no reason. That launched an investigation into the cause of his unsteadiness.

As usual, at the motel meeting Walt adamantly denied he had any sort of problem, but the decision had been made.

He was given an offer he could not refuse: Take a financial severance package worth more than $400,000, and get help for a substance-abuse problem. The package consisted of the final two years of his $130,000-a-year salary, and an additional $60,000 a year for the following three years.

The next day the Jets issued a terse statement, presumably dictated by Michaels. Michaels had said that he didn't want the word "burnout" used in the statement, the word popularized by the Eagles' Dick Vermeil, who had quit just weeks before as a result of his own self-imposed pressure. Michaels simply said he was resigning, explaining that he had never taken a vacation. It was 17 days after he had led the Jets to the conference championship.

Walton, the Jets said, would be the new coach.

The news shocked defensive-line coach Dan Sekanovich, whom Michaels had hired the very first year he became head coach. It was Sekanovich's first NFL job and followed a stint in the Canadian Football League. Sekanovich had helped mold the Sack Exchange. Of the four, only Abdul Salaam had known a pro line coach other than Sekanovich.

Sekanovich had been looking forward to 1983 after having seen his team get to the conference title game.

"It would have been unbelievable," he says now, from a distance in Buffalo, where he eventually went on to coach under Marv Levy on the Bills.

"I was shocked, shocked, when I heard the man was let go."

Sekanovich was so dismayed that he quit the Jets.

"There are some things you have to do. You go home with the one that brought you to the dance. A guy brings you into the league, it means something."

Sekanovich also considered the fact that Dan Henning had offered him the assistant head coach's job with Atlanta.

Sekanovich believes he understands a major and overlooked reason the Jets then collapsed: Not only did he leave, but so did Bob Fry, who had been the offensive line coach since 1974, and had tutored Powell and Ward and Fields and Alexander. Then Bob Ledbetter, the running backs coach, who had brought along McNeil and who had a special relationship with his players, left to join the Giants for more pay.

"Look, here's what happens," explains Sekanovich as he contemplated the changes. "New people come in. They're good. But the personality of the team changes—and I didn't think the team at that time needed any changes."

So it wasn't only Walt that was leaving. Perhaps the three most important position coaches—the offensive and defensive lines, and running backs—were suddenly gone.

"All I can say is that Walt Michaels was a hell of a football coach," concludes Sekanovich. "He took the Jets from mediocrity to winner. Who else did that? Only Walt and Weeb."

. . .

Fifteen years later, Michaels was still wondering if he had been blacklisted—why, in all that time had no one from the National Football League even inquired whether he would be interested in so much as an assistant's job? Michaels was reflecting on that even as Vermeil returned to the NFL, and as Mike Ditka ascended, left, and came back as well. But Walt's only connection to football, other than being paid to give gambling tips over a 1-900 phone number, had been a fling a few years later with Donald Trump's New Jersey Generals of the USFL, the league that was supposed to rival the NFL. Walt's Generals teams did well, but when the league folded, Walt was out of football again.

The irony, of course, was that the Jets had to fire the best coach they ever had after Weeb.

"What I can say about Walt now," says Richard Todd with the perspective of time, "is that teams go out of their way for players who have problems. So why couldn't they help him?"

11

The Sack Exchange

The most famous take-no-crap, take-no-prisoners performer for Walt Michaels was Joe Klecko, the heart of the defensive line that was dubbed the New York Sack Exchange.

Klecko didn't get there first, but he was the foundation and he presided over a group that, together, actually had a starring run of only two years. He had a long Jets career, though, and his presence kept alive the hope that maybe, just maybe, the Jets would be able to recreate another golden moment.

Joe was part of Walt's first draft group, and he was one tough guy. Players on the team were actually afraid of him. Not that he threatened them (well, at least only some of the time), but he exuded violence.

He had a little joke. Making believe he was about to punch you, he would hold up his right fist and say, "Do you want six months?" and then he would hold up his left hand and add, "or life?"

The first time I saw him I thought the Jets had robbed the world's biggest cradle. He had a pink face and pug nose, was barely six foot two inches, and weighed about 250 pounds, all of it round.

He was the Jets' sixth-round draft choice of 1977, a legend of the Philadelphia sandlots but from Temple University, which made him suspect.

I once asked him to describe his life to me, for he had always dropped hints about unsavory associations, odd jobs, little suggestions that he had flirted with the other side of the law. I'm sure he did, but not in a bad way, you understand. He used to hint playfully that he used to collect debts—or break windows, and threaten to break arms—for "some guys you wouldn't want to know." Was Joe fooling around? Perhaps he was. I always felt that he liked leaving you wondering.

Joe liked to drive. In a car, he would be reflective, telling me about his street-thug adolescence, and then suddenly talk about what being a father meant to him. He was proud of the things he had to do to get to his status in the NFL. Once, as we drove along Hempstead Turnpike not far from the Jets' practice facility, I suggested where he turn to get onto the Meadowbrook Parkway.

"Don't ever tell me anything when it comes to driving," he said, with the merest hint of menace.

Brought up in Chester, Pennsylvania, he worked as a truck driver, part-time boxer, and semipro football player. He suited up on weekends under the name of Jim Jones for the Aston Knights.

Temple offered him a scholarship, which he decided to take "after a couple of years of getting up at five, six o'clock in the morning for my jobs." The Jets discovered him at Temple. He became a football player of profound courage, and despite repeated knee surgery, and game-day hangovers, he remains the only defensive player in league history to go to the Pro Bowl at three different positions. Of course, that didn't help him escape a prison term for auto-insurance fraud after he retired.

Klecko led the league in sacks in 1981 with 20½ as the Jets came of age. But he was also a devastating tackler and blocker. He cleared out swaths of players, allowing the linebacker behind him, Lance Mehl, unobstructed paths to the ballcarrier. All Mehl had to do was avoid stepping over the bodies Klecko had leveled. Mehl produced 168 tackles that year—47 more than the middle linebacker, Stan Blinka.

Klecko's buddy was his alter ego, the grumbler Joe Fields. Fields was the team's center, so they went up against each other in practice every day from 1977 to 1987. It got more intense when Klecko shifted to nose guard and was directly opposite Fields.

They shared a house in Point Lookout, Long Island, during the season while their families were back home. Sometimes around midnight, they'd have a discussion about a football move.

"What would you do," said Klecko, "if I did this?"

"I'd do this," claimed Fields.

"No fucking way," replied Klecko.

"So show me," retorted Fields.

They cleared the furniture to the side of the room. There in the middle of the living room, the pair of 250-pounders would hurl themselves at each other. They broke more than one table.

From his humble beginnings as the 14th-round pick of 1975, when the Jets chose offensive linemen named Joe Wysock, Tom Alward, and Dan Spivey ahead of him, Fields had worked his way to the top.

They caught each other's eye: low-round players with tremendous work habits, no-nonsense approaches to the game, and a certain toughness. They also liked to share a brew.

They'd sit in a bar until 3:00 A.M. and talk about their fathers. Klecko told Fields how his father rarely gave him recognition, of how after one baseball game that 12-year-old Joe won with a home run, his father asked him, "How come you booted the ball at short?"

As the 1980s progressed, Fields and Klecko became team icons, although both ended their careers in misery and anger. At the start of the 1986 season, Klecko was football's highest-paid defensive lineman at about $700,000 while Fields was the game's top-paid offensive lineman at $400,000. Yet, if you looked at them in their T-shirts proclaiming the name of some bar in Philly or South Jersey, wearing their outsized blue jeans, you would have thought you'd fallen in with a construction crew. And you would have been right.

Joe Fields was doing welding on top of a water tower in the middle of winter of 1981 when he suddenly realized—"What the hell am I doing here? In three days I'm going to Hawaii for the Pro Bowl!"

That epiphany for Fields allowed him to give up metalworking in the offseason—but not offseason work. He went on to earn a real-estate license, a stockbroker's license, an insurance license. He was a certified financial planner.

The pair shared businesses. They owned four restaurants and some real estate. Klecko also had a piece of a popular Long Island bar-restaurant.

And yet, when their careers ended, both suffered major business setbacks. Everything they had done as players—including crossing picket lines—had been geared to amassing money for retirement. Essentially, they lost everything through bad business decisions or bad luck or timing in the real-estate market.

Of course, Klecko's pals will tell you that it was his loyalty to friends that led to his prison sentence. Ironically, it revolved around a truck and an oil company.

"You know Joe, he's always trying to help people," one member of the Jets family explained to me. And in a sense, he was right.

Klecko was indicted in 1992 as part of huge scheme in which 67 people were named. The conspirators were part of a three-year auto-insurance scam that targeted a Sun Oil Company refinery. The 67 were charged with conspiring to collect on car damages that never occurred—damage that supposedly resulted from emissions from the oil company operation and ruined the finish on hundreds of vehicles.

Two of the men made false claims on a pickup truck owned by Klecko. Later, in front of a grand jury, Klecko vouched for the claim. So while Klecko didn't actually initiate the scheme or move it along, he was caught lying about his minor role in the whole affair. Privately, he told friends he had lied to the grand jury because he thought he could help out his friends, that he hadn't even been aware they were putting in false insurance claims in his name.

He got a fairly stiff sentence in 1993: three months in prison for lying to a federal grand jury. He served his time at Allenwood, the white-collar federal penitentiary in Pennsylvania where so many of President Nixon's associates had also stayed. In addition, the judge ordered 39-year-old Joe to remain under home detention for three months after he served his time. He was also hit with a $3,000 fine and ordered to perform 150 hours of community service.

"I am sorry not only for myself but I am more deeply sorry for the pain and the embarrassment that it has caused everyone in my family," Klecko told the court. The troubled United States economy destroyed two restaurant companies he backed and cost him his home in one of the tonier townships in Pennsylvania, Chester County. His 10-acre spread went on the sheriff's auction block after a bank foreclosed on Klecko, who along with business associates had borrowed $1.7 million. The home had been used as collateral along with his restaurants and a gym. The name of one of his companies was Jets Group Inc.

We spoke about his life since then.

"Everything's going great," he said one day in 1997. "I've got three young kids and they're keeping me busy. Nothing like it."

Three young kids? Well, I figured, this is a typical nineties kind of thing. Older guy marries younger woman.

"No," he said. "I'm still married to Debbie. We're practicing Catholics. We had the three kids while I was playing, and then we didn't have any for a long time. And then we got three more, one after the other, just like that. I love it."

Joe said he was so busy once again that he didn't have any time to talk during the week.

"Love to talk to you on either Saturday nights, or any time Sunday. But I've just got no time the rest of the week," he explained.

.   .   .

Once upon a time, Marty Lyons had looked up to Klecko. Marty played tackle alongside him as a Sack Exchange legend.

Lyons was the first player the Jets drafted in 1979 as they closed out the decade—a time that had come to symbolize despair and defeat for the Jets and Giants as well. Yet the Jets had finished at 8–8 the year before, and in Lyons on the first round, and then Gastineau on the second, they appeared to have plugged in the defensive line. The previous two drafts had brought them the offensive line bookends, Powell and Ward. Clearly, the Jets were ending the 1970s as New York's better team.

The year looked so promising for the Jets that for the first time, New York was allowed to be the site of a *Monday Night Football* game.

Lyons came onto a team on which Klecko already had established himself as the strongman, emotionally and physically. It was to be Lyons's legacy one day, but not quite yet. Although he had come from Alabama, a national power, and was the third top draft pick the Jets had chosen from the school (after Namath and Todd), he was merely a rookie. He didn't want to say much in front of Klecko or Buttle, the outspoken linebacker. Lyons, an emotional, outgoing guy, became the quiet rookie.

"I remember my first night off, I was going to the city. And you know that spot on the Grand Central Parkway where it splits off and you're supposed to continue westbound? I didn't take it and I wound up on the Interboro Parkway and the next thing I knew I was in Brooklyn."

The six-foot-five-inch, 255-pound Lyons survived the ordeal of actually driving in the place I used to call home. But he was so shaken and confused that he said the heck with it, and eschewed Manhattan that particular night. He found his way back to the leafy safety of Long Island.

"No one said much to you in those days," he said of 1979, as if it was another America. "I got on an elevator once in Baltimore with Walt, and he said nothing the whole ride down."

But Walt did speak to him enough once to give him the only bit of advice he was to offer the lad that rookie year: "The name of the game is get to the quarterback."

As a rookie, Lyons was tested as a pass-rushing defensive end. Klecko was on the other side of the line and was the team's best quarterback-chaser.

"I went into the weight room and Joe was there lifting along with John Roman and Stan Waldemore. They were offensive linemen and traditionally, they were the weight guys. Defensive linemen were supposed to be quicker. They didn't spend as much time lifting, but there was Joe in the middle with them."

"Where you going?" Klecko asked Lyons.

"I'm finished," replied Marty.

"Listen," Klecko retorted. "You and I are going to be playing together a long time, and if you want to stay with me, you're not going to leave until I'm finished." Marty got undressed, put his shorts and T-shirt back on, and returned to the weight room to lift with Klecko.

They stayed together for eight years, long after the Sack Exchange had burned itself out, and deep into the failed Walton era.

"We should have been able to build from one year to the next, and whenever it seemed we could, a piece of the puzzle was missing," laments Lyons. He is sitting now in the boardroom at a Long Island office of Paine Webber. He joined the brokerage firm after repeated attempts to get a Jets assistant-coaching job following his 1991 retirement.

"I told them all I'd work for nothing just to get the experience," he says. "I asked Bruce Coslet, I asked Pete Carroll, I asked Rich Kotite, I asked Bill Parcells."

As for the name "the Sack Exchange," it probably was invented by a fan once the team got good in 1981.

Marty remembers that Pepper Burruss, who was the assistant trainer, had started to chart the defensive line's sacks. Burruss was so proud of their deeds, he put the chart on a wall. In fact, it looked like a stock chart.

Meanwhile, at one of the games, Ramos saw a fan holding up a bedsheet on which he had scrawled "New York Sack Exchange."

"Say, that's not a bad name for them," Ramos said. In his next press release, he began to chronicle the unit he dubbed the "New York Sack Exchange."

Those of us in the press quickly adopted it. The nickname fit well, it gave the group a ready identity, and it caught on instantly. Helped by that sonorous nickname, they became the toast of New York. They seemed ready to follow other great teams with a great defensive front and a nickname that defined them perfectly: the Steel Curtain, the Purple People Eaters, the Fearsome Foursome.

Klecko was the right end, Lyons the right tackle, Abdul Salaam the left tackle, and Mark Gastineau the left end.

When the four appeared on the floor of the New York Stock Exchange one day in October 1981, trading stopped. They received a sustained ovation. The team was just breaking out after its 0–3 start and was routinely recording five and six sacks a game. They were famous.

"That name gave us recognition," says Lyons. "All Abdul and I had to do was keep the middle occupied and Joe and Mark went one-on-one—and they could beat anyone one-on-one."

Sixteen years later, himself a stockbroker now, Lyons returned to the floor of the exchange.

"And you know what, there were a few people there who still recognized us," he said, proudly.

Spearheaded by the Sack Exchange, the 1981 Jets recorded 66 sacks, then the second-greatest total in NFL history. Lyons, who was to undergo eight operations in his career, missed most of 1982 with a hamstring injury, then came on in the playoffs to generate three sacks in three games.

His pregame performance before the 1982 playoff against the Raiders in the Los Angeles Coliseum was an extension of his raucous and histrionic nature. By then, he had long sloughed off his rookie fears and reluctance to go nuts. He had always wanted to do wild and crazy things before a game, but Buttle used to take over the locker room with his wild-eyed and oratorical exhortations. Buttle would get him so worked up, Lyons's body shook.

"Between my second and third year, it was like the torch was passed," he recalls. "I got up and said something and the adrenaline wouldn't stop."

If the team needed a lift, Marty would provide it with some outrageous action. He would split a table in half, he would scream obscenities—goaded on by his teammates, who couldn't wait to see what he had in store for them this time.

Away from the game, Lyons had a traumatic and yet cathartic experience before the team's seminal 1982 season. He had become a volunteer Big Brother to a six-year-old boy named Keith, who had a terminal illness. In a six-day span in March, Lyons's wife, Kelley, gave birth to a son named Rocky; Lyons's father, Leo, died; and then Keith died.

"I never got to enjoy the birth of my son," Marty recalls. Emotional about the tumbling events, and wanting to keep his father and Keith alive in his memory, he started the Marty Lyons Foundation. Its premise was simple and wonderful: to grant a wish to a child diagnosed with a terminal or chronic life-threatening illness. Helped by his celebrity status, it grew to encompass several states, and now helps more than 200 children a year, raising half a million dollars annually.

When the four players who were to become the Sack Exchange were united in 1980, only one player was at his accustomed position: Abdul Salaam, left tackle.

He was the quiet rookie named Larry Faulk out of Kent State in 1976, and I don't think any of us in the press room had ever said a word to him. We said even less when he showed up in 1977 and said his name was now Abdul Salaam.

There was in those days something menacing about the group generally referred to as the Black Muslims. Yet, while Abdul rarely smiled, seemingly always serious, he didn't growl either.

His name meant "Soldier of Peace," which intrigued me. So I broke the ice one day and started to talk to him.

He smiled and seemed anxious to talk about himself and his religion. In fact, as time went on, as we got to know each other, he often would ask me why I didn't write more about him. The quiet man actually liked a little publicity.

"I am a Muslim," he said when I asked him about the name. "In changing my name, I chose one that best fits my character."

He explained that he had decided on "Soldier of Peace" because he had fought all his life. He was a tough kid back in Cincinnati.

"So to reach the stage where I can find peace, I adopted the religion. When I was younger, all I did was fight. I grew up in a tough neighborhood in Cincinnati. You take the meanest guy there is—he's mean because he wants some peace around his environment."

Klecko was listening to this in the next locker.

"Oh, bullshit!" said Klecko.

Boy, I thought, this is a pretty scene: Good ole truck-driving Joe, making fun of Abdul's religion. What would happen next?

Abdul started to laugh.

His tenure on the Sack Exchange was the shortest of the four, and it was never the same after he left. He was dealt after the 1983 season to the Chargers, a move that stunned and dismayed him. Uncharacteristically, he complained.

"I've got some more wars in me, and I'm looking forward to 'em," the Soldier of Peace said.

Like the others on that famous line, he was done in by injuries. All their careers—although long by NFL standards and certainly distinguished—were abbreviated when they couldn't overcome serious hurts. Each of them left the Jets with hard feelings—even Lyons, the only one of the group who was given an official retirement sendoff.

Abdul had suffered such a serious rotator-cuff injury in 1983, Walton's first season, that he was in on only two defensive plays, plus a field-goal attempt, all year.

"The reason I didn't play," he claimed, "was that they probably were concerned that I would hurt myself again and have grounds for a suit. That's what the defensive coordinator told me, anyhow."

Perhaps he did, and perhaps he didn't. Football players forever fantasize about the reasons they were screwed. It's always, "Someone told me . . ." or, "I heard that . . ."

Yet, Salaam was philosophical at bottom about the trade: "I didn't want to spend all my career in New York," he claimed. "You only have one career, and you like to realize other ambitions, achieve other goals, and see other places."

We spoke again 10 years later. He said he was surprised to hear about Klecko's troubles. "Will he be all right?" Salaam asked.

"What is Mark doing?" he wondered. "Is he serious about boxing? I hear Marty's fine."

Abdul was working with youth groups in Cincinnati, and sounded as if he had made a comfortable niche for himself. Nothing dramatic, for that wasn't his style, but solid, a nine-to-five job that he enjoyed and that he felt was having an impact on kids.

After a while, though, everyone lost touch with him. The Jets would call him from time to time to see what he was up to, but he wasn't at his old phone number. His mailing address had become a PO box number. Even the Players Association pension fund couldn't reach him.

"I haven't heard from him in years," said Lyons. "From time to time we get offers to do Sack Exchange card shows and autograph sessions, and Abdul is never there. The last I heard, he was working in security for some famous singer."

.   .   .

The last time I spoke to Mark Gastineau, late in 1988, he offered to bring a bathroom scale to a diner on Long Island on a Sunday morning. He told me he would get on that scale to refute a published story that he had gained weight because he was on steroids.

Something went out of the newspaper business when Mark and football parted company. He was, in Lyons's words, "a football player, and an entertainer." I'm not sure Mark ever understood what each role was supposed to be, or how they could be separated.

Some years after his retirement, when I was also writing about boxing, I climbed the rickety stairs in a gym off Times Square. It was the kind of place fit for an old black-and-white movie about that punishing business. The punching bag hung from a beam that cracked the ceiling. In fact, all the walls were cracked and peeling, somewhat like the fighters and managers there.

Mark had been trying to become a boxer and produced a 15–1 record with 15 knockouts at one point. It was a dubious record. One of his opponents claimed that he had been paid to take a dive, falling like a tree struck by lightning after Mark hit him. At the age of 39 in 1996, he tried a comeback after two years away from the ring. He was knocked out in the second round by the former Oilers running back Alonzo Highsmith. It was payback time for all those players on offense who had always wanted to flatten Gastineau on the field.

The millions Gastineau had made in salary disappeared. I heard talk of failed wildcat oil deals, of bad investments involving family members. I heard he was living in someone's garage, or in the bedroom of a friend on Long Island, or someplace in Brooklyn. When he came around to the Jets one day in 1996, two people told me he hit on them for money.

Atop the black pay phone in the gym was this sign: "If there is a call for Mark Gastineau, he is never here."

As a football player, he was the purest pass-rusher anyone had ever seen, and was a credit to Walt Michaels's astuteness as well as that of draft director Hickey. It was the Jets' turn to coach the college all-star game in 1979, and Walt was impressed with this specimen from East Central Oklahoma named Mark Gastineau. They took him on the second round after having selected Lyons as their top pick.

Gastineau heard only his own voices. They got louder once he got famous. Every summer he redefined his body: Once he showed up after a winter-long diet of fresh fruit. His body fat had dwindled to an incredible 4 percent, actually trimmer than the cornerbacks.

He was so proud of that body that he sought me out and said, "You ought to do a story on my new body." I thought it was a good idea and I got my photographer and went up to his dorm room at Hofstra.

Mark was grumpy. He called me aside.

"I didn't shave my body and I don't have any oil to spread on me for the pictures," he said. "But look at this." He pulled out a color photo of an oiled and shaved Gastineau, his six-foot-five-inch, 280-pound bod glistening and hairless.

"Maybe you can use this in the paper," he said.

I tried to explain to him that my photographer was a union man. *The New York Times* couldn't go around using posed photos of their subjects when there was a photographer available.

He was crestfallen. We did the story, but his hair upset him no end.

Another year he had his thighs sculpted. This was 1986, and he wanted to get back his lost sack title. He bulked up to 280 pounds. To improve his thighs, which he believed helped him push off to begin his charge at the quarterback, he started to work with a West Coast legs guru known as Doctor Squat.

Gastineau came to camp able to squat 700 pounds—that is, having a 700-pound barbell nestling on his shoulder, and then squatting. He worked out twice a day, and then spent two and a half hours in his dormitory with equipment that a gym company sent him. He signed a $50,000 deal with Jack LaLanne, joining the singer-actress Cher as a spokesperson.

Mark also used to walk around in shorts, and had a T-shirt sliced at the bottom so his navel showed. He was the only player on the Jets whose "six-pack," that group of abdominal muscles, showed when he donned his uniform. That was another part of his body he once spent an offseason developing.

"All strength comes from your stomach," he announced, as if quoting a mystic shaman. Actually, there was a bit of the fourth dimension about Mark. He was fascinated with American Indian lore and artifacts, and often went hiking in the Arizona hills looking for arrowheads and pottery shards.

And yet, as much of an outcast to his teammates as he became, as much as they hated him for his selfishness, his individuality, his tardiness, I always had the feeling that there was something lost about him and that New York would never be the place where he could find it. Indeed, New York and the Jets and fame were, ultimately, the last thing he could handle.

"When I was younger I knew that if I looked different, it would give me credibility," he explained, not quite understanding the depth of what he really said.

But those 700-pound squats were healing for him. He was going through a divorce from his wife, Lisa, who had given birth to a baby girl whose name they had decided to spell as Brittny.

I don't recall the moment he began his Sack Dance. But Gastineau may have been the first pro football player singled out for celebrating—certainly, the first white one. When he got to the quarterback he would start to twirl, and from the stands he appeared to be an Indian brave celebrating around a campfire in his enthusiasm.

By 1984, the NFL passed a rule—it came to be known as the Gastineau Rule—that prohibited prolonged celebrations on the field. Even the Jets hierarchy voted for it at a league meeting. Essentially, they had voted against their own player. It didn't stop him much; he got into fights on the field all the time over it. And yet, he didn't understand what the problem was.

"I don't hurt anybody with it. It's me," he claimed. When teammates growled, he took it as jealousy.

"The situation with Gastineau was a constant problem," recalls Walton.

Lyons and Klecko, the essence of Middle America blue-collar beer-and-a-shot traditional values, hated his showboating. Only Salaam was understanding.

"If there was a clash of personalities, it didn't matter in a game," suggests Dan Sekanovich, their line coach who wound up with the Bills. "I didn't care about Mark's Sack Dance. I told him, 'If that's the way you feel, fine. If you're doing it because you're genuinely caught up in the moment, I don't have a problem.' You've got to give them their head."

The sack was to be the vehicle of Mark's fame and destruction as a football player. He soon became the first celebrity Jet since Joe Namath. Just as he went through physical-culture phases, he went through his materialistic phases.

There was the mink coat. He looked great in it, a full-length job provided by a Long Island furrier who subsequently got indicted for handling stolen furs. Obviously, Mark couldn't have known this. But then again, those were the kind of people who found themselves hovering around Mark. Or vice versa. He craved attention.

We were in a hotel in Seattle one Monday afternoon and I was in the lobby talking to Howard Cosell. Mark walked out on a balcony overlooking the lobby, saw me, and then noticed whom I was speaking to. Gastineau waved.

A minute later, Gastineau appeared on the balcony in his mink and shouted, "Hey, Jerry, how ya doing?" Cosell looked up. That night, on *Monday Night Football,* Cosell conducted a taped interview with Gastineau wearing his mink.

Then there was his Rolls-Royce. One day he showed up driving it to camp. He sort of claimed to own it. Actually, he was vague on the question, just as he was about his ownership of the mink.

Someone used to drive the Rolls to the Jets' parking lot and Harry the Cop would give it a salute, like a soldier honoring a four-star general's car.

The thing about Mark, though, is that he was good. On the 1980 team that was only 4–12, he led with 11½ sacks (one more than Klecko, who had so much more to do). In 1981, Klecko led the league with 20½ sacks, a half more than Gastineau (shared sacks count ½). In the strike-shortened 1982 campaign, Gastineau led with 6. But he truly flowered under Walton when he led the league in sacks in 1983 with 19, while Klecko was on the decline. Mark became a full-fledged star in 1984 when he set the NFL record of 22.

Look at what Walton had to look forward to.

12

Once You Cross

the River . . .

There is another major undercurrent to the 1980s in our quest
to trace what went wrong with the Jets. Sometimes the unseen is
palpable in sports, which deals with feelings that can't be charted,
emotion that can't be measured.

For many players and Jets fans, the loss of Shea Stadium—not
the acquisition of Giants Stadium—is a trauma from which the
whole organization has never recovered.

Yes, ugly, leaking, poorly run Shea Stadium, the place run by the
Parks Department, a city agency that can't figure out how to have
a pothole in Central Park filled. It was the Jets' home, however,
and it defined the team's history. It wasn't in Giants Stadium that
Namath made his stretch run, that Riggins became the first 1,000-
yard rusher in team history, that Walker loped. It was what Ken
O'Brien was designed and drafted for, and it was where Jerry Rice
would have played as a Jet because of its natural grass.

"Hey, if we played in Shea Stadium instead of Giants Stadium,
we take Jerry Rice instead of Al Toon [in the 1985 draft]. Rice was
a better grass player," explains Hickey.

"Before the draft, we watched Rice's greatest game. I asked Richie Kotite, 'So what do you guys think?' Kotite says, 'Ah, I don't know if Rice can get away from the press.' He didn't mean the media, he meant the defensive players on the other team."

If you like, blame Mayor Ed Koch for the Jets' losing Jerry Rice. Maybe if they had been at Shea Stadium, they would have drafted him.

Instead, in one of the more intriguing secret battles in the history of New York City politics, the New York Jets wound up in New Jersey. And it happened at one of those critical moments when the Jets once again were poised to do good things. Suddenly, there was a halt to that progression.

The Jets went not only to New Jersey, but to the stadium that Sonny Werblin built. For Werblin had been the head in the 1970s of the New Jersey Sports and Exposition Authority that created Giants Stadium, its adjacent race track, its nearby arena. Thus Sonny, the front-office architect of the Jets' moment of success in the 1960s, became the instrument for luring them away from the city that had defined them. And to the suburbs yet.

Ironically, in his Jets' years Sonny liked to say, "When you're leaving New York, everyplace else is Philadelphia." Or, "When you leave New York, you're camping out." Suddenly, though, Sonny latched onto a word: "megalopolis." The tri-state area was simply an extension of New York. What was the difference if you were on 42nd Street or in Secaucus? It was a straight east-west line between them. When you left the Lincoln Tunnel headed west, you weren't leaving New York. You still were in the megalopolis.

The Escape from New York had been on Hess's mind from the moment Giants Stadium opened in 1976 and while Shea Stadium suffered continued deterioration and neglect. It's interesting to note that much is made of the fact that now the Jets are the only team in all of sports that plays in a stadium named for another club. Whenever things go bad—that is, when the Jets are having their usual season—everyone says how different it would be if the Jets had a home of their own. Of course, that never can be proved.

But Shea never was quite that, either. Even at Shea, the Jets were known as the team that played a full schedule on the road. The Jets didn't train at Shea, they didn't keep their equipment at

Shea, they bundled up all their stuff and brought it there on Saturdays and took it back Sunday nights, when they had to get back to their Long Island training complex so Bill Hampton could do the laundry.

Yet the Jets had such a long and emotional connection with Shea that once they left it seemed as if they were indeed wanderers. Shea with its swirling winds was where they had moved in their Jets infancy, and where Namath and Snell and Riggins had romped. The Jets had a Queens–Brooklyn–Long Island identity. They were wedded to the Mets as the anti-Yankee, anti-Giants tandem, anti-Manhattan and the Bronx. The Jets, the Mets, and their fans were the New Breed.

These fans were younger, hipper, less entrenched, more grateful. They had been jilted once before by the Brooklyn Dodgers, then the Giants, and now were grateful for teams that stayed. The Jets had become part of a place in New York City. Okay, so their home had problems. So did many apartments in Flushing and Flatbush. On Sundays, though, Jets fans were entwined in camaraderie. It was fun to be at Shea. Still, it was not a continual love-fest. About 15 percent of Jets season-ticket-holders never showed up at Shea, either. While their fans loved them, they didn't seem to be wedded to them as tightly as those rich, button-down followers of the Giants.

The other thing about Shea was that it was run by the city, and Leon Hess enjoyed the power he had over politicians, accustomed to getting them to go along with his will. But his sway was limited. Mayor Ed Koch had other things on his mind, such as rescuing New York City from bankruptcy. The Jets? Ed Koch knew diddly about sports, didn't know and didn't care. He attended only one football game at Shea Stadium in his mayoral tenure.

In the early 1980s, Hess embarked on a long series of secret talks with the city and with the Meadowlands. The foolish people who ran the Mets had sold out to Fred Wilpon and Nelson Doubleday, both of whom were willing to discuss an accommodation with the Jets. They talked of closing the stadium's open end so that thousands more seats could be added, they talked of yielding hot dog and soda sales percentages to the Jets, and they even discussed artificial turf. All this, the Mets and the city would do.

Leon, meanwhile, had decided to move his team if he couldn't get what he wanted. He even refused to allow anyone on the Jets to sit in a luxury box the new Mets owners had built for the Jets as a peace offering. It was done in soft brown colors. It was carpeted, had paneled walls, air-conditioning, swivel chairs, and a bar.

But Hess not only refused to allow any Jets employee to use the box during baseball season, he kept it under lock and key during the football season, not even permitting Mets management to sit there. He told the Mets it had been constructed without his consent. Hess found many things wrong in dealing with New York City.

He knew that New York City didn't always deliver on its promises. Some time in the late 1970s, I noticed a water drip in the press box after it rained. The drip wore a rust spot on my desk. The water dripped directly over the seats assigned to *The New York Times*. I called everyone I could think of. No one fixed it. Finally, offhandedly, I mentioned it to Hess.

He took out a pad and pen and said, "I'll take care of it." Two years later, it was fixed. No wonder Leon didn't believe what the city told him. By then, however, his ego had also gotten in the way, as did his penchant for secrecy.

Someone working both sides of the negotiations—New York and New Jersey—told me, "This is Leon's style. He told each side that if any of their discussions leaked out to the press, he would go to the other side. When you've got a billion dollars, you can frighten people." So New Jersey was scared he'd stay in New York, and New York was worried he'd go to New Jersey. It was difficult as a reporter to get even off-the-record stuff.

The move to renovate Shea Stadium and keep the Jets heated up at just about the same time that Hess fired Michaels in February 1983. Remember, the Jets had just gone to the conference championship, Michaels was running a team on an upward curve, and the future looked bright.

Perhaps Hess thought he had more leverage just at this moment. For years he had chafed at the lease in which the Jets paid more rent for eight home games, about $500,000 a year, than the Mets did for 81 home games. And even though the new Mets management understood the Jets' problems, Hess felt that the stadium's deterioration would not be halted by a $43 million planned renovation—even if the city were able to implement it.

Thus, Hess sounded dubious in a letter dated February 25 when he told Koch he would give the city until March 15 to submit its proposal for renovating Shea. That was also the date he had given the Meadowlands people to hand him a Giants Stadium proposal.

In a letter that began, "Dear Ed," Hess, who along with his family had just contributed $48,000 to Koch's unsuccessful run for governor, wrote, "During your five years in office you attended only one JETS' game, in the company of Governor Carey, and then only stayed for a brief period."

Clearly, Hess was petulant. Even Koch's reply that the city planned to add 10,000 seats by enclosing the stadium, and to add 98 luxury boxes on the press level, did not seem good enough or even feasible.

The city did meet the deadline in submitting a proposal, but it was weak and imprecise. Meanwhile, Hess had a clear-cut invitation from Giants Stadium, with its 76,000 seats—8,000 more than Shea even after its proposed renovation to 68,000. On seating alone, the Jets would gross $2 million a year more in New Jersey, not including income from concessions, parking, and luxury boxes.

New York was fighting a losing battle with the wealthy suburbs, and Koch knew it. But Koch, with big-city sensibilities, who liked to describe himself as "a liberal with sanity," couldn't see his city being held hostage by one of the world's wealthiest men who wanted a bigger personal playpen. And that is really the way Koch saw it.

Because the mayor of the World's Greatest City couldn't understand the hold that a sports team has on those who follow it, the special angst a fan suffers in defeat, or the sense of sharing in victory, he failed to appreciate how much a part of a city the team —any team—was. Still, he responded to Hess in an urgent tone, arguing that the city's proposal was "first-rate," even though it would take 18 months to implement.

"Let me say again," the mayor stressed, "that New Yorkers in general—and I in particular—very much want you to stay. . . . On the verge of another real shot at the Super Bowl, we are particularly anxious to continue together with the Jets. New York City will not ever be without an NFL team and the Jets are our favorites." He ended with a handwritten, "Hope to see you soon."

It dragged and dragged and suddenly Joe Walton's first season, the new Jets era, was upon them. In a dramatic grandstand move, Doubleday and Wilpon offered to buy the Jets. Their messenger? Ex-governor Carey, who had become head of a committee to keep the Jets in New York. Five days before the home opener, the two wealthy Mets owners gave Carey the letter, which he hand-delivered to Hess. That angered Hess even more, and he told a friend, "Can you imagine the nerve of these guys, making a grandstand move like that?"

Still, Hess as usual made opening day a gala social affair for his family and friends. It was a warm Sunday, and those pesky Seahawks were coming to town. He brought in his usual circle. They began with a pregame buffet, but were dismayed to find that the air-conditioning was out in the private dining lounge that Hess used near the Diamond Club.

After Hess led them to his box to watch the game, he looked down on a torn-up grass baseball field that had cost him $200,000 to convert to football.

"That day was a microcosm of the whole time we were at Shea," Helen Dillon recalled. "After all those years, nothing had really changed."

More than a week later, Hess, at a college football reception, said, "The mayor never even comes to my games. He goes to the opening of the Mets, but he never comes to Shea Stadium to see my team play. Now he asks me to keep my team here."

But the dark comedy of errors and misinformation and ego continued. When city officials learned that Hess believed the mayor was snubbing him, they decided to change that image. That Sunday the Jets were playing the Los Angeles Rams at Shea. Why, Mayor Koch himself was going to attend the game, his associates said. That should heal the rift with Leon.

But the mayor never went. His deputies had forgotten that his brother was getting married that day.

The Jets beat the Rams. They were 2–2 after four games and headed for the road, to Buffalo. When they returned, though, they were to learn that their tenure as the Jets of New York was about to end.

At the next meeting with Hess, the city marshaled its forces: Koch, Carey, and the corporation counsel F.A.O. Schwarz, Jr. (yes, of the toy store F.A.O. Schwarz). Rather than respond to the city's belated offer, Hess for the first time told them he was moving to New Jersey.

But he also told them, in a *Field of Dreams* scenario: If you build me a stadium, I will come back. The important thing, though, was that he was leaving. Still, he contended, he would be willing to forfeit $10 million to New Jersey by breaking his new lease if the city could build him a new place within five years.

The proposal angered Koch so much that he publicly announced the Jets' move to Jersey before the Jets did, a few days before their game against the Bills at Buffalo. Essentially, that announcement by Koch terminated Hess's relationship with New York City. An angry Hess didn't respond immediately; he waited till after the Buffalo game, which the Jets won. They now were 3–2 and poised again as major players in the NFL.

The Mayor had angered Hess. So he publicly confirmed that the Jets would play out the 1983 season at Shea, and then be gone.

How badly did the news affect the team? Greatly. Players had made a home for themselves on Long Island and in Queens. They were the New York Jets, winners again, and suddenly they learned they would be playing in a place named for their most annoying neighbors, the ones who had been the big kids on the block. The Jets lost their next three games.

They struggled to get back to .500, only to drop their final two games of the season. In Joe Walton's first year at the helm, in their post-championship-game season, the Jets had fallen to 7–9 and were leaving town.

Some time later, I was working on a story to put the move in perspective. I called the mayor's office and asked to speak to Koch alone. He granted me an interview in his office. He made no apologies for the city's foot-dragging, but he did blame Hess and accused him of double-dealing.

"He knew all along he wasn't staying in New York," claimed Koch. And then the mayor told me something they should teach in public school.

"Billionaires," said Mayor Koch, "aren't stupid."

13

Joe Walton and the
Era That Never Was

Joe Walton seemed to have been blessed with a fine inheritance: a core of outstanding players, five of whom had gone to the Pro Bowl. The Jets were no longer a joke and no longer were defined only by that long-ago Super Bowl. The Jets of the 1980s had created their own identity and had a hip offense to go with a stinging, stingy defense.

How could the Jets' upward trend not continue, especially now with the stable Walton in charge?

Talk to Joe Walton these days and once again you're talking to the youthful, enthusiastic offensive coordinator, and not the often-troubled head coach who presided over so much frustration that overshadowed success.

Walton is back in college—in fact, just 22 miles from where he grew up in Beaver Falls, Pennsylvania, and used to watch a kid named Namath star on the Little League baseball team.

In 1993 Robert Morris College wanted to start a football program and Walton wanted to be near home. So Walton returned to his Pennsylvania roots as head coach, equipment designer, locker-room carpenter, chief recruiter, and number-one booster of the Robert Morris football team. They don't give scholarships there. In his first three seasons they were 22–7–1, and went to the post-season game known ironically as the Nonscholarship Bowl.

Walton, relaxed these days, is very willing to talk about his Jets years—the longest tenure of any coach except for Weeb Ewbank. He even knows something about the Jets' first head coach.

"You know, my dad played with Sammy Baugh's Redskins during the war," says Joe. "Tiger Walton. He had flat feet or something and so he was 4-F and didn't get drafted. I have an autographed picture of Sammy Baugh in my den. I haven't seen him for a long time, but he was a big hero of mine. I was 11 years old at the time. I used to sit on a towel on the sidelines at the old Griffith Stadium. You could do that in those days."

Of Joe's seven Jets years . . . well, he has tried to remain coolly objective: "I look at it like the rest of my coaching career—you have good times and bad times. We had some good football teams, and we had some bad teams. You stay in the game long enough, you'll have that."

As for taking over the Jets, he was faced with a dilemma, in retrospect:

"There's always a period of changeover," he explained before the 1997 season. "One of the hardest things in sports is to take over a team that's been successful. I really believe that. We had lost to Miami in the championship game. You have to make some changes on a team that was successful. The best jobs are the ones where you take over a club that has no success.

"Look at Coach Parcells [in 1997]—he wins five or six games, he'll be a hero. Once you win a Super Bowl, everyone thinks you know how to do it. And he is a good coach."

Walton's first major coaching change was dropping McCulley as the receivers' coach. In his place, he hired Rich Kotite, who had been with the Browns for five seasons. Kotite, like Walton, was a former overachieving Giants' tight end.

Joe, who had been my favorite of assistant coaches under Michaels before he took over in 1983, quickly viewed me as an antagonist. Perhaps it was because a few days before his first regular-season game, I telephoned him at midnight, after I had learned that one of his key players, cornerback Jerry Holmes, was going to jump to the new United States Football League after the season. A midnight call is part of the business. I didn't even think twice about it, nor would he, I figured.

I had known Walton for two years as the Jets' offensive coordinator. He was one of the most popular guys on the staff. But while Joe was the most affable of men, he had never gotten a late-night call from me before.

When he heard my voice and question, he said, "Jerry, I'm going to do two things. I'm going to hang up now, and in the morning I'm going to change my telephone number." Which he did.

The next day at the Jets' camp I saw the grandmotherly Elsie Cohen, who was the head coach's secretary. She was a fine woman and always perplexed by the insanity sometimes exhibited by her bosses. Before Walton, there was Walt. In Elsie Cohen's world away from football, men didn't walk the halls at night mumbling that people were against them.

I said offhandedly to her, "Elsie, anything unusual going on today?"

"Why, yes," she replied. "It was very strange. Joe came in and the first thing he did was tell me to call the phone company to change his number."

Boy, did the other reporters hate me for that one. All the writers always had the home phone numbers of the Jets coaches. The Jets were the most open team in the league, maybe the most available in all of pro sports. But Joe Walton quickly put the clamp on that tradition.

Besides making personnel changes, Walton stunned the players when he instituted rigorous workout procedures that were very different from the Michaels style. Players belted one another in pads constantly when Joe took over. Very likely, this constant pounding took its toll late in the season, when the Walton-coached Jets invariably collapsed.

While Joe never admitted that his rough workouts—starting in the brutal summer's heat—may have drained his smallish players by crunch time, he did change the way he did things after several yearly collapses.

But first, he suffered through two disappointing years in 1983 and 1984 that left him desperate. At one point in the '84 season the Jets were 6–2. They lost seven of their final eight games, and he dismissed every defensive coach who had been a holdover from the Michaels era: coordinator Joe Gardi, linebacker coach Ralph Baker, defensive backs coach Bill Baird. Walton and Gardi had driven in to work together every day for years. Then one day Walton told Gardi, "You're gone."

"I got fired the day before Christmas," recalls Baker, still bitter. "And five years later Joe Walton himself got fired the day after Christmas." Baker doesn't say it, but it is obvious the irony is not lost on him. What bothered Baker so much about his dismissal was that he was led to believe he would be returning. And in any event, of course, he doesn't believe the defense was that bad. It was the offense that was really the culprit—it never scored more than three touchdowns in a game the second half of the year. Tired? Worn out? If so, Walton didn't admit it.

"The weirdest thing was the timing of getting fired," says Baker. "We had meetings after the season and we made plans about what we were going to do when we got back." And then Baker got that phone call.

"I always thought we had some tremendous bad luck at the end of the year with injuries," says Baker now, from the safety of the Long Island office where he works for an auto-insurance conglomerate. "We always had small defensive backs and it just caught up with them. I remember once starting Buttle, who was a linebacker, at strong safety. But Joe Walton's practices were so long and so brutal, they took their toll on the smaller guys."

Those practices, in fact, were famous beyond the confines of the Jets' boot camp. Players around the league remarked at how Walton abused his men in those punishing summer days.

Yet many in the press, and the uninformed public, believed it was Walton's arrival two years earlier that had actually led to the Jets' revival. We celebrated Joe, who got repeated credit for the Jets' winning seasons of 1981 and 1982. There were some moments —not many, mind you—when Walt Michaels would make a joke about it, saying something like, "I guess I just didn't know how to coach until Joe Walton got here." But Walt never expressed any bitterness toward Joe.

My feeling was that, whatever Walton's attributes, and they were considerable, if you were to blame head coach Michaels for four years of mediocrity before Walton, then you had to credit Walt Michaels when the team achieved success. You couldn't simply say, well, Joe Walton's arrival has made the Jets a winner.

Still, Walton was the brains behind the Jets' offense, a stable guy who was taking over a team that had gotten as far as the conference championship. The Jets could only be better with him running the entire show, right?

He had established a terrific rapport with Todd, helping to turn him into one of the most efficient quarterbacks in football. Richard, in turn, was loyal to Joe. Remember, Richard didn't say a word about Walton's offense in the mud debacle at Miami.

Nonetheless, the first player drafted in the Joe Walton regime was to be Todd's successor: quarterback Ken O'Brien. He came from California-Davis, a Division II school more noted for its wine-tasting classes than its football players. The news of his drafting made Richard Todd a very glum young man. Richard figured that was the end of his Jets' career, and he was right.

O'Brien became a pretty good quarterback for a number of years. The problem that Jets fans have with his pick, though, is monumental: The Jets passed over Dan Marino to take O'Brien.

That act has haunted the Jets since, and has created a what-if longing for something that never happened:

What if the Jets had chosen Dan Marino?

That question is one of those mantralike murmurings that Jets followers have repeated over the years, as if the Jets were too stupid to realize that Dan Marino was a better quarterback—no, a greater quarterback—than Ken O'Brien. It will never go away and will remain in Jets consciousness forever—just as Red Sox fans still think unkindly of Babe Ruth's trade to the Yankees, which happened just after World War I—until a championship is won.

So I asked the man who chose O'Brien over Marino, Mike Hickey. Hickey ran the Jets' draft from 1978, Michaels's second season, until 1989, Walton's last. Hickey's drafts included a second-rounder in 1979 named Gastineau and a third-round pickup named Mickey Shuler. There were also the Hickey busts that were beauts—the dual first-round 1984 picks of Russell Carter and Ron Faurot, or the odd choice in 1986 of guard Mike Haight of Iowa, who was so surprised he admitted he expected to go in a later round.

"That Hickey," the Patriots' personnel director at the time, Dick Steinberg, said, "doesn't follow the crowd."

Another front-office executive, commenting on Hickey's style and the Jets in general during the 1980s, suggested, "They think their shit don't stink. Every other club, you talk to the GM or the personnel director and there's a give-and-take. But the Jets think they've got something special that no one else has—even though they've never won anything. When you talk to them, they're very secretive, like they've got some great talent there they don't want you to know about."

The Jets gave out that aura, intentionally or not. They'd had nobody you could call a football man directing the entire operation since Weeb in 1974. As a result, there was no give-and-take, the sharing of opinions and values that were most obvious in the exchanges among the Giants' George Young, the Skins' Bobby Beathard, the Pats' Dick Steinberg—all of them part of a virtual round table.

The Jets, in fact, had been run by a four-headed committee since 1978: Kensil, the administrator (followed by Gutman); Hickey, who ran the draft; Walton, the head coach; and Jim Royer, who was in charge of pro personnel—that is, acquiring players from other teams, or assessing players other teams dropped.

"It's not rocket science," Royer used to say self-deprecatingly of the entire NFL roster. "You need a tight end, you look at who's out there, for a guy six-four, 245, can run the 40 in 4.8 seconds, got good hands, can block."

If it were that simple, of course, you could program your laptop computer to pick a tight end out of the bunch. But when Steinberg took over the Jets' operation in 1990 after leaving the Patriots, he was appalled by what he found in Royer's files and how the Jets' pro-scouting operation worked.

"I wasn't happy with it," explained Steinberg. "Just waivers, news of injuries, that sort of thing. It was the kind of stuff you could almost get from the *Football Register.*" The *Register* is a book you can buy on the newsstands for about $16.

Royer was a graduate of the Naval Academy, and a confirmed grouch. I enjoyed jousting with him verbally. He used to like to munch nuts. Once, I bought him a bag of nuts and left them with his secretary.

A few minutes later he came down to the press room. Unsmiling, he handed me back the bag and said, "If I took these it could be construed as a conflict of interest." Rocket science, indeed.

Hickey, meanwhile, was a lightning rod around the league. The son of Red Hickey, a famed head coach of an earlier era, Mike was vilified or praised, depending on the current state of the Jets. He was a big red-haired guy who had a quick wit and temper, was feared by the secretarial staff (as was Royer), and who liked to lace his conversation with polysyllabic words.

If his one, two choices in the first round in 1984 were busts, consider that his more enduring 1984 picks were plucked from the second (Jim Sweeney) and third (Kyle Clifton) rounds, players who lasted into the 1990s.

"Ken O'Brien was my decision," said Hickey, reflecting on the controversial choice that kicked off the Walton era. "We had three players we thought could be our first pick. We had a strong team, a balanced team, and if you have a team like that you could take a player who wouldn't help you immediately, but you could develop for the long haul.

"I knew Joe's offense was complicated. I called around the league and asked about Joe and other people told me to make sure our quarterback was very, very smart—if not, he wouldn't get it. Walt had tried to keep Joe restrained, but couldn't do it."

Hickey also had personally discovered O'Brien, who had an IQ greater than 130 but who was playing for a nonfootball power. So perhaps some of Mike's ego went into the appraisal *(I've got something no one else has the smarts to have)*. And also Mike, as we know, "didn't follow the crowd." Perhaps there was something in that coloring his choices, his sense that he was a tad smarter than all those other personnel directors out there. He seemed to revel in shocking everyone on draft day.

"We saw Ken with his high IQ and incredible size and strength —but we were also looking at Darrell Green, a cornerback," recalls Hickey. "It was a question of whether we would take the cornerback or the quarterback."

Green was still with the Redskins 14 years later—when he signed a five-year contract. And Marino, who also was playing 14 years later?

"He was not a Jet because of his IQ and a bad knee," explains Hickey. "He wouldn't have learned Joe's offense and he would have been hit often and never made the Hall of Fame. People keep talking about not selecting Marino—hey, we were drafting 26th. Everyone else had a shot at him before us. I asked Bobby Beathard, 'Would you have taken Marino?' and he said 'No.' People forget there was only one team that did—and they took him on the 27th pick."

When I told Todd of Hickey's contention that Marino didn't have the smarts to be a Jets quarterback, he was incredulous:

"Hickey said what? Maybe I should have played in Miami, too," suggested Richard with a laugh.

Marino was one of two from that famed Quarterback Class of '83 still playing when Bill Parcells stormed back to New York 14 years later. That class sent six quarterbacks to the NFL on the first round, starting with Stanford's John Elway, the first overall pick. The Baltimore Colts took him and he promptly announced he would play baseball for the Yankees rather than go to such a lousy team. His strategy eventually worked and he was dealt to the Broncos.

Jim Kelly and Tony Eason and Todd Blackledge also went, and then Marino and O'Brien were still there. The Bills had elected to take Kelly over Marino, the Patriots preferred Eason, the Chiefs were more enamored of Blackledge. In other words, every other team bypassed Marino.

"Marino's reactive IQ and his other talents were off the charts— but how could he learn the playbook?" argues Hickey. "I will go to my grave saying, 'Should we have taken him? No—he also didn't do well on our physical.' I saw our quarterbacks being rushed. But if you're bringing in someone and he's not smart enough, how's he going to learn?"

O'Brien might have been smarter, and he didn't have a gimpy knee, but he also became the most-sacked quarterback in NFL history in 1985. He would get dumped once for every seven passes he threw. If O'Brien, who mastered Joe's cerebral offense, still couldn't find receivers in time, Hickey might say, imagine how much more often Marino would have gotten sacked.

Somehow, though, I can't buy that argument. Maybe he would not have become the great Dan Marino with the Jets, but he certainly would have been a heck of a player.

There was another factor in why the Jets liked O'Brien—his arm. He could gun it with a beautifully tight spiral that Hickey and Walton thought would offset Shea's swirling wind conditions.

How could they know that O'Brien would never throw a pass at Shea Stadium? For 1983 turned out to be the Jets' last year there. The next season, they moved to Giants Stadium.

We'll never know how much O'Brien's progress was slowed because of another glitch in the Jets' march to excellence—Studio 54 and the drunken brawl that led to one of the longest misdemeanor trials in New York City history. It also permanently changed Ken O'Brien's outlook on New York, and perhaps on people in general.

O'Brien's arrival had stunned Todd. Here he was coming off a marvelous season, a few inches of rain away from a Super Bowl, and his guru went ahead and selected the heir apparent.

"So you want to stir up some stuff?" Richard asked me one day 15 years later, when we spoke about his Jets' career and Joe Walton. Richard laughs easily now about the near-misses and peccadilloes of Walt Michaels and Joe Walton and even the bitterness he often felt.

Of course, Richard can afford to laugh these days. He is a big shot with Bear Stearns. He is the managing director and a principal in their fixed-income office in Atlanta. Fifteen people work under him. Lulu, his wife, and their three children live in Florence, Alabama, and Richard commutes to them on weekends in his twin-engine Cessna.

He became a full-time broker after his career ended with the

Saints. He had a final brief fling with the Jets as a backup years later. "When New Orleans gets rid of you," he explains, "then you know it's time to get out of football."

Life as the quarterback of the New York Jets never seemed to consume him. He couldn't understand the vagaries of fans, but then again few players in New York ever do. He always put more store in his family than the team. He always had a life off the field. Still, I always had the sense in talking to Richard that there was one bit of unfinished business to his life—that 1982 season.

"I think they sort of panicked," he suggests, thinking of Hess and Kensil. "I think if Walt Michaels had stayed the head coach it wouldn't have been that big a change. The next year Freeman and Wesley got hurt, and you have a new head coach. If you look at Joe Walton's situation—he's inheriting a team one game from a Super Bowl, and then you fail. You know who everybody's gonna blame: the coach.

"Was I surprised when the Jets took O'Brien? A little bit—especially when Marino was out there. He was the best I saw. But you can't dog them. Everyone else passed him up."

As for Walton's ascension, Todd is not so kind.

"I didn't think we were that old. When Walton was named head coach I thought it was the greatest thing. And in hindsight I think it was the worst thing. He had so many allies on that team, guys who really liked him. But it was like the Peter Principle—he was promoted to the level of incompetence. He was a great offensive coordinator. He treated you fairly. I learned so much. But now when I talk to some of the guys who stayed with him, I hear them badmouth him."

. . .

Todd wasn't the only one who began the 1983 season out of sorts. So did Walton. And so did many players. We saw how Walton reacted when I quizzed him on Jerry Holmes's eventual defection to the rival league. That news broke on the eve of the season.

When Bobby Jackson, the team's best defensive back, heard that Holmes was going to get a small fortune by jumping teams, he was stunned. Jackson was a better player than Holmes and couldn't understand how so much money was changing hands.

It became the talk of the locker room—when what should have been on their minds was the fact they were going into a new era after having just been 60 minutes and a tarpaulin away from the Super Bowl.

Over the next two years, the threat of the rival league was to form a strong undercurrent on the Jets, with some players threatening to jump and others holding out. In the background the New Jersey Generals' owner, Donald Trump, was spreading around his money and coveting Jets: young, up-and-coming players who already had met with some success.

When cornerback Johnny Lynn and defensive lineman Ben Rudolph (who endeared himself to us grammarians in the press room by saying, "I've got big feets") signed agreements to jump to the USFL, the Jets moved quickly to better the offers and keep them.

When Mehl, Klecko, and Gastineau were courted by Trump and his lieutenants, the Jets more than doubled their salaries. The Jets suddenly became the highest-salaried team in pro football.

The Jets succumbed further in 1985, when McElroy and Powell held out. The Jets were forced to play their opening game without their offensive tackles against the sack-happy Raiders. The result was such a disaster, it made players wonder just what the Jets' management's commitment was to winning. To some players, it appeared that Kensil and Gutman and Hess and even Walton were more concerned with winning strategic negotiating points than winning a football game.

Not even in immobile Joe Namath's final days in New York had a quarterback been greeted with the assault that the Raiders leveled against O'Brien to start the season. They sacked him 10 times, the most ever recorded against a Jet quarterback. And there were several other times when he was dumped just after releasing the ball. The result was a 31–0 defeat, matching the most decisive opening-day loss in Jets history.

Lyle Alzado, the wild man who was matched against a converted, smallish guard, Guy Bingham, was to gloat, "We were ready and the Jets weren't."

It got so awful for the Jets that McNeil even believed the Raiders had somehow stolen the signals. They jumped on every play with anticipation, as if knowing where it was heading.

Within three days, the Jets signed Powell and McElroy and, for good measure, Al Toon, their acclaimed first-round rookie receiver whom they'd had extreme difficulty negotiating with.

These problems were typical of the Walton era, which nevertheless produced three winning seasons out of seven. But Walton is remembered more for failed hopes than achieved goals. Todd alternated through the highs and lows of 1983, which came crashing down on the Jets as they lost their final two games to finish Walton's first season at 7–9. Soon Richard was gone, traded to the Saints, and O'Brien was anointed his replacement even though he hadn't gotten into a game as a rookie.

But before O'Brien could take over in 1984, he had to go to court—and the time he spent there ruined his chances to become the immediate starter to replace Todd. For in an incident in 1983, O'Brien's rookie season, he and Gastineau and friends had spent much of the night at Studio 54. It was a place of gender-bending and pot, of celebrity-gawking, of back rooms, of balcony-smooching, of Andy and Bianca—and on this night, Mark and Ken.

In the course of drinking and revelry, Gastineau got into an arm-wrestling match with a bartender-cum-male-model. The bartender, about five inches shorter and 100 pounds lighter than Gastineau, won, and Gastineau reacted violently.

Soon, there was pushing and shoving and someone said Gastineau threw a punch. Another man charged that O'Brien landed a right that broke his nose. O'Brien, or a look-alike, had gotten involved (a friend of O'Brien's claimed he really was the guy who broke the other fellow's nose).

It took a year for the case to come to trial, and when it did, it was a big one. It was also at the exact moment when O'Brien should have been preparing and ready to step in as the Jets' quarterback.

The city's news media marshaled their forces and laid siege to the courthouse. The trial took three and a half weeks. Unfortunately for O'Brien, it began just as the exhibition season was to start. He was in court every day and Walton had no choice: He nominated career backup Pat Ryan as the Jets starter.

By the time the trial ended, the Jets had started the 1984 season

1–1 under Ryan, the Bengals were coming in a few days, and it was O'Brien who became the backup. It affected the easygoing O'Brien in ways that surprised even him.

There was this about O'Brien: Even Reese, who prided himself as being a father-confessor to the players, couldn't get a handle on him. O'Brien kept things to himself. Jim Nicholas admired O'Brien's grit but couldn't break through his emotional wall. Even his coaches couldn't tell—was he angry? was he in pain?

"Both my parents are very intelligent people and know how to control their emotions," Kenny explained. "Negatives are something for me to work out."

The one window into his life that he allowed to open even slightly was the Studio 54 affair and how it affected him. His surfer's-blue eyes would narrow when he thought about what happened.

"There's no doubt it changed me in what I show people," he admitted. "Did it make me more cynical? It was just a nasty situation. It sets things straight. It lets you know how things will be. Your friends are your friends, but you just can't trust people. I'll never forget it."

While O'Brien was struggling with his emotions and with running Walton's offense, Hickey was struggling with Walton. Joe had started to second-guess Hickey. Walton wanted players who were quick learners and whose attitude harkened back to the 1950s. But that was almost 30 years before. Walton ran out of patience if Hickey's draft picks weren't making an immediate impact.

"With Joe it seemed fine—all of it seemed fine—until it came to cutdown time," says Hickey. "He wanted to cut Johnny Hector the first year," Hickey says of the useful running back who was to produce a nice career. "I went to Jim Kensil and said, 'Is Joe kidding?' " Michaels, on the other hand, had patience with a player. He allowed him to develop, at least in Hickey's view.

"The difference between Walt and Joe is so obvious and no one has homed in on it: We had Jim Kensil, a George Young type, as a backstop, but once Kensil was gone, a foundation was missing."

Perhaps. Certainly the timing of Kensil's departure is interesting. A few months before the 1988 season, the heavy-smoking, overweight Kensil, bothered by a host of medical problems, retired after 11 seasons as team president. Gutman, who had been the club's corporate treasurer and administrative manager since 1977, was named to succeed Kensil.

The announcement had an unusual undercurrent: For the first time in his long business career, Hess actually presided over a news conference and fielded questions. Most of my colleagues were so stunned, they couldn't come up with anything to ask the man, whose perpetual silence—as far as the news media were concerned—made him something of a mysterious figure. Around the NFL it was hardly unusual for owners to become central figures, to speak to the public, to be reachable by the press: the Giants' Wellington Mara, the Cowboys' Jerry Jones, the Chiefs' Lamar Hunt, the Dolphins' Joe Robbie, the Broncos' Pat Bowlen, the 49ers' Ed DeBartolo, Jr., the Steelers' Art Rooney.

But Hess was determined to stay in the background most of the time. It was as if he were playing the oil game in football as well, somehow believing secrecy with the press was crucial to success.

"In 1933, during the Depression, I started out with one small 615-gallon truck delivering home heating oil in Asbury Park," he told a stockholders' meeting in 1995, when, at the age of 81, he announced he was stepping down as chief executive officer of Amerada Hess. The company had $7 billion in sales.

He was a man whose father had been trained as a kosher butcher in Lithuania. Instead, his father pursued the American Dream, came here, and began a fuel-delivery business. But it went broke in 1933. His son Leon, 18, started driving the truck.

That experience was invaluable during World War II as Leon became General George S. Patton's oil-supply officer, a critical key in running the mechanized Third Army.

In the 1950s and 1960s he consolidated his business with a major merger and then broadened it with some unique corporate and tax games-playing. He had also married into one of New Jersey's first families. His wife, Norma, was the daughter of David Wilentz, a national figure in the Democratic party, but more widely known as the man who successfully prosecuted the Lindbergh-baby kidnapper, Bruno Richard Hauptmann.

When the shah of Iran came to New York, guess whose Park Avenue apartment he stayed in? Hess also dealt with other Middle East oil barons—with Moammar Qadaffi, for example. Once, during a negotiation over oil, Leon was surprised to see someone from the other side put a pistol on the table.

"And I'm still here," Hess was to quip with a wry smile years later.

Hess was always in those special issues of business magazines like *Forbes* or *Fortune* that ranked the world's richest people. Yet, I remember his odd reaction to being in the public eye. One of the first times I spoke to him was back in 1976, at Richard Todd's first workout. Hess saw me there, and I was surprised to see him walking toward me on the field.

"Please don't put in the paper that I'm here," he said. "I'm supposed to be at the office."

To say the least, it evoked a chuckle. The only people who had ever told me that before were bettors I'd interviewed at race tracks. It hardly befitted the head of a billion-dollar empire who didn't have to worry about what any of his employees thought. But that was Leon. Velvet glove–iron fist. Lips sealed.

Hess's oil company received extraordinarily favorable tax breaks for putting up refineries in the Virgin Islands. He was involved heavily in the Alaskan Pipeline. His employees included people intimately involved and connected with the oil industry—among them, former senator Henry M. (Scoop) Jackson, one-time head of the Senate's committee on energy, and Interior Secretary Stewart L. Udall.

Once, driving around on the Caribbean island of St. Lucia, I passed a schoolyard with a nice new building. It was called "The Leon Hess School."

Above all, Hess demanded loyalty. Thus, he overpaid his loyal employees. And if that happened to include beefy football players who didn't know North Sea Crude from 3-In-One oil, fine. But when it came to dealing with the Mets and New York City, Leon Hess as head of the Jets couldn't wield power. His oil smarts helped him hardly at all.

In Gutman, Hess had another loyal employee to replace Kensil.

Rightly or not, Gutman became a vilified nonfootball man in a football world. For he was the one who ran the Jets.

From 1988 to 1996, Gutman's first nine seasons at the helm produced one playoff-game appearance. The team posted 48 victories, 96 losses, and 1 tie. It is hard to believe any other chief executive in pro sports ever was given nine years and showed twice as many losses as victories. No wonder Parcells was given the store when he rode into town in 1997.

I asked Gutman about that record. He was self-effacing and honest.

"I think the Jets have had an unusually difficult time in finding the winning formula, and some decisions didn't work out," he conceded.

At moments like these, when he wanted to be diplomatic yet felt obliged to respond, the often-affable Gutman lapsed into formal locutions. He was perhaps the most well-spoken sports executive I have ever met, blessed with a precision of speech. He had a playful side, liked to go to practice and banter with the players and coaches. He was a museum-goer and an avid reader, and on vacation he was as likely to go to the Galapagos Islands as Paris. Indeed, strike up a conversation with the man and you would wind up discussing the Broadway theater rather than Broadway Joe.

Unlike other officials in power, Gutman had no illusions about his limitations in matters of football. He was raised in the Bronx—but, ever contentious, was a Brooklyn Dodgers fan. With a master's degree in corporate finance from New York University, he was the administrator for a string of mental-health facilities in Westchester County before joining the Jets as the team's financial officer (and wasn't his mental-health experience a perfect training ground for Jets football?). He admitted he had no play-calling acumen, but always said that did not stop him from being able to choose the people who did know the game.

His unfamiliarity with football seemed crystallized to me when we would get into discussions early in his career about paying number-one draft picks.

"It goes against everything my background has taught me: that you reward seniority and success. How can you pay someone a million dollars when he has never played a down for your team?" he wondered during the height of the Al Toon negotiations. "How can you make a 21-year-old the highest-paid member of your team?"

Gutman also knew that the hydra-headed Jets operation wouldn't work and hadn't worked. A year after he became president he realized the team needed a strong football man at the helm. That is when the Jets hired Dick Steinberg following the 1989 season, Hickey's last.

By then, Hickey's feelings about Walton had deteriorated irreparably. It galls him even now that Walton would think his coaches knew talent as well as Hickey.

"Joe Walton didn't understand personnel," Hickey says now. "Invariably, he'd fall back on his coaches, and they didn't know as much as he did.

"When you look back, it was the foretelling. The late Howard Cosell used to call me regularly. When Walton got the job I got a call from Howard and he said, 'Mike, you've got to get out of town. Walton will ruin you and your reputation.' Don't ask me how he knew, but the guy called it."

Cosell, enamored of Hickey, once did a television profile of him and asked Walton how he liked the job his draft guru was doing. Walton replied laconically to the camera, "He's doing a good job."

Cosell, his ego damaged by the Jets' failures, hated the team.

"They're ruining our ratings!" he once wailed to me.

With Howard, everything was internalized. The Jets may have helped *Monday Night Football* debut way back in 1970, but they were an embarrassment to him in later years. Thus his calls to Hickey, consoling the big redhead. And Cosell did this even while professing friendship for Hess and other members of the Jets' hierarchy.

As the years went by, Walton and Hickey's differences became more pronounced. Hickey used to say that Walton would love him to draft a whole team of pint-sized underachievers with character —just the sort of player Walton was.

Hickey was especially incensed when Walton would ask Kotite for his opinion of a player. Hickey did not believe that Kotite could possibly have anything to add to anything Mike believed.

"The biggest mistake I made—but I would do it again—was that I never looked for another job when I was with the Jets, and maybe in retrospect I should have. But I was brought up to be loyal to the people who are loyal to you," said Hickey, who never got back into football. His first job after the Jets? It was with Blue Cross.

Hickey couldn't understand why other clubs didn't offer him a job. He had, after all, been the point man in drafting players that formed the nucleus of solid Jets teams in the 1980s.

"A knowledgeable union guy told me, 'It's simple—you guys were blackballed.' It is very strange. Walt and I. Hey, the great Buddy Ryan was running Walt's defense on the Bears. But Buddy never credited Walt. Now it's too late for Walt to get a coaching job. A week and a half after I left the Jets I was in graduate school working on an M.B.A."

> .   .   .

Joe Walton's Jets put together two outstanding seasons—1985 and 1986. O'Brien came of age. Pat Leahy was one of football's best kickers. Mickey Shuler and Al Toon caught everything. McNeil continued to burst for big yardage.

The Jets under Walton became habitual front-runners—and habitual losers in the stretch. Their last season at Shea was followed in 1984 by their first at Giants Stadium, where they started 6–2. They wound up at 7–9 again—one victory the entire second half of the season. But at least Walton locked in on O'Brien as his quarterback.

The Jets' problematic bistate marriage with Giants Stadium had begun. They found acceptance at Giants Stadium hard going. They attracted 70,000-plus fans for their home opener against the Steelers, and then again for the Dolphins and Giants (who were the visiting team!). But the other five home games began a pattern of thousands of no-shows. It was not an easy move to the new neighborhood.

Many of the fans came from Long Island, which had meant a 20- or 30-minute commute to Shea. Crossing to New Jersey, though, made it an all-day affair, having to leave home two or three hours before a game, often not getting back until four hours after the game ended. Many of the Giants' fans had come from New

Jersey or Westchester, so following the Giants from Yankee Stadium to the New Jersey Meadowlands was neither a hardship nor a psychological jolt. But to Jets followers, going across the Hudson was a major decision. For a New Yorker, going to Jersey was not something usually done, unless you had a job there. They didn't go there for shopping, or for entertainment, or for a stroll.

Giants Stadium was an odd place for the players to call home, too. The walls inside the stadium hallways were painted Giants blue. The stadium itself had an overall blue color, offset by red. There was nothing Jets-green about the place. Even the big logo in the center of the field that read "Giants Stadium" reminded the Jets of their second-class status.

In fact, the Jets were to become one of the worst home teams in football over the years, and their search for an identity even led to the land of dreams.

Five years after they moved in, during Joe Walton's last season, they hired a California company that dealt in creating mirage environments for shopping malls, to alter the look of Giants Stadium for Jets home games. Bunting and banners were hung and draped and strung.

The blue wall beneath the stands the length of both sidelines was draped in green-and-white nylon eight feet high. It included three-quarters of a mile of fabric. It bore the Jets name and logo and vaguely had the feel of an airplane mock-up.

In addition, the company put Jets banners atop the 12 flagpoles near the Stadium Club entrance. The effect on the outside was more of a jousting tournament than a football stadium. The Jets even stopped calling the place Giants Stadium; in their official press guide and yearbook, they called the stadium the "Meadowlands." In the Giants yearbook, the same place was called "Giants Stadium."

"I was trying to create a sense of identity for the Jets when they're playing at the Meadowlands," the firm's head explained. "It seems there's an identity crisis for Jets fans at a Giants-blue stadium."

It didn't help. From 1987 to 1996, under four coaches, their home record for the decade was football's worst, 29–50–1. They could claim it wasn't the stadium, it wasn't the fans, it was them.

But the karma was so bad there, it was as if a mystical force had wafted through the place, attaching itself to anything in green.

Reflecting one day in 1997 on the Jets playing in a place named for their overshadowing neighbors, Ewbank suggested, "The Jets playing in Giants Stadium—it sounds like you're a second-rate team. I know Leon tried to get it together, but . . ."

"I definitely feel it's made an impact on the Jets' problems," says Ralph Baker. "You can't go there every week and play in a place called Giants Stadium and feels it's your place. I'm not sure they'll ever be champions, no matter who the coach is—until they have their home stadium. You go there one day a week, you pack a bag to go, and you pack and leave."

In fact, five former Jets head coaches I spoke to believe Giants Stadium is bad for the Jets.

"That was another thing we went through—the move to Giants Stadium," says Walton. "I don't care how many banners they put up or how many signs. It's like playing 16 away games. The problem is that many times the Jets will get home quicker from an away game than a home game. It takes almost three hours, especially early in the season.

"Another thing I think is a factor: When the team moved to Giants Stadium, after a couple of years, their big fan base from Long Island left, dropped out. A lot of the people who have tickets now for the Jets are Jersey people. And a lot of those are Giants fans. Remember that last game of 1988, when we knocked them out of the playoffs? The fan base had to be 50–50.

"No matter how many banners you put up, it's still Giants Stadium."

Bruce Coslet, the man who followed Walton, echoed him.

"One factor in the Jets' long-term problems, and I know what it can do, is the stadium problem," contends Coslet. "Giants Stadium is not Jets Stadium. I tried 'Let's go Jets.' I told management we have to get a homefield advantage.

"You know, it was easier to go on the road. We'd go up to play New England, we'd be home sooner than if we played them at Giants Stadium. It was like the Bataan Death March. We tried things, but they were like Band-Aids. We changed the uniform our first year. We tried to do some cosmetic things. I drove Bill Hampton crazy in the equipment room. You do things you hope will help the atmosphere, to help the players' psyches. I instituted bringing lunches in."

To this day, Coslet remains shocked that he never got to finish what he started. The culture of the Jets, Coslet felt, was changing and he was responsible. And then one day he was told to leave, and the turmoil continued.

. . .

There was another constant: Mark Gastineau's antics. And yet, the outrageous and the flamboyant were tolerated by Walton and the players—until the one moment when Gastineau screwed with their history. Thanks to his unbridled enthusiasm, we will never know whether another Super Bowl was in the Jets' future.

The 1986 Jets were the team poised to go all the way, just as the 1982 team had seemed destined to break the mold.

That 1986 squad started 10–1 with an offense so powerful that four of the victories produced more than 30 points apiece. They had won nine straight games in surging to the NFL's best record. Walton's offense and defense had come together in ways that made Jets fans anticipate each Sunday. It was time for me to do one of those rare stories: how the Jets got so good. And how was Hess reacting to all this good fortune?

I called him at the Amerada Hess Corporation offices and, as usual, left a number. Whenever you called, his secretary always said, "Mr. Hess is in a meeting." She took your phone number. This time he actually called me back.

I told him I was writing a story about Walton and the Jets, their 10–1 record, and was wondering how Hess was feeling about his coach these days. His answer surprised me:

"I'd rather not say anything right now. My heart's been broken too many times. But, Jerry, if we go to the Super Bowl, I promise you an interview."

The Jets lost their last five games of the 1986 regular season. Leon still hasn't called me back.

If you really thought about it, you could see the collapse coming. In Game 6 of the winning streak, Mehl was lost for the season with a knee injury. Even in their ninth straight victory, over the Colts,

Gastineau got it in the knee and he was to be out for most of the remaining games.

The defense collapsed, and the offense followed. The team yielded 45 points to the Dolphins as the winning streak ended, then 17, then 24, then 45 to the Steelers. Klecko and McElroy, the starting offensive tackle, were injured so badly in the rout by the Steelers that each required reconstructive knee surgery. The Jets ended their regular season by giving up 52 points to the Bengals.

What terrible irony that this was the team that had pioneered, with Nicholas's help, the study and science of sports medicine in America.

Nicholas created, helped by Hess's backing, the Institute of Sports Medicine at Lenox Hill Hospital. Nicholas brought the latest techniques to the Jets, in surgery and rehab. Nicholas had outfitted Namath with what was called the Lenox Hill Derotation Brace, and Namath's fame had made the contraption the brace of choice for sore-kneed weekend tennis players everywhere. Like Joe's, their knees didn't wobble side to side any longer.

The Jets in the late 1970s also pioneered predraft physicals of collegians. They brought in as many as 100 players for exams following a series of bad drafts.

"Let's bring them in and look at them," Hess had told Nicholas following drafts when the Jets took gimpy-kneed or ineffective players.

"We established five criteria to rank players' health," says Nicholas. " 'HP' was the highest priority—it meant the player had never been hurt. Then there was P1—he had been hurt in the past but it shouldn't affect his career. A P2 was someone who had an injury that could shorten his career. A P3 was a player we couldn't rate either because he needed an operation or was recovering from an operation. Then there was a P4—outright failure of the physical.

"I remember I made Ronnie Lott a P2-minus when he was in college. He had a separated shoulder. He still had a long career. I missed that one. But I was also accused of failing Anthony Munoz. Actually, I didn't, but I couldn't rate him because he had just undergone surgery."

Even after all these years, Dr. Nicholas can rattle off the injuries that afflicted the 1986 Jets—"The linebackers Mehl and Crable,

Klecko hurt before then, O'Brien scope of shoulder, Marty Lyons hand in cast, Gastineau hurt. Beyond that, we had guys hurt who were playing."

Here was the team that probably was the most noted in all of sports for its medical research and acumen—and it was one big hospital case. Many players believed it was because of Walton's strenuous workouts that started in the summer and depleted them by the time they got into the long days of the autumn and winter. Others felt his practices were too long once the season started. And of course there was the AstroTurf of Giants Stadium—that was the culprit, said some.

"When I look back to Joe Walton's time, the pre- and postpractices were longer than the practices," recalls Baker. "You ended up being out there three and a half hours. I think that was one of the reasons we faded the latter part of the season. Our defensive backs were small—it seemed they ran out of gas.

"I always thought Joe Walton had our team ahead of schedule for the preparation for the week. He'd give these great pep talks early in the week, and by the time we got to the game it was almost anticlimactic. By game day we were on the decline."

Reese the trainer and Nicholas the orthopedist charted and studied the injuries.

"There was no way of analyzing why they got hurt," Nicholas still concludes today.

Instead of finishing first, the Jets got into the playoffs as a wild-card team. Walton decided to bench O'Brien and started Ryan against the Chiefs, who had been slumping themselves. The Jets won and faced the Browns.

A victory over Cleveland would have propelled the Jets to the conference championship—60 minutes from a Super Bowl again. They seemed to be headed in that direction as Ryan directed them to a 20–10 lead with only 4 minutes 14 seconds remaining. These Jets had been doing everything right in the clutch: Holmes, the cornerback who would be leaving in a few weeks to jump to the USFL, had intercepted Bernie Kosar, the first time he had been picked off in 134 passes. The interception set up a Freeman McNeil touchdown.

Now Kosar had a second-and-24 after being sacked by Lyons.

Kosar was all the way back on his own 18-yard line. It was an untenable situation. He went back to pass and threw it incomplete as the Jets defense formed an umbrella around the receivers. But moments after Kosar unloaded the pass, Gastineau appeared out of nowhere. He hit Kosar from behind and that was the start of the Jets' problems. That late hit produced a roughing-the-passer penalty on Gastineau, an automatic first down, and kept alive the Browns' slender chance.

From there, they drove for a touchdown, then the tying field goal —and in double overtime, they crushed the Jets on another field goal from Mark Moseley. It ended the third-longest game ever played. It was to result in a $2,500 fine for Gastineau's flagrant late hit.

That was only money. But more than that, it set him in stone as the teammate who had cost the Jets their last great chance at the Super Bowl. Their anger festered the next day when Denver beat the Patriots to face the Browns in the championship game. The Jets knew they could beat the Broncos; they had already done it that season, quite easily, by 22–10. Even today, fans talk about the late Gastineau hit on Kosar. Even Kosar brought that up when we met a dozen years later.

Before that hit, teammates had grudgingly accepted what Lyons described as "Gastineau Rules."

If the players were allowed to wear dress jeans on a road trip, Gastineau would show up in faded jeans. That defiance led to a Gastineau rule: On the next road trip, no jeans were allowed for anyone. When he wore shorts in a hotel lobby on a road trip, that created another Gastineau rule: no shorts in a hotel lobby. And when he was often the last player to arrive at the airport for a road trip, a Gastineau rule was created: Every player must be at the airport half an hour before the scheduled departure time. He even had his own rules on the field: tackle a running back? Naah, not Gastineau.

Even now, so many years later, as Nicholas contemplates the unending and unpredictable series of injuries, he thinks of what he describes as "Gastineau's recklessness" in halting the Jets' season.

And that teamwide anger against him turned into a lingering despair when the Broncos defeated Cleveland and went on to the

Super Bowl to face . . . the Giants, of all people. There was no way, the Jets believed, they would have lost to the Giants in Super Bowl XXI. Imagine—a Jets-Giants Super Bowl. Imagine the Jets the winners. The Giants, though, were the toast of New York, back in a championship game for the first time since the 1960s, while the Jets contemplated the late hit and what might have been.

Give Walton credit for resiliency, though. He kept the team to-gether—for a while. The Jets even began 1987 at 2–0. They crushed the Patriots in a *Monday Night Football* game to give them 74 points in two games, and the old visions returned. Even Walton was upbeat.

"They showed," he claimed, "that the New York Jets have a good future." But not in football, he might have added.

At that point in his Jets career, Walton's teams had posted a 37–31 record. With that "good future" ahead, we started to write about his won-lost record and how he could be the first Jets coach to post a winning career mark with the team.

Instead, Walton's career never went so well again: His Jets teams went on to produce a 16–26–1 record before he finally was canned in 1989.

When I mentioned to Joe years later that for a while he had the only winning career record of any Jets coach, he let his hair down briefly and admitted it was important to him: "I still would have had a winning record if it wasn't for the last year," he said.

Then he became practical again and reflected on how it felt to be fired.

"If you stay around long enough and you don't win the Super Bowl, you get fired," he said. "And sometimes when you win the Super Bowl, you get fired."

. . .

Gastineau helped do him in with a final blow. Just a few days after 1987's major Monday night victory, the NFL went on strike. Gastineau was the only Jet to cross the picket line that first day when camp reopened for the so-called "replacement" players.

There was no game the Sunday after the strike began. But a week later, in one of the strangest and most ill-conceived projects in the history of pro football, the NFL decided to put together "replacement" teams. Their records would count for that season, and for all time.

At 9:15 in the morning, Gastineau attempted to drive his Mercedes-Benz into the Jets complex, accompanied by a woman. When he stopped his car to get a pass at the security gate, he was heckled by the 25 Jets who were on the picket line. They shouted "Scab!" and cursed. Someone pelted the car with eggs.

One of the players started to rock Gastineau's car. And when Mark rolled down the window to get his pass from security, Bingham, the backup center, spat in his face.

Gastineau flung open the door and charged Bingham. The pair fought. A photographer from *Newsday* attempted to get a picture of the brawl, but Mickey Shuler, the taciturn tight end, held his hand up in front of the camera. Lyons separated Gastineau and Bingham, and the Nassau County police showed up to calm things down. Meanwhile, Gastineau and McElroy and Tom Baldwin exchanged curses and shouts.

Why would Gastineau show up to break a strike? Money. It was the same reason that Klecko, and then Fields, and then Lyons, eventually would. All had become fat on the Hess payroll. All had seen their incomes increase almost five times in the last two years thanks to the threat of the USFL. Whenever these guys spoke, the first words out of their mouths were a homage to Hess.

Gastineau's excuse for breaking the picket line was that he had just signed a five-year, $3.7 million contact—and he needed the money for support payments to Lisa, from whom he was estranged.

That parking lot had seen its share of weird Gastineau moments. One was the time he tooled around in his Rolls while the Studio 54 trial was at its height. Or the moment he took off, tires screeching, and scared the shit out of McNeil, who was wearing a neck brace from an injury. Freeman turned quickly to see what was happening—and reinjured his neck.

The spitting incident would never be resolved, nor would Gastineau's relationship with his teammates. And the splits became worse the next day. Klecko, whose career was threatened by a season-ending knee surgery the year before, and who still couldn't play, nevertheless had a salary of $812,000. In order for him to collect it, though, he had to report to the Jets training room for therapy. He explained that to the players at a team meeting. They let him go with their blessing.

Lyons, meanwhile, spoke of his financial obligation to his family. In other words, he didn't want to give up $600,000 a year. He crossed. A day after him, so did Fields, who was earning $400,000.

The Jets had been separated into the haves and have-nots, and three of the guys who were the heart and soul of the team—Klecko, Lyons, and Fields, along with the outcast Gastineau—had left their teammates on the sidewalk for the big bucks.

The future that Walton had envisioned became a joke, and a sick one at that.

They went on to lose their two strike games and saw their record fall to 2–2. When real play resumed, the Jets won only four of their remaining 11 games. They dropped their final four, all in December. The 1987 Jets were a 6–9 team, and last in their division.

The strike of 1987 dimmed the Jets' future and Walton's irreversibly.

"I've admitted I probably didn't handle it very well," concedes Walton now. "The strike probably hurt our team. I should have done what some other coaches around the league did. It was a difficult time, and some of the coaches just let the new guys who came in do it by themselves, didn't even coach them. My mistake was trying to coach the kids who came in, and some of the veterans resented that.

"What happens during a strike is that different leaders come to the fore, and people who are marginal players become important in the strike, and when they come back there's a division there. We had people like Guy Bingham, and that guy who returned punts and was a receiver. Yeah, Kurt Sohn. When they came back they had to go back to their football role, which was that of marginal players who should have just been happy to be there."

It was time for another Walton housecleaning, and this time he dumped Klecko and Fields. Gastineau's future was in doubt as well following consecutive injury-plagued seasons in which he produced a total of six and a half sacks.

"As we got into the late eighties we had to start rebuilding," says

Walton. "We did a pretty good job in '88 with a bunch of young guys, " he says of the team that would be the last winning squad for a long time. And even that 1988 team barely made it over .500 with an 8–7–1 record. Three different head coaches followed Walton and couldn't win, leading to Parcells in 1997. "They took a couple of steps backward in 1989. I think any time you're playing with young people, they might go backwards. But who knows? We got into a losing mode in '89 and couldn't get out of it," says Walton.

But in 1987 Gastineau was not finished as a Jet, nor was he finished making headlines. He had become deeply involved with Brigitte Nielsen, the sculpted six-foot-two-inch actress who made *Rocky IV* with Sylvester Stallone (and even married him) and *Beverly Hills Cop II* with Eddie Murphy. Mark and Brigitte met in the offseason, how being a matter of gossip-column fodder.

She supposedly had met Stallone by sending nude photos of herself up to his hotel room. She had met Gastineau after seeing him, scantily clad, doing a postgame locker-room interview. Her people called his people.

Brigitte's first appearance at summer camp saw her wearing a teeny black-leather miniskirt and white sweater. But she stayed in the background, sitting on a bench off to the side, where family and friends of the players used to watch practice.

Then she came to the scrimmage.

The Jets and Redskins used to meet every summer at Lafayette College, in the hills of Easton, Pennsylvania. There, Jack Kent Cooke, the padrone of the Redskins and one of the world's wealthiest men (his holdings included the Chrysler Building), presided over a minor version of his famous Washington pregame celebrity cocktail parties.

Suddenly, the scrimmage down below shifted its attention when a charcoal-gray limousine pulled up to the sidelines—the sidelines!—and out stepped Brigitte. She emerged wearing shorts, a halter top, and boots, and was immediately followed by television cameras and photographers.

While players thudded and collided on the field, the movie actress was prancing on the sidelines. At first the players couldn't understand what the commotion was about. But when they saw the limo, some immediately grasped the fact that Gastineau somehow was involved.

When the scrimmage ended, and, as usual, players from opposing teams shook hands and patted one another on the back, Brigitte came onto the field and she and Mark embraced—and kissed.

Her appearance again became an issue during the season—not for showing up again on the sidelines, but on Mark's butt.

Gastineau, who always liked to show off his body, started to walk naked through the locker room, the better to display his new tattoo. It said "Gitte," and was encircled with roses. Meanwhile, she bragged of having "Mark" tattooed on *her* rear.

His teammates decided to have some fun. One day a bunch of them paraded nude through the locker room to the shower—and each one of them had the word "Gitte" tattooed on his ass.

Despite all the commotion, something special was happening to Gastineau—he was sacking quarterbacks again. Indeed, he forged to the lead in the NFL as the Jets had an early three-game winning streak in 1988. The return of Mark Gastineau was certainly worth a full-blown story, and I got the sports editor, my boss Joe Vecchione, to agree to let me take Mark and Brigitte out to dinner. It turned out better than I expected.

Because I wanted to write about them as a couple, I figured that if I brought my wife, Rosalind, it would help them to open up, to talk about themselves. I made reservations at a restaurant in Locust Valley, one of the toniest sections of Long Island's North Shore. It wasn't far from where they were renting a house.

We met them at the front door of the restaurant. Brigitte wore tight jeans and a simple white sweater. I held the door open for her and we walked in together. It opened onto the dining room, and as I stood next to this six-two Scandinavian blonde, I noticed everyone in the restaurant staring at us. But especially, I noticed one guy with his mouth open. He was a dentist who lived in the neighborhood, and we had had a problem that escalated to the point where he had threatened to punch me. And now I was walking in with this blonde movie star and the dentist couldn't close his mouth. It was one of life's golden moments.

We were led to an alcove, where I saw another couple sitting at our table. Mark had invited along his sister and her boyfriend. Both of them loved to eat, it turned out.

In any event, it was a surprisingly muted dinner. Hollywood talk? Not really. Brigitte explained she wanted to go to this local restaurant because "Mark has to work on Monday night." The Jets were to play the Bills on *Monday Night Football.*

"You know, I've turned down two movie offers so I could be with Mark during the season," Nielsen claimed. "People won't believe this, but I'm down on all fours cleaning the house." Well, sure, I could picture that.

She also told of being on her own from the time she was 16, when she went to Rome to become a fashion model. Of how she married, had a son (who didn't live with her). She told of how she was kidnapped for 36 hours during an uprising in the Seychelles, how she was almost trampled by crowds in Rome, where they tend to live life like a Fellini movie.

We talked a little football and she displayed a surprising amount of insight into her Mark and the game he played ("At first I thought it was insanity. Forty helmeted men trying to reach that little pigskin ball. How dumb"). At one point, Gastineau said, "We may have something important to say in a few days," but she quickly shushed him.

Brigitte invited us back to their house. She fumbled for the keys. She couldn't find them.

"Did you look under the mat, honey?" Gastineau asked. Still no keys. He went around the back way and somehow got in through a window. Then he opened the front door, saying, "Well, what do you think?"

The house mirrored their personalities. On a wall overseeing the front room were two huge portraits—one of Nielsen's face, the other of Mark's nude torso.

"Come here, I want to show you something," Gastineau said. He took out a huge basket of yarn, enough to make a horse blanket. It contained a tiny pink sweater and a tiny blue sweater with a matching blue hat.

"Brigitte's knitting," he said with a wink.

She led us into their bedroom. The huge pine bed was so high off the floor there was a small ladder at its foot. Brigitte didn't need it. She dived onto the bed, started to roll around, and proclaimed, "This is where Mark and I spend all our time!"

My wife and I decided it was the best and most unusual interview I had ever done.

Three days later, Gastineau, accompanied by Nielsen, told Walton he was going to retire.

Walton talked him out of it at a meeting on Tuesday night. The next day, Mark announced to the players, "I'm dedicating my season to you guys for the way you supported me." But usually, at emotional times like these, Mark swore on the life of his daughter or mother to punctuate his truthfulness. He didn't this time.

The next day, however, Brigitte got a doctor's report that she misinterpreted. Some believed she did so intentionally. She told me she had cancer of the uterus. A day later, he announced he was quitting football.

The twin stories—her illness, his retirement—made front-page news in America and in Europe. It turned out that what she had was a more common precancerous condition, and whether they both knew that is hard to figure.

But Gastineau's decision to retire two days before facing the Dolphins really got under the skin of Walton and his players. They just didn't believe Gastineau was retiring. Walton, in fact, said that if Mark changed his mind and wanted to play again, it would be up to the players to decide if they wanted him back, for he had deserted them in midseason.

His desertion also sparked an outpouring of medical investigation that rivaled the search for the cure to Yellow Fever. Paul Needell of the *News* and Greg Logan of *Newsday*, no fans of Gastineau and my rivals in the press room, set out to prove that Gitte didn't have cancer at all. They just didn't believe anything that Mark said, even when his girlfriend said it. With the doggedness that has marked their careers, they called friends of Gastineau who knew her medical history. Thus, New Yorkers were treated to days of hearsay medical stories about the condition of an international movie star in the sports pages of two of the better tabloids in the United States. It was tabloid journalism at its finest.

Ultimately, Mark never came back. The Jets concluded 1988 with an 8–7–1 record, while various Mark sightings were reported: He was in Vancouver, ready to play in the Canadian Football League; he was going to box; he was going to Hollywood.

She recovered, and gave birth to his baby. But in time there were also some legal problems alleging violence on his part, one of her lawyers confided. They parted. And I've never seen Brigitte, Mark, or the dentist again.

14

The Nineties and the
Football Man

When the Jets hired Dick Steinberg as general manager in 1990, they at last put at the helm the football man whom everyone had longed for. He was credited with helping turn the Patriots into a (briefly) respectable team, good enough to get to the Super Bowl against the Bears. Hess and Gutman gave Steinberg the ultimate hiring and firing powers and control of the college draft. Finally, the four-headed Jets boss had become a single strongman.

The 1989 campaign not only marked the end of the decade, but seared forever in the public's mind—and the players'—the image of the Jets as bumblers and losers, performers who failed to win the big game and failed to win in the cold. It was the end of the Joe Walton era, too; you know a coach is finished when the players can't hear the signals because of the deafening chant of "Joe Must Go!"

So I stopped covering them after '89, when they went 4–12 and lost, of course, their final three December games. Joe Walton was fired, along with his staff, in one of Steinberg's first moves.

I wondered about Joe's record. He had lasted seven seasons and at one point actually had a winning mark. His teams posted three winning seasons. But he was bitter at the end and so were his players, who were sick of his constant threats.

In his seven years, his team never finished first. I wondered about that. It just seemed to me that seven years was a long time to stay with a coach who never brought any sort of significant success. I checked the record books going back to the 1930s, and I could find only one other instance of a coach lasting that long without a first-place finish—Bart Starr of the Packers. And of course, he was a legend in Green Bay and difficult to fire.

The realization that the Jets had stayed so long with one coach made me understand that this was a team that seemed to be constructed around the myth of family. On other clubs there usually was a son of a bitch for an owner or a chief executive. Coaches or assistants or scouts were gone after a while. But under Hess's ownership, there was a comfort factor that settled in the front office, the coaches, the players. You could screw up and Mr. Hess's millions still were there. No wonder this patient man was praised so often by everyone who was taking his munificent salaries. The Jets got along, needing to impress no one.

It was up to Dick Steinberg to change that. Accordingly, much attention would be paid to his choice of Walton's successor.

Steinberg didn't get his first choice, or even second choice, as coach. In fact, Steinberg ultimately failed to get, or keep, the three key elements he knew were needed to turn around the franchise. Those three elements all happened to wind up at Green Bay, where Ron Wolf (whom Steinberg had hired as his assistant on the Jets) became general manager; where Mike Holmgren (whom Steinberg failed to land as head coach) became the coach; and where Brett Favre (whom Steinberg failed to make a makeable deal for) became the quarterback of his era.

Dick had wanted George Perles, Michigan State's coach, who had a history of capitulating to a suitor—and then backing out. He did it again, this time to the Jets.

Perles had even come to New York to meet with Steinberg and Gutman and to agree on a contract. But Perles either played the Jets for fools, or found out to his dismay that the president of a great school like Michigan State had less power than the board of trustees.

After Perles had agreed to take over the Jets for at least four years, Steinberg said to him, "Before we go further, find out if you can get a written release from Michigan State."

That shouldn't have been a problem. The school's president, John DiBiaggio, had gone on television after Michigan State played in the Aloha Bowl and said he would not object to Perles's seeking a pro job.

Perles supposedly called the chairman of the board of trustees after leaving Steinberg. When Perles returned, his ruddy face was ashen. The board, he told Steinberg, would not let him out of his contract. Oh, and by the way, the trustees also offered Perles the athletic director's job to sweeten his contract.

This infuriated DiBiaggio, who contended, "You can't be your employer and employee at the same time."

There are some who believed that Perles had suckered the Jets as well as the Spartans, and had used the Jets as leverage to wrest the athletic director's job as well.

In any event, it left the Jets still without a head coach.

The next day, I got a call from DiBiaggio's wife. She was standing by her man, an academic who she felt had been undermined by the politics of big-time athletics and a board of trustees more concerned with a winning football team than Rhodes Scholars.

"You don't know everything that they did behind the scenes," she told me. "My husband's supposed to be the president of a prestigious Big Ten college, but the athletic people undermine him. He doesn't want Perles to have both jobs. Who does Perles answer to?" The board of trustees had more to say about the direction of Michigan State's operations than the president of the school.

So now the head of Michigan State and the Jets were both upset with George Perles.

Steinberg was then interested in hiring the 49ers' Holmgren. But Holmgren was not quite interested enough in the Jets. And anyway, he was the offensive coordinator for the best team in football. The 49ers upped his contract, and he stayed with them until 1992, when he left for the Packers.

The Jets also coveted Bruce Coslet, though, and Steinberg got him. Coslet knew how to run an offense; he had been the Bengals' offensive coordinator, and twice in the previous four years they had the top-ranked offense in the entire league.

Bruce was a wise-ass. His favorite movie was *Caddyshack,* so you knew he enjoyed a whimsical sense of humor. When he booked tickets to New York for a salary discussion with Steinberg, he did it under the alias of Dan Rowan, half of the comedy team of Rowan and Martin. At Indianapolis the previous week, for a secret meeting with Steinberg, Coslet had checked into a hotel under the name of Dick Martin.

Bruce had little patience with fools or people who didn't know as much football as he did—which, to his way of thinking, was about the same thing.

He was a good football man and he made the Jets respectable. He had made the most of his own talents as a player, becoming a Bengals special-teams daredevil when he was unable to crack the starting lineup as a tight end.

Coslet, though, gave up on football after his playing career ended.

"When I retired from the Bengals in 1976, I was an ordinary player," he explains. "I was a building contractor in California in the offseason, and I was making more money doing that. Plus I'd had three knee operations and I was taking Darvon and three aspirins just to go to practice. So my wife and I decided to go to California. I did some real-estate deals. I owned seven delicatessens and some restaurants. Then Bill Walsh called me and asked if I'd like to help him with his special teams at San Francisco, never for one moment dreaming I'd go back to coaching.

"He had started an intern program in San Francisco. I went through training camp and he asked me to stay the season, and so I coached the tight ends, and by then I knew I liked doing what I was doing. Then I bumped into Paul Brown, who was scouting the East-West game along with Forrest Gregg. They said they wanted to talk to me about special teams. We went to Paul's place in La Jolla, and we're pushing chairs in different formations. And I notice Paul is standing at the window, and we ask, 'What are you doing?' and he's watching the whales going by. He had this huge window that took up an entire wall. So we stood there for 15 minutes and we watched the whales, and I got the job as special teams and tight-end coach."

Coslet remains a bright, sharp fellow. No sooner was he out of a Jets job than he landed back in Cincinnati, first as offensive coordinator and then as head coach. When he first arrived in New York, though, he thought he understood what it meant to coach in New York, and specifically to coach the New York Jets. Of course, he had no illusions about the difficulty of being a head coach anyplace. But New York, he knew, would challenge him.

"But you don't pick and choose when you're in my position. This was the opportunity to become a head coach, and unless you're a Mike Holmgren you don't have all the options. I was in the running for the Arizona job, and Steinberg called me back first. I called Bill Walsh and some other head coaches I knew, and they said that until you experience being head coach, you won't know what it's like."

Nor did he know exactly what the Jets and the mass confrontation by the media would be like.

"You know and you don't know what the Big Apple is like," he says. Did he agree with Boomer Esiason's description of the New York Jets/Giants Stadium crowd as emitting one big sucking sound, the air being deflated, when things go badly? "You don't want to blame everything on that factor but I understand what he's talking about. It's easy to explain about the karma. Situations crop up where they bite the Jets in the ass."

Then Coslet had an afterthought. "But do me a favor," he added. "I don't want this sounding like sour grapes, because it isn't. I wound up in a great situation here. There are certain principles I have and I just won't deviate from them."

His problem with the Jets might have been Steinberg. We'll never know. Coslet always hinted he suffered from Steinberg's unproductive drafts. At least, they failed to give Coslet his quarterback or his running back.

Steinberg's first pick of his first draft became one of those continuing symbols of the Jets' failed hopes: Blair Thomas. He was a Penn State running back who most NFL teams believed was the top rusher in college ball. The Jets chose him as the second player in the entire draft. He had a decent, unproductive, unspectacular

Jets career and was cut before the 1994 season started and was picked up by Bill Parcells at New England.

"What happened to him over in New York?" a Penn State official once asked me. "Blair was such a great player here. Never hurt. Great attitude."

What happened to him was New York, and the fact he was the player the club was supposed to go into the nineties with. He was the second player chosen in the entire draft. As he read and failed to digest the negative tabloid headlines, Blair became embittered about the entire atmosphere. He couldn't understand how he had become the scapegoat for a franchise still trying to get it right. In his rookie season the Jets went 6–10 under Coslet and he averaged a healthy five yards a run. But he scored only one touchdown rushing, and his total ground gains were merely 620 yards. He was injured four times—a hamstring, an elbow, a rib, a heel. Four injuries, all on the practice field.

When the season ended, Coslet asked the medical staff to analyze why Thomas was so healthy in college and so injury-plagued in the pros. They had no answer, at least none that wasn't metaphysical.

One day, several years after Thomas was out of football and running a health club in New Jersey, his agent Tony Agnone asked me, "What happened with Blair?" Might as well ask that of anyone else on the Jets.

Rich Cimini, who left *Newsday* to report on the Jets for the *Daily News,* believes the turning point in Blair's career came in Chicago, where the Jets appeared ready to halt a two-game losing streak in his second season. On the national stage of a prime-time game in Chicago, Thomas blew his career and became another symbol of Jets failure. On a simple running play to chew up the clock, he was hit and he fumbled it away.

"His fumble, running down the clock with the lead, changed him," said Cimini. "He got stripped by Dan Hampton. The Bears tied it and the Jets lost in overtime. It was a Monday Night game," recalls Cimini. "He went into a shell and never recovered."

After Coslet's first season, I spoke privately to him about the team and he hinted that he was doing the best he could with what Steinberg had given him. He had wanted to put in his famed and copied no-huddle offense, "But it didn't fit Ken O'Brien and we weren't ready for it," he said. He compared his former Bengals quarterback Boomer Esiason with the Jets' O'Brien this way:

"If we were an NBA team, we'd have the half-court offense while Boomer was Magic Johnson leading a fast break."

And of his problems with the reporters, he said in exasperation, "People don't know me here. They see my sense of humor as sarcastic. What should I do, go to media school?"

Of course, Bruce also had some diplomatic problems with the officials, fans, and opposing players. The man had breadth.

Early in his first season, the television cameras caught him making an obscene gesture to the officials. He had a shouting match with some fans. He used a couple of four-letter words in a live postgame radio interview.

There were also his hints that the Jets lacked talent—but boy, did he coach good.

Responding to the fact that his team outscored its opponents by 192–138 in the opening half, but then were trounced by 207–103 in the second half, he claimed: "You have our 250-pound defensive linemen while other teams have 280-pounders. We get tired. We get injuries."

He also had a problem with O'Brien, his half-court basketball player. Coslet couldn't open up the Jets' attack, he claimed, because he needed to keep a tight end back to protect the immobile, slow-reacting O'Brien.

"We beat every other team that had a first-year coach," he said, "including Houston, which has made the playoffs the last four years. How many other coaches do you think could have won six games?"

He might have won seven if his boys were luckier in the season's opener. For dramatic effect, the league scheduled the first game for the Coslet Jets against his former team, the Bengals, at Cincinnati.

The key moment came in the third quarter. The Jets were leading by 17–10 and facing a third down on the Bengals' one-yard line. A touchdown would have forced the Bengals to produce at least two touchdowns merely to tie. Suddenly, Doug Wellsandt, a rookie who had been cut by the Bengals and picked up by the Jets only a few days earlier, came off the bench and onto the field.

Sure enough, Wellsandt got the ball on an end-around play—and was tossed for a three-yard loss. The Jets settled for a field goal that put them up by 20–10. The Bengals rallied for 15 consecutive points to win.

The next day, several Bengals players told *Newsday*'s Greg Logan that Wellsandt had inadvertently tipped the play. According to the story, Wellsandt was gabbing with some of his former Bengals teammates during warmups. He told one of them that he was going to be involved in a trick play. Then, said the story, he bragged that when he scored he would hand the ball to Mike Brown, the Bengals general manager and presumably the man who cut him off the squad. The Bengal player then alerted Sam Wyche, the Cincinnati coach.

Unbelievable, if true.

Then again, if you understood what kinds of things happen to the Jets, why not this latest assault on their attempts to win, even under a new coach, even by one of their own players?

Wellsandt denied it the next day. Maybe, he said, he did talk to some of the players, "But I never said anything about that."

And a look at the films confirmed for Coslet the fact that, if they had had their men blocked, Wellsandt would have walked in. Guard Dave Cadigan, a former number-one Jets draft pick, stumbled on a blocking attempt, and the Bengals' Barney Bussey got past him to tackle Wellsandt.

In fact, Coslet might have tipped the play himself by using Wellsandt. Coslet's former boss, Wyche, had told his players that if Wellsandt came into the game, they should be alert for the end-around.

"Wellsandt's running out on the field for that goal-line play is actually what tipped us," explained Wyche. "Usually if a player is only with a team for a few days, he knows only a few plays."

Midway through the season, the Jets defeated the Dallas Cowboys for the first time in franchise history. At halftime, Coslet clashed with Jim Jeffcoat, the Cowboys' six-foot-five-inch, 265-pound defensive end.

Jeffcoat confronted Coslet in the tunnel leading to the dressing room. Jeffcoat complained that Wellsandt (a fellow who figured in an awful lot of controversy for a backup) had thrown a cut block at his knees. Wellsandt indeed had been penalized on the play. Defensive players look at the block, which is legal only within five yards of scrimmage, as a deliberate attempt to injure. And Coslet's Jets had been getting something of an outlaw reputation. Even at Cincinnati, Coslet had been accused by other teams of teaching that tactic.

Coslet had left the field at halftime and was engrossed in looking down at his play sheet when suddenly Jeffcoat came up and stuck his finger in the coach's face. Coslet denied that any blows were struck.

"I parried," claimed Coslet.

But other than Coslet's pushing away Jeffcoat's hand, there was no contact. Still, Jeffcoat did not get satisfaction. Late in the game, Jeffcoat was penalized for spearing O'Brien.

Although Coslet's introduction to the New York media was problematic, as time went by they came to enjoy his wry humor, and he trusted them with off-the-record analysis and comments.

Such as?

One day after a press conference with the local writers, he said, "Okay, put away your tape recorders and pencils. This is off the record."

Some of the writers had been blasting Coslet's offense for its inability to score in the Red Zone—the area inside the opponents' 20-yard line. Coslet assailed O'Brien.

"You guys are writing about us not scoring in the Red Zone. You know why we're not scoring in the Red Zone? It's because our quarterback stinks. You know it, I know it, everyone knows it."

Even O'Brien knew how Coslet felt, although that tirade never was published. Coslet never hid his feelings too well from the quarterback.

Coslet was stuck with him, though, because the heir apparent wasn't ready and Brett Favre was someplace else. Yes, Brett Favre. The Jets had passed up the quarterback of the eighties in taking O'Brien over Marino, and they couldn't pull the trigger in the draft to get the quarterback of the nineties, Favre.

Instead, they had Browning Nagle.

After the Jets took Blair Thomas, they made some decent picks through the rest of that 1990 draft—Terance Mathis, a wide receiver, on the sixth round; guard Dwayne White on the seventh; center Roger Duffy on the eighth. Then Steinberg made a bold move in the following supplemental draft: He went after Rob Moore, the Syracuse wide receiver who had gone to high school in Hempstead, not far from the Jets' camp. But in taking Moore, Steinberg yielded his 1991 first-round pick.

So in 1991, the Jets had no first-round choice. Instead, they began picking in the second round.

How Jets history might have been different: On the second round, the Cardinals were picking 32nd, the Falcons 33rd, the Jets 34th.

The Jets had graded a player they wanted as the top pick in the draft: Brett Favre. Actually, Steinberg liked Rocket Ismail of Notre Dame better, but the Rocket was lifting off to Canada. So the top-rated player on the Jets' board was Favre. Yet, the Jets still thought they might get him, because Southern Mississippi quarterbacks generally do not go high in the draft—and anyway, this Favre (and how did you pronounce his name anyway?) had a reputation as a hard-living party animal.

The Jets thought they had a draft-day deal with the Cardinals, who drafted ahead of Atlanta on the second round; with the Cardinals' pick, the Jets were going to take Favre. That was fine with Wolf, the Jets' assistant general manager, who was among those who considered Favre the best player in the draft.

The Jets were poised to draft Favre. But the Cardinals backed out of the deal. They were nervous about Mike Jones, a defensive tackle, going to Atlanta, so the Cardinals took Jones, and that left Atlanta sitting there and taking Favre with no hesitation. The Jets had to settle for Nagle, the strong-armed gunner from Louisville.

"I don't know if Dick had made a deal for Favre," contends Wolf now from his perch in Titletown U.S.A., also known as Green Bay. "Dick was a very secretive person and he'd go off in a room by himself to make a deal.

"But my thought was Favre was the best player in the whole thing—that's why when I had a chance to get him after I went to Green Bay, I did. I know Dick had him second on the board—the top player Ismail had already gone off the board because he had gone to Canada."

Late that year, Wolf left the Jets for the Packers, and "as luck would have it for me, ironically, the Packers were playing the Falcons. They told me, 'If you want to see Favre throw you better do it now.'"

Thus, in a matter of weeks starting with the end of the 1991 season, a bizarre series of missed connections by the Jets helped transform the Green Bay Packers into a Super Bowl team.

Wolf's first big deal was to convince Mike Holmgren, who had eschewed the Jets two years earlier, to leave the 49ers and become the Packers' head coach. Wolf's second big deal was to trade for Favre, the quarterback the Jets didn't get—a deal that held Wolf up to ridicule, since he dealt away a first-round pick to acquire the second-rounder Favre. Moreover, as a Falcons rookie Favre had thrown only five passes, completing none; two were intercepted.

Thus, Wolf, Holmgren, and Favre—general manager, coach, and quarterback, all of whom might have been part of Jets history—were helping another downtrodden franchise return to excellence. Within five years, the Packers had their own Super Bowl victory for the first time in almost 30 years.

By then, Steinberg, bravely, quietly, had succumbed to cancer. Coslet had been fired and gone back to Cincinnati, first as offensive coordinator, then as head coach. Nagle fizzled and was off to Indianapolis and then Atlanta, where he was used hardly at all.

Dick Haley joined the Jets from the Steelers after Wolf left. Haley had run the Steelers' draft for more than two decades and had made some legendary picks that helped them capture their four Super Bowls of the seventies.

Haley and Steinberg once discussed the draft in which Favre got away.

"It confuses me, because usually to move up a little number, the way the Jets could have, doesn't take much of a deal," says Haley. "You give them something like a third-round draft choice. Anyway, that's what I thought when Steinberg said they tried to make a deal for Favre. It's easy in hindsight to say you should have tried harder."

Coslet never had a coterie of topflight players. Only one player he inherited even got to the Pro Bowl during Bruce's four seasons.

(In Coslet's last year, 1993, the newly acquired Boomer Esiason also made it.)

Coslet's great moment in terms of wins and losses occurred in the 1991 season, the playoff-saving overtime victory over the Dolphins on the final day of the season.

The 7–8 Jets needed a placekicker. Leahy, who seemed to be about 68 years old, had played what was to be his last game. He was injured. The Tuesday before the Dolphins game, the club picked up another ancient, Raul Allegre.

Allegre booted a 44-yard field goal to force the overtime, and then his 30-yarder gave his new teammates a 23–20 victory. That boot lifted them to the playoffs against the Oilers.

It was the Jets' first playoff appearance since the 1986 season, and only the seventh time in team history they made the postseason. They battled the Oilers, an offensive powerhouse, and even had a desperation chance to tie with two Hail Mary bombs in the final 20 seconds. One missed, the other was intercepted, and the Jets lost by 17–10.

When Bill Parcells took over six seasons later, he inherited a Jets team that had only three players—Mo Lewis, Roger Duffy, and Marvin Washington—who had ever seen playoff action with the Jets.

If anyone thought the Coslet era was going to soar . . . well, he was facing the same historic hurdle as his predecessors. From 8–8 the Jets went to 4–12. That was a shocker in two ways. Everyone thought they would build on 1991. They even produced a 5–0 record in the 1992 exhibition season, which seemed to confirm it.

The 1992 campaign was going to be Nagle's and the new Jets'. It actually started brightly, but with a loss. They were beaten in Atlanta, 20–17, but Nagle showed some guts and a willingness to propel the ball downfield. All those months of offseason work with the young quarterback coach, Walt Harris, might have been paying off.

The problem for Nagle was that he simply couldn't digest all the mental gymnastics of quarterbacking in the big time. Those hundreds of hours with Harris in the classroom didn't synthesize on the field. Before you knew it, the Jets of '92 were 0–4. And their troubles were just starting.

Before the season ended, the careers of their most dangerous offensive and defensive players were to end: Al Toon retired following what he described as the ninth concussion of his career, while Dennis Byrd's near-tragedy closed out his stint as a football player.

Toon was no Rice, but who was? Al was a topflight receiver, though, and his 517 receptions trailed only Maynard as the Jets' career leader. Toon was a remarkably agile athlete, good enough to be a triple-jump star at Wisconsin, and that body control exhibited itself in his contortionist catches.

One of his coaches told me that the only problem they found with Toon was his distaste for contact.

"He looks at his face in the mirror after every game to see if he got any cuts or bruises," the coach explained. It reminded me of young Muhammad Ali, who used to probe the skin on his face to check for bruises or swelling. When he didn't find any, he could utter, with satisfaction, "I'm so pretty."

Perhaps Al indeed was concerned about his looks, but his career became defined by his catches in a crowd rather than the deep passes. Somewhere along the way he became a possession receiver, and that lowered his yards-per-attempt dramatically. He led the league in number of catches with 93 in 1988, but averaged only 11.5 yards. One year Toon snared 74 passes and didn't have a touchdown among them.

Ironically, Toon, who was supposedly so concerned with what the pounding he received was doing to his face, ultimately retired because of what was happening to his head. He suffered from headaches and he had memory lapses, even while he continued to play. The term "postconcussion syndrome" had come into prominence, and players in several sports were beginning to describe their problems with this newest term. In the ninth game of the season, he suffered still another concussion at Denver. He waited for the nausea and headaches and memory loss to abate. They didn't. Finally, two days before the Jets were to face the Chiefs, he retired. He had caught passes in 101 consecutive games.

By 1992, I had stopped covering the Jets for the *Times*. The 1989 season was my last. I used to tell people I was taking time off for good behavior. I returned to the Jets' wars in 1994, just in time for Pete Carroll's brief fling.

Still I was at the Jets-Chiefs game on November 29, 1992, to do a sidebar. It had been a miserable Jets season and I was glad I had decided not to cover them on a regular basis anymore.

Earlier that week, Rich Cimini of *Newsday* had telephoned Dennis Byrd. It happened to be Thanksgiving, and Byrd was watching the Lions in their traditional holiday appearance.

"It was halftime," recalls Cimini, "and they were honoring Mike Utley in a ceremony. And Byrd is going on and on about how strong Utley was, and saying, 'God can you imagine what that must be like? Spending the rest of your life in a wheelchair?'"

Three days later, Byrd faced that same future.

The third quarter was only a few seconds old when it happened. Byrd, the left end, looped in toward Chiefs quarterback Dave Krieg's right. Scott Mersereau, the nose tackle, charged from Krieg's left as they bore in on the quarterback in a second-and-10 situation, knowing he would pass.

But as soon as Krieg saw Mersereau coming, he ducked under his grasp and then fumbled the ball. In a sense, Krieg fell out of the way of the oncoming linemen. They couldn't stop and they collided.

The 266-pound Byrd drove his helmet into Mersereau's chest, knocking him backward with such force that the 275-pound Mersereau was down for two minutes. Byrd lay motionless on the turf for several minutes, as medical personnel surrounded him, alarmed at his lack of movement.

"I happened to be standing on the 35-yard line, on the east end, and Bob Reese was standing on the western end of the 35," recalls Pepper Burruss from his home now with the Packers.

"The way the play started was not unusual for any of us to see: Byrd coming from one end, Scott Mersereau from the other, converging. I saw them hit and I said, 'Oh, my God.' As fate would have it, I ran to the closest guy to me, who was Dennis. Bob ran to Mersereau.

"My recollection of what happened next is quite clear. He was one of the people who chose to call me 'Peppy.' And as soon as I got there he said, 'Peppy—I can't move my legs, I broke my neck.' I said, 'OK.' And that OK was volumes—it meant I understood, that I was here and I would take care of you.

"I slid my left hand up to his neck—I've got the poster of this on my wall, my hand sliding to stabilize his face mask."

Players started to mill around. Coslet ran out to the scene.

"It was devastating," recalls Coslet, still chilled by it. "To hear him say, 'My neck is broken.' I tried to shoo the players away."

Reese by now had joined Burruss, along with Jim Nicholas and the assistant trainer, Jim Patten. Reese held Byrd's neck while Burruss and Patten secured the backboard. Burress recalls how everyone "meticulously" put Byrd on the backboard. Then Doctors Steve Nicholas and Elliot Pellman and Burruss got aboard the golf cart with Dennis and took him off the field, driving through the tunnel under the hushed crowd to the waiting ambulance.

There, his wife, Angela, wearing a long fur coat, and daughter, Ashton, met them.

"I'll never forget what he said at that moment," remembers Burruss. "He said, 'I just want to be able to hold the two of you again.'"

Ask Burruss about the next 45 minutes and he recalls it as if watching the scene unfold again in front of his eyes:

"It's a very mystical picture to me . . . we go across Route 3, siren blaring . . . Steve wanted to get an IV started, but it was bumpy, so we pulled over and he got the IV . . . she's holding Dennis's left hand, which was flaccid, and the three of us were praying out loud . . . rather bold thing of us to do in front of three people . . . we didn't know their faith, but it was nothing for us to pray . . . the astounding thing was, Dennis said, 'Thank you, Lord Jesus, for putting me in this position because you know I'm strong enough to stand it.'"

They drove through the Lincoln Tunnel and on to Lenox Hill Hospital.

"Within 45 minutes he started getting steroids. This was an anti-inflammatory, not the kind for muscle-building. This was one of the remarkable things about the whole episode—these were given 45 minutes after injury."

All this time, Byrd still had his helmet on.

As Burruss had piled onto the golf cart with Byrd, he realized he had left a tool to remove the screws from the face guard in a bag on the field. So he shouted to Hampton to give him a screwdriver.

"I figured I'd just unscrew the bolts. There's four that hold the face mask on. You can't take off the helmet without unscrewing the mask. It pinches the helmet tight. Once you do that, then you just have to spread the helmet and it lifts off the head easily. Well, lo and behold, the first screw comes out fine and the next three were corroded shut."

So they wheeled Byrd in with his helmet firmly on his head. At the X-ray table, Burruss got a saw used to remove casts; he placed a towel over Byrd's eyes so the dust wouldn't fly in and sawed off the grommets. Steve Nicholas slipped his hand behind Byrd's head and the helmet came right off.

The Burruss began a vigil into the night. "I took over control of his head," is the way he describes it.

This was 1992, but Lenox Hill did not yet have an MRI machine. So Byrd was loaded again into an ambulance, taken a block away to a building where there was one. They had to maneuver him through narrow hallways until they were able to get him to the room. Then they reloaded him back to Lenox Hill.

In the long hours that followed, Byrd threw up several times. Often he would soil Burruss. Someone asked Pepper if he wanted to wear gloves or a towel, and he said, "Don't worry, he's my friend."

Back at the stadium, Mersereau was stunned but otherwise healthy. He and Byrd had known each other since Byrd's rookie season of 1989. Mersereau, a Long Islander from Riverhead, and Byrd, an Oklahoman, had adjacent lockers. They had become friends.

After Mersereau was able to compose himself and found out what happened to Byrd, he still wanted to return to the game, and did so while his friend was taken to Lenox Hill Hospital.

Later, of course, we all wanted to ask Mersereau about it. That is a particularly distasteful part of the newspaper business, talking to people about tragedy. It doesn't happen often in sports, but this time it seemed that something really serious had taken place, a young man suffering a paralyzing accident.

Mersereau didn't want to be interviewed, and dressed alone by himself adjacent to the locker room. Since I knew him, I suggested to Ramos that I act as pool reporter. Mersereau consented.

He had tears in his eyes when I sat down next to him. He was just starting to comprehend the incomprehensible, that his good buddy, a deeply religious 26-year-old, was in a hospital room, that they were drilling a "halo" into his skull, that he might not ever walk again, might not even have the use of his limbs.

"I didn't know until later, when I was on the sidelines, when I saw them take him away," said Mersereau. He reflected on the fact that despite all the hard hitting in a football game, tragedy rarely becomes part of it.

"It happens," he said. "You're looking at the quarterback. That's all you have on your mind."

Because Byrd had gotten such extraordinary emergency care—the Jets trainers had stabilized him immediately in assessing the problem—and there was a top orthopedic surgeon on hand in Dr. Elliott Hershman, Byrd had gotten to the hospital without undergoing any additional trauma. The steroids the hospital staff had given him were part of a new medicating technique that had proved successful when administered within the first hours of paralysis.

A few days later Byrd took experimental drugs—since he was not part of a test, there was no chance of his receiving a placebo—and he also had surgery to stabilize his spine.

"Often, the one thing, as I looked back over the six or seven hours of his care that was so important—he was never handed off from the moment he was hurt until the moment he was stabilized," explains Burruss. "An average person gets in an accident and gets handed off, I don't know how many times. He was never handed off once. I never left his side. Steve Nicholas never left his side. The timing was just so perfect. You just wish that for every person who gets into this kind of accident, it could work like this."

Byrd's injury traumatized the team. The club's internist, Dr. Elliot Pellman, addressed the players the next day and offered them special counseling, which many of them took. Players cried when they learned the seriousness of his injury.

My son Mark was at New York University Medical School then, but had been doing an internship in sports medicine at Lenox Hill under Dr. Jim Nicholas. I was not even aware that Mark was part of a team of doctors that had gone to see Byrd. I never asked Mark about any dealings he might have had with the Jets, and he never mentioned them to me.

Some of the reporters staked out the hospital, hoping for word from the players who regularly visited Byrd. Among the writers was the *News*'s Needell, one of the most aggressive and innovative hard-news hounds. Indeed, Paul had managed to work his way onto the same floor as Byrd's room.

Paul had an idea, albeit a somewhat unorthodox one. He could not go into Byrd's room, of course. But he had a special relationship with Byrd and with teammate Marvin Washington. Paul routinely spoke with each of them about their families and they always exchanged stories about how the kids were growing up. Now, standing near Byrd's room, Needell decided to ask Washington to interview Byrd for him.

"I handed Marvin my tape recorder," Needell recalls. "I said, 'Marvin, can you do me a favor? Here's my tape recorder and here are five questions. People want to know how he's doing, how his spirits are.'

"Marvin said, 'Fine,' but when he got to the room there were too many players and family members. So he never broached it, and rightfully so."

Meanwhile, Needell felt pretty confident he would have any inside stories about Byrd's condition or what went on in his room. And then Needell saw my son Mark, wearing his hospital togs, coming out of Byrd's room with a bunch of doctors. Needell's spirits sagged. With his tabloid sensibilities, he was convinced that Mark would share with me all the information from inside that room. It never happened.

Byrd went on to make a truly remarkable recovery, cheered constantly by teammates and buoyed by his deep religious beliefs, which helped him interpret his injury as being divinely inspired, a test. The title of the book he wrote about the incident and his recovery was the Biblical-sounding *Rise and Walk*.

Of all the reporters around the Jets, Byrd's healing was most precious to Needell.

"A year later," Needell remembers, "I got a call back from him

on Thanksgiving. I asked him, 'Are you going to carve the turkey?' "
Byrd replied:

" 'Me standing at the head of the table carving the turkey. Who
would have thunk it?' "

There are moments in the sporting life when an athlete feels he
is possessed with powers beyond his normal range. Some think of
it as Zenlike, as "being in the zone." I once heard a receiver describe a day in which he had caught a passel of passes, some from
difficult positions, as being "out of my mind." It was as if outside
forces were pushing him to remarkable feats.

Some Jets believed a higher power helped them a week after
Byrd's injury in their game against the Bills.

It was a week of incredible roller-coaster emotions, players sob-
bing at team meetings yet somehow preparing to face the Bills,
who were headed for another Super Bowl. The Jets? They had lost
10 straight games to the Bills going back to 1987. The Jets season
had collapsed as they won only once in their first seven games.

They had come close to even more tragedies in the days before
the Byrd injury. Erik McMillan, who had a shooting-star career as
the Jets' safety, was relaxing at home in Baldwin, Long Island, one
evening when he heard a commotion downstairs. He ran to the
hallway and saw a hooded man fighting with his girlfriend. Erik
jumped the man and started flailing. Suddenly, a gun appeared in
the hands of another man.

The way Erik remembered it, "I was a black man living in a nice
white neighborhood, and they must have thought I had drugs."

When he told them he was a Jets football player, the men, who
never removed their hoods, left. He never heard from them again.

Then there was the near-tragic van accident involving Glen Cadrez, a linebacker. Cadrez was driving several teammates and his
wife and child when he spotted a disabled car in the middle of the
road. He swerved to avoid it and the van toppled over. Remarkably,
no one was injured.

Burruss remembers several players sitting around saying, in the
wake of the Cadrez, the McMillan, and the Toon incidents, "How
much can a team take?"

And then came Byrd's accident.

All week the players were getting contradictory reports about Byrd's condition. Did he really feel sensation in his toe? Was that a voluntary or involuntary movement in the left hand? The team was a jumble of nerves.

And then, on the flight to Buffalo, something extraordinary happened. Steve Nicholas made an announcement that Dennis had moved his big toe. The players cheered, and by the time they arrived there was a feeling of goodwill and confidence.

"It was almost a lock we were going to beat 'em, and I think Buffalo knew," says Burruss. On game day, cornerback James Hasty told Kyle Clifton, "It's in God's plan for us to win today."

I consider Bruce Coslet's performance holding his team's fragile emotional state that week together to be his greatest moment as the Jets' coach. Then, before the game, Coslet told the players, "Dennis wants us to go on." It was what Byrd had told Coslet repeatedly. And, Coslet recalls, "The guys picked it up. They bought into it. Quite frankly, Buffalo had better players than we did."

The inspired performance by the Jets was punctuated by safety Brian Washington. With the game tied, he intercepted Jim Kelly's pass in the final two minutes and zigzagged 23 yards through the outstretched arms of Buffalo players to score the winning touchdown. As he landed in the end zone, he shouted "Yes!" as he thought of Byrd, who promised to be watching. The Jets, 17-point underdogs and a mess emotionally, had engineered a wonderful victory. They had played the game "whacked out," in the words of defensive tackle Mario Johnson. "It was nothing but emotion."

In some ways, that victory was to be as meaningful to the lives of the players who performed it as was the Super Bowl triumph 23 years earlier. Indeed, if this had been a Jets team that was going somewhere, with the victory having some importance in standings, it might have reached the status of NFL legend.

Instead, it remains a small Jets miracle, but no less so for its happening in a losing season.

At game's end, players from the Jets and Bills held hands on the field and knelt in prayer. Then two dozen Jets and Coslet squeezed into a small room off the locker room and spoke to Byrd by conference call.

That night, when the charter flight arrived back at LaGuardia, Gutman and Nicholas brought a package to Lenox Hill Hospital: the game ball. They delivered it to Dennis Byrd.

. . .

The 1993 season was promising. Boomer Esiason was arriving at quarterback to be reunited with Coslet. The Browning Nagle experiment was dead; Boomer was coming home to Long Island following an often-brilliant career with the Bengals, where Coslet had been his offensive coordinator.

Boomer was a big, blond left-hander who had a sweet touch on the ball. He knew New York and New York sports like few players before him. He had been a high-school hero on the Island, a habi-tue of the Knicks and Rangers, and he could talk to you about Stanley Cups and Super Bowls. He had seen championship hockey games and he had played in Super Bowl XXIII.

"I was very excited about coming to the New York Jets," he re-calls. "I was like a kid in a candy store. All I wanted to do was just get out of Cincinnati alive. I liked the Jets' chances. I figured all they needed was a veteran quarterback. It wasn't going to be Kenny O'Brien—somebody didn't like him. But I was coming home to my hometown team and reuniting with Bruce Coslet. They were my number-one choice."

His first moments on the field, though, proved to be darkly trou-bling.

"I was in New York for the first minicamp; I had taken the 6:00 A.M. flight from Cincinnati. I had gotten a call from my wife when I was on the field about 11. After I got off the field I called her, and she said Gunnar went into the hospital. I got the diagnosis that Friday."

Little Gunnar had been tested for cystic fibrosis when he was a year old, but the result at that time came back a false negative.

"I called Bruce the next day and broke down and told him my son was diagnosed with cystic fibrosis. That really dampened the whole thing, returning to New York. But maybe his being diag-nosed and me being in New York was a godsend. We've raised well over $4 million for my foundation. I have three people working for me."

Because Boomer's father had lavished so much attention on him —Boomer's mother died when he was six years old—he found it natural to start to spend all his energy and free time working with Gunnar, and also trying to find a cure for the disease that cuts down young people.

"There's a certain amount of guilt with every parent," says Boomer, "and the guilt you feel when you've brought a child into the world and they've inherited something you've given them . . ."

Like his own father, he became Super-Dad. He remembers his father, who used to watch Jets practices sitting in a folding chair, never dating another woman after his wife's death. Instead, his free time was spent taking young Boomer to see the Mets or Knicks or Rangers or Jets.

"That's a great thing about coming to New York," says Boomer, "and that's what my father did for me, and what I do for my son."

In that emotional cauldron for Esiason, the Jets also appeared to have gotten better by picking up a couple of fellows with Super Bowl rings—Leonard Marshall from the Giants and Ronnie Lott, who had starred all those years with the 49ers. In all, the Jets committed $17 million in offseason free-agent contracts.

It was going great as the Jets produced an 8–5 record with three games remaining. Then came consecutive losses to the Cowboys and Bills, both Super Bowl–bound teams. No disgrace there. Still, even today Coslet says wryly, "The guy who became the best kicker in the NFL missed them for us."

Cary Blanchard blew three field-goal attempts against the Bills, all wide left, as the Jets lost by two points. Two points! Some right windage would have put them into the playoffs.

Still, the Jets entered the final day of the season at 8–7, needing a Miami loss to position them into the playoffs. If that happened, and the Jets defeated the Oilers on Sunday night, they'd get in as a wild card.

It had been quite a season for Boomer, whose career was revived and who was headed for the Pro Bowl. He completed more than 60 percent of his passes.

Everything seemed to be unfolding perfectly that final Sunday, as the Dolphins lost to the Patriots in overtime. The Jets, though, had a problem with the Oilers' defense. It was terrific. And Coslet's offense hadn't been doing much for a protracted stretch, scoring more than a single touchdown only once in the previous five games.

Boomer was harassed into four sacks and an interception, completing fewer than half his passes.

Despite the shutout his charges were throwing, the Oilers' defensive coordinator, Buddy Ryan, the old Jets coach, went berserk just before halftime. His problem was the Oilers' offense; nursing a 14–0 lead with 24 seconds left before intermission, quarterback Cody Carlson was sacked, fumbled the ball, and the Jets recovered.

It was a stupid call by the Oilers' offensive coordinator, Kevin Gilbride, an angry Ryan screamed. He yelled that Gilbride should have ordered Carlson merely to sit on the ball for the final seconds.

Gilbride strode toward Ryan and told him to mind his own business. Ryan responded by throwing a right-handed punch that clipped Gilbride on the side of the face. Players jumped in and separated them.

Meanwhile, the confrontation on the field led to sympathetic fighting up above in the coaches box, as a pair of Oilers assistants started to fight. The Oilers' general manager, Mike Holovak, the ex-Jet coach and front-office official, stepped in to break this one up.

The weird battles almost overshadowed the Jets' 24–0 defeat that kept them out of the playoffs. Almost, but not quite.

"If anybody doesn't think this was an embarrassment," said the outspoken cornerback, James Hasty, "I'll slap their face."

The next morning I showed up at the Jets' camp. I felt I was in a time warp.

As I looked around the room I realized I had written this scene many times before. Players were loading their things in outsized plastic trash bags. It was something they always seemed to be doing the day after the regular season ended. Indeed, it was the 20th time in 25 years that the Jets were leaving town while other teams were preparing for the playoffs. I knew the routine so well, I would immediately alert our photographer to head for the parking lot and get a picture of a Jet with the massive trash bag slung over his shoulder, walking toward his car. What surprised me in this scene was that some of the players had actually packed before leaving for Houston. They had expected to lose.

And the players spoke in the same old way about how close they had come, and what it would take to get to the next level. Even Boomer, the most media-savvy guy I'd ever been around, and (I had thought) a realist, said, "I know we're at the Giants' level. They just happen to be winning the games we're losing." The Giants had done very well, 11–5 their first season under Dan Reeves.

"This is not like the other Jet teams that used to collapse in December," claimed Scott Mersereau, who had been hammered over the head with the Jets' 13–30 post-November record in the years since Walt Michaels was fired.

Steinberg dropped the first hint that morning. He told me he was considering bringing in someone "who will contribute to the offense." In other words, an offensive coordinator to take over that role from Coslet. In the Jets' last six games they had scored three touchdowns.

The way the story has usually come out is like this. Two days after the season ended, Steinberg met with Coslet and essentially gave him an ultimatum: Cede control of the weekly game-planning and play-calling for the offense on game days, or else. Coslet refused. Immediately, Steinberg met with Gutman and consulted with Dick Haley. Steinberg felt that Coslet's intransigence was a serious block to the success of the team.

Suddenly, three days later, Steinberg fired Coslet.

The reason, said Dick, was that Bruce refused to hire an offensive coordinator and insisted on calling his own plays. The game, said Steinberg, was becoming too complicated for that. Steinberg was unhappy with the way Coslet managed a game. But Coslet's ego was getting in the way, and he didn't realize he was unable to handle both jobs.

Coslet has always claimed that this was not true, that he would have been willing to consider hiring an offensive coordinator. His backers believe that Coslet became a scapegoat for the failed Steinberg administration. In four years Steinberg (and Coslet) had produced a 26–38 record with one playoff appearance. Steinberg's four drafts had not yielded a game-breaker. In 1992 there was tight end Johnny Mitchell, who failed to block and couldn't learn his routes, although he was still spoken of as potentially the most dangerous player on offense. And the 1993 top pick, linebacker Marvin Jones, suffered a serious hip injury that cut his rookie season in half.

Coslet still gets worked up when he thinks about getting fired and the lingering reports that he allowed his ego to get in the way.

"The Tuesday and Wednesday after the last game of the season we would review things," he explains. "They told me the contention of Mr. Hess was that I hire an offensive coordinator. I told them, yes, I have people on my staff who can do it but they can't do it as well as I can. I'm not bragging, but that's the way it is.

"I was ready to get an offensive coordinator for the next year. I stated that in the meeting with Steve Gutman and Dick Steinberg. The next day they fired me. Steinberg said he was going to give me an explanation. I said, 'Wait a minute, Dick, I'm fired, right?' And he said, 'Yeah,' and I said, 'I don't need an explanation.'" And Coslet got up and left.

You could be cynical and say that Steinberg was merely protecting his failed administration and needed to pass around the blame. Or it is possible that Coslet's hubris kept him in two jobs that, increasingly around the league, had been divided among two people.

"The thing that puzzled me was, if it's broken, fix it, but how were we doing offensively?" asks Coslet rhetorically. "We were always among the top producers."

So another coaching administration was over. As he has looked over the Jets, in the years since, did Coslet see anything that infects this organization? Was there something that could have been done differently?

"You mean, is there a mystique?" he asks. "You have to take it year by year. I don't think there's one thing, because if there is one thing someone would have figured it out. I know one thing I'll go to my grave believing is this: Instability won't work."

When things go bad, everyone's to blame. Rob Moore blamed Boomer Esiason for not getting the ball to him and Mitchell in the closing weeks of the season. And he blamed Coslet for departing from the game plan.

"Every week the game plan would include passes downfield," Moore said. "But when the game came around they wouldn't throw the ball downfield. I kept running those slants across the middle. We had these great ideas in the game plan, but during the game we just kept trying to fool people. We need someone who's going to look at the talent we have and tell the players on offense to just go out and beat your man. That's what the Cowboys tell Michael Irvin and Emmitt Smith."

It seemed elementary to Moore.

15

The Nineties and the
Nice Man

Pete Carroll, the boyish but respected defensive coordinator, was
Steinberg's choice to replace Coslet. It was logical, too; he had
helped produce a demon Jets defense in his four years under Coslet.

And Pete Carroll was not the sort of guy who would be cowed by
the weight of Jets history. He was a product of the 1960s and he
didn't appear to have the heavy-handed approach to football that
infects so many head coaches. Every one of them always says the
game should be fun, yet they go right out and make it anything but.

Carroll had some immediate plans. He was going to know players on both sides of the ball. He didn't want to have the inevitable
schism on a team that separates the offense and the defense—
especially when the head coach specializes in one aspect of the
game. Carroll, who had helped the team achieve a reputation for
creating turnovers, not only was hiring an offensive coordinator,
he was going to hire someone to replace himself at defensive coordinator.

Thus, the very qualities that helped elevate Carroll to the head-
coaching post—his skill at managing a defense, getting it to play

smart and to play tough enough to recover fumbles and produce interceptions—would not be used in the same way. By replacing himself, he rid the Jets of one of their great assets.

One thing Carroll vowed he would not change, and to his credit he didn't, was his playful side. He organized touch football games after practice, or he would stand under the goalposts while the field-goal kicker was trying to boot the ball over the crossbar—and Carroll would toss up a football and knock it away.

Carroll knew he had a daunting task. It wasn't just getting players to perform; it was clearing their heads so that they could play well at the place they called home. In four years at Giants Stadium under Coslet the Jets were 12–20. Their road record was better.

His hope for the offense was to make it multidimensional. The East Coast Jets were to get the West Coast offense. He fired the Jets offensive coaches and hired Ray Sherman, who had been the 49ers' receivers coach, to direct the offense. Harris probably was Coslet's choice to succeed him as offensive coordinator, but he was gone, too. Boomer and the entire offense were starting over.

This was sort of a revival for me, too. Since I'd last written about the Jets on a daily basis in 1989, I had done quite a lot of Giants stories, and had seen life from both sides. The Giants' good seasons had been with strongman Parcells as coach and strongman George Young as general manager. There was something new and refreshing about Carroll, though, and I thought, "Here's a guy who has got it right. He laughs at history."

Carroll's summer camp was like an old-fashioned kids' summer camp: games, storytelling time, planned activities.

After one practice, he allowed a would-be placekicker, Tony Meola—who had been America's World Cup goalie—back in the nets for some fun. They had a shootout, with the players contributing to charity for every miss. Meola put on a show and the players were delighted. They whooped and hollered and acted like they were college kids again.

There were old-fashioned grass drills that tested the players' stamina, too. The rookies ran in place in one torturous drill, chanted, and then threw themselves facedown onto the grass. Then up they came, everyone humming a mantra, and down they went. Half a dozen times. Then they ran. When it was over, they were high-fived by the old-timers, everyone screaming, "Jets '94!"

Two nights earlier, when the summer's first meeting was held, there was a reverential silence as Hess strode to the podium. He delivered a rousing pep talk. They had the ability to make the playoffs, Hess told them, and in new coach Pete Carroll and in the quality of the personnel, there was a real chance at postseason play. And finally, Hess liked the camaraderie among coaches and players that Carroll was instilling.

Two years earlier, he had made a similar speech boosting Coslet, informing the players, "Bruce will be here as long as I'm here."

Well, now it was Pete's turn, and the atmosphere was of a bright new beginning—but don't lose sight of what the Jets once were. To instill this historical perspective, the Jets called on Dr. Nicholas. He explained how the Jets were a guiding force in the merger of the NFL and AFL. He spoke of the Titans years and Namath and the Super Bowl.

What a time it was for the Jets. They roared through training camp. They stormed to a 3–1 exhibition record. And they opened on the road at Buffalo, home of the defending AFC champions, and they quieted the crowd.

Stunned silence by almost 80,000 fans greeted the rampaging Jets. Bills backers couldn't believe what they were seeing from the Jets, this perennial group of also-rans. The Jets thumped the Bills by 23–3.

A week later the Jets were greeted by their largest home crowd since 1986, and this time they swatted the Broncos by a field goal in overtime.

The Pete Carroll–led Jets were 2–0 against the AFC elite teams that had been in seven of the previous eight Super Bowls.

It's easy enough to look back and say those victories were not quite what they seemed. The 2–0 record had been inflated, for the Bills' and Broncos' eras were ending. Each of them went on to post a losing 7–9 record that season.

Ah, but who was cruel enough then to harp on the other teams' poor play? The Jets had quickly become New York's darlings. Carroll, with his enthusiasm, with the one-on-one basketball games he played with the other young coaches on a minicourt right near the practice field, with the college-inspired cheering that punctuated practices—it was wonderful. The secretaries on the second floor always knew when Pete was about. They heard him bouncing the basketball in the halls.

One day during practice I was discussing Carroll with Gutman. We talked about how football coaches often had multiple personalities, and how some of them were hardly stellar characters.

"As a father, as a husband, as a coach, Pete is one of the best people I've ever been around in football," said Gutman. Gutman was also a person to whom these qualities mattered. There are front-office executives who either look the other way, or don't even notice, when their head coach starts acting like a martinet, or treats his family in a bizarre fashion. But football never robbed Gutman of his humanity. Given the team's consistently poor record under his presidency, this may say something about what qualities it takes to be a chief executive in pro football.

Pete's humanity and enthusiasm and inexperience as a head coach conspired to produce an up-and-down season after that opening euphoria. They dropped three in a row, then won three in a row, and Pete was constantly retooling his approach, learning to become more demanding.

Some of my colleagues in the press room didn't share my (naive?) enthusiasm for what was happening. Remember, they had been there the previous four seasons every day in the Coslet regime. They had seen the club come close. They had seen the bizarre. I had been away, although I, too, had been observing the bizarre; I was covering boxing and the return of Mike Tyson.

Here were my two assignments: the buccaneering, out-of-control world-without-rules of boxing, and the almost-fascist, tight orb of football. It was a delicious contrast. And for a writer, it didn't get any better. If I made an appointment with Pete Carroll, I knew he'd be there. If I made an appointment with Don King, I had backup plans to go to lunch. Go to a Tyson news conference, and you wondered whether he'd leave the podium and jump into the front row and smite you if he didn't like your question. In football, they always answered your question, no matter how dumb or provocative.

The cynicism in the Jets press room was palpable. "Just wait," more than one colleague told me.

Inevitably, they felt, the Jets would do something to self-destruct. That incident, whenever it came, would be known as a "Jets moment." It was a phrase we all came to use, and it was apt. There were many Jets moments. There had to be one coming, even during this period of plenty.

The "spike" was it.

Journalism and the American sporting scene had changed significantly and dramatically during the early nineties while I was away. There was the rise of sports-talk radio, a phenomenon that infected and infused all aspects of the sporting life. In New York, there was radio station WFAN. For the first time, virtual round-the-clock sports news was being disseminated and dissected.

Often, an outrageous statement by a caller would be heard over the airwaves, and the host had neither the inclination nor the smarts to refute it. So wild rumors, trade talk, misinformation, and ignorance began to rule the airwaves. It all got sent out, uncritically.

This was going on all over America, and was coupled with the rise of the magazine television shows in which anything goes. Suddenly, citizens and fans would talk about any aspect of a person's life, and once all those parts of an athlete's persona were opened, the entire way of reporting sports changed. It was all fair game. An athlete started to be known for his quirky off-the-field shenanigans, or his bizarre personality, as much as for what he did on the field.

I'll say this for the Jets: Because of the aura surrounding Hess, and Gutman's sensibilities, the team probably drafted or acquired fewer truly bad characters than most clubs. Even though neither man had a thing to do with personnel choices, it was clear to those under them how they felt about rapists and druggies and wife-beaters and shoplifters who also happened to be able to run with a football. They didn't want them.

The '94 season bumped along and suddenly the Jets, with a 6–5 record, were meeting the Dolphins. A victory for New York would put them in a first-place tie. Five games remained and the Jets seemed to be surging, seemed to have found their voice.

It was Thanksgiving weekend, and as usual Hess showed up on Thanksgiving Day to address the troops. He had nothing but good feelings for Carroll.

"I'm more optimistic now than at any time I can remember," said the patriarch who 11 years earlier had refused to revel in a 10–1 start.

But now, he stood out on the field and told the players, "It's Pete's team now."

The game against the Dolphins attracted the largest Jets home crowd in the team's history. Wouldn't you know it—instead of having more than 75,000 people leave with fond memories and heightened expectations, the Jets picked this time to begin their latest three-year ruin?

They led by 17–0 and then 24–6. They even led by 24–14 early in the fourth quarter. But then Esiason tossed his first interception of the game, and two minutes later Dan Marino hooked up with Mark Ingram to cut the edge to 24–21.

Then Boomer's protection shattered. He was hit three straight times and fumbled each time. The Jets recovered every time, but they had to punt, and got a break when the Dolphins fumbled. The Jets recovered, and with six minutes remaining had the ball on the Dolphins' 38. Boomer was picked off again. The Jets held.

Now fast-forward. There is 2:34 remaining and Marino gets the ball back on his own 16. He is trailing by three points. He whips the Dolphins downfield. They get down to the Jets' eight-yard line with about 25 seconds remaining. Marino needs a timeout, needs to stop the clock.

Tens of thousands of fans stand screaming, trying to outroar Marino's throaty commands to his Dolphins. Marino stares at Ingram, who is matched against the Jets' rookie cornerback Aaron Glenn, their first-round draft pick.

"Clock! Clock! Clock!" Marino barks. He makes a spiking motion with his right hand, as if he is going to spike the ball and stop the clock. Ingram knows, but the rookie cornerback doesn't.

For a moment—a Jets' moment?—Glenn holds up, thinking play will stop. Instead, the ball is snapped and Ingram heads for a corner of the end zone. Too late, Glenn chases Ingram. Marino passes the ball instead of spiking it. Ingram grasps it for his fourth touchdown of the day. Twenty-two seconds show on the clock—but another era has just ended for the Jets.

"A staggering defeat," Carroll called it. He didn't know how staggering.

The Jets lost all their remaining games. And the legacy of that somber stretch carried over the next two years under Rich Kotite's aegis. The team went 4–28 under Richie, but was actually 4–33 from the moment Marino found Ingram. One game seamlessly went into the other, one regime into the other, one "Same Old Jets" retort into the next.

Carroll never was prepared for how his players or the public reacted. The familiar cry, "Same old Jets," replaced "J-E-T-S! Jets! Jets! Jets!" Everyone came down on the Jets. The losses tumbled over one another: New England, Detroit, San Diego. Carroll couldn't stop it.

Meanwhile, he had a serious locker-room problem. Brian Washington and James Hasty, two of his better defensive backs, had started to question what was going on, started to wonder what was wrong with this franchise. Johnny Mitchell asked if there was some sort of hex over this team.

After one practice I got into a discussion about the team with Carroll. For the first time, I sensed his bitterness at what was unfolding, the unfairness of how we in the media were reacting to it, and how the fans were looking at the Jets. This was not something the normally sunny Californian had ever experienced.

"I can't believe how everyone's turning on us," he said. "It's almost as if they couldn't wait. I never expected such a reaction."

His time ended at the Astrodome, the season's last game, when the Jets also announced that Steinberg was suffering from cancer. The Jets' collapse was total, a 24–10 defeat.

So the Jets ended the year with five straight losses, starting with the stunning defeat at the hands of Marino.

Hess had given Carroll only one season, but Hess had had enough. What galled Hess was the lack of character, he believed, the team had shown in losing. They had given up, especially against the Oilers.

"I couldn't forgive that," Hess explained.

"My three years there were probably the most volatile of all,"

Boomer reflected. "Three years. Three head coaches. Three systems. Consistency. Maybe now they'll have it with one leader. He's been anointed. When Bruce got fired, I was devastated. It's one thing when it's done for the right reasons. It took me three weeks to get over it, and if it hadn't been for him calling me, I don't know if I would've gotten through it. He revived my career. I went back to the Pro Bowl."

Boomer is trying to put into perspective what had infected and affected the club. But as with all the others who try, it is elusive:

"So many things were done the three years I was there to appease . . . I don't know who they were trying to appease. You know, I was equally devastated the day Pete Carroll got fired. I had come in to pick up my bonus check, and I saw Rich Kotite walking around the building, and I said, 'What's Rich Kotite doing here?' I thought he was angling for an assistant coach's job. And when they told me, I said, 'What!' "

16

Rock Bottom

While Hess was on vacation in the Caribbean, he made his decision. And the man he wanted to see replace Carroll was Kotite, a former Jets assistant. Richie had gone on to four seasons with the Eagles, bringing them to the playoffs once and compiling an overall winning record.

But Kotite had just been fired by the Eagles' rookie owner. Richie had seen the Eagles collapse from a 7–2 start to lose their final seven games. He was having a farewell-to-Philadelphia dinner in famed Bookbinder's restaurant when the long-distance call came to his table.

Hess told him he wanted to speak to him.

A few days later, in one of the more novel events in team history, Leon Hess presided over a news conference. It was only the second one he had ever staged, and it was a beaut. He was anointing Kotite "the head of the Jets' family."

Richie was, in Hess's words, a "dese, dems, and dose" guy. Hess was enamored of Rich's loyalty, his Jets connection, his sidewalks of New York demeanor, his winning Eagles record despite those seven straight losses that ended his career there.

"I'm 80 years old," growled Hess. "I want results now."

Carroll, of course, was devastated by his dismissal. Pete attacked Hasty and Washington. But Pete also realized he had lost control of the team at the end, had too late exercised his will to halt a deteriorating locker-room situation.

The thing is, I believe Pete would have learned. I think he was bright enough to know what had to be done. His biggest failing was that he had never been a head coach before, and perhaps that was really the fault of the people who hired him to do a job that few can master instantly. Leon Hess's being embarrassed because "the team quit" may not be reason enough to make such a dramatic change—especially after there had seemed to be a genuinely new direction.

Here's the kind of guy Rich Kotite is. When he calls, he says, "It's Richie."

He came to the Jets with powers no head coach had enjoyed since Ewbank. Essentially, he was the general manager as well, although the ailing Steinberg still held that title. In a terrible way, Dick's illness was to freeze the Jets that entire year. Who was controlling the operation? Who would make the moves? It was Richie who did, but with a savvy front-office head too ill to assist him.

It would be a year in which everyone in the front office tiptoed around Dick's dying. His deteriorating condition kept him from actually making moves, although he did attend meetings on personnel and drafts and was consulted.

Kotite, meanwhile, was home—not that he ever really left, even while he was in Philadelphia. His wife, Liz, was brought up in Staten Island, while he was a Brooklynite. Richie and Liz and their daughter, Alexandra, lived about 30 feet from where Liz grew up, virtually sharing a backyard with her mother. When he became Jets head coach, he was renovating his two-bedroom Cape Cod–style home, gutting it, making a big house out of a little house.

Why not simply move to a bigger house? Out of the question. Even when he was in Philadelphia, he often commuted to Staten Island, or stayed in a motel.

Everyone in New York liked him.

"Do I know Rich Kotite? Size 18 shoes," said Mike Cosby, whose father founded Gerry Cosby's, the landmark sports-equipment store abutting Madison Square Garden. "He used to come to us all the time at the old Garden when he went to Poly Prep. He had big feet and couldn't find shoes that fit."

"Rich Kotite?" said Don Turner, trainer of heavyweight champion Evander Holyfield. "Are you kidding? I used to spar with him at Gleason's Gym in the Bronx."

Kotite became the first home-grown coach to lead the Jets. (The man who replaced him, Parcells, was the second.) Kotite had put in seven seasons with the Jets. From 1983 to 1985 he had been Walton's receivers coach, then was elevated to offensive coordinator.

From there he had gone to the Eagles, where Buddy Ryan made him the offensive coordinator. The day Ryan was fired by Eagles owner Norman Braman, Kotite was summoned to the office.

"I thought," said Kotite, "Braman was calling me in to fire me."

Instead, he was offered the head-coaching post.

But now he was with the Jets again. And what about that Jets history? How was he going to address it? Those season-ending five straight losses still were on everyone's mind. (By switching teams, Kotite had actually shortened his team's active losing streak by two.) Think of the Jets, and you thought of collapse.

There were three things Kotite said he would never comment on: "The weather, injuries, the Meadowlands." No Jets player would have an excuse if it was windy, if injuries depleted the team, if they were playing at home in a place most refer to as Giants Stadium.

"When you win in New York," he told his new team, "there's no place like it."

Neither he nor they ever got to find out.

I don't think it was the unique New York pressure that did Rich in. Certainly, there were enough other problems with his tenure. But he thrived on being a New Yorker. Or, as some players said, imitating his Brooklyn pronunciation, "Noo Yawkkuh."

He could remember when he was a chubby, privileged kid in Bay Ridge, Brooklyn, whose father owned a huge commercial printing operation in midtown Manhattan. His father also managed prize fighters, and that association transformed the son.

"I was a very heavy kid, and lethargic, when I was 13 or 14," Kotite recalled. "Boxing became a means of exercise and working out for me." He became the only youngster allowed to work out at the legendary Stillman's Gym on the West Side, where the world's great fighters used to train. His father and Lou Stillman were friends.

Every Friday after school he worked out there, and when Stillman's shut down, he moved up to Gleason's in the Bronx. He went to the University of Miami, which wasn't far from Angelo Dundee's famed Fifth Street Gym, where Muhammad Ali trained. Kotite sparred with Ali and also became the school's heavyweight boxing champion while a freshman.

Kotite eventually transferred to Wagner College on Staten Island and was voted to the Little All-America team as a tight end. ("I was the only one—and still am—from Wagner College to play in the NFL," he notes.) He became something of a local celebrity in 1967 when he made it to the Giants, the team he had rooted for.

His career mostly saw him on special teams, and then he got into coaching. When he was an assistant with the Browns in 1981, he underwent surgery for a brain tumor. It left a permanent medical problem; every year he has to return to a Cleveland hospital for hormone shots.

Perhaps it was his own work habits, perhaps it was his reaction to nearly succumbing to a tumor, perhaps it was any of the dozen or hundred things that make up a personality. But Rich Kotite had a misplaced faith in football players: He thought they all tried as hard as he did. He failed to recognize the difference when others did not.

In his 4–28, two-year Jets' tenure, he seemed content if his players "tried hawd." His two-year record equaled the worst such stretch in at least the last 50 years. His Jets of 1996, which were 1–15, produced the poorest record in club history. That followed 1995's mark of 3–13. Overall, his head-coaching career came crashing down. In his last 39 games his record was 4–35 when you factor in his seven-game Eagles losing streak. It is probably the worst won-lost coaching stretch in league history.

"He never spoke to me for two months after he got the job. That was kind of bizarre," says Esiason of Kotite's early Jets days. As the incumbent quarterback and leader of the offense, Boomer saw himself as the symbol of authority on the field. According to Boomer, "Zeke Bratkowski acted as offensive coordinator, but from everything I saw or heard he had nothing to do with it. I used to come in on Tuesday nights for the game plan, and I'd say, 'Zeke, what's this?' And he'd give me his name, rank, and serial number."

Kotite's Jets opened with a 1–3 record and then prepared to play the Raiders.

This was the beginning of the one-two knockout punch that symbolized Kotite's regime. Anyone who was around the Jets then still recalls and recoils at the memory.

Two days before the Raiders game, the Jets discovered that the rookie they hoped to start at cornerback, Carl Greenwood, had not been eating properly. He was dehydrated.

"He's living by himself and just wasn't taking care of himself," explained Peter Giunta, who coached the defensive backs.

Greenwood had simply skipped too many meals ("I didn't eat the proper foods," he conceded). On Wednesday he was nominated to play right corner, but on Thursday he stopped practicing after a few plays.

And that led to the debut of Vance Joseph. It wasn't merely Joseph's pro debut at cornerback. It was his career debut there. In college he was a backup quarterback and running back. And who would he be matched against in his first appearance on defense—and in an NFL game, at that? His teammates quickly let him in on it:

"You're going up against Tim Brown—a Heisman Trophy winner, you know?"

"Hey, I played some big games," he countered. "I was in the Big Eight. We played Texas."

Of course he did. But until two weeks earlier, Joseph, a bright kid with a sense of humor, had been on the practice squad. Now he suddenly had to contend with Brown, a Pro Bowl performer, as well as Raghib Ismail and quarterback Jeff Hostetler.

Joseph didn't even know how to run backward, which defensive backs must do, since the receivers are running forward, until minicamp. He had joined the Jets as a walk-on. No one drafted him out of college.

"Nervous is good," he said of his first impending start.

The whole scene blended into one of the most disgraceful moments any Jet has ever experienced. And their fans didn't cover themselves with glory either: It was a Sunday night game, and the only chance all year for the Jets to flex their muscles on nighttime television. They were not ready for prime time.

"I have never felt so utterly embarrassed in my football career," said Esiason of the 47–10 defeat.

And what happened to Joseph? Brown beat him for two touchdowns. He gave Brown such a huge "cushion"—the space between defender and receiver—that Brown could have spent all game just standing in front of Joseph, catching passes untouched. Ismail also snared a 48-yard pass among defenders, including Joseph.

Some of his teammates wondered privately how it was possible to put the kid in that situation.

Matt Willig, the offensive tackle, shook his head and said, "Joseph against Brown?"

Joseph had more sense than any of the coaching staff.

"I played that position like a quarterback," he admitted. "You see a rookie out there, you throw at him."

The largest home crowd of the season turned out, and it is possible that it never came back to the Jets for the rest of Kotite's tenure. By the end of the third quarter, fans started cheering "Let's Go Raiders!" And at the end, much of the remaining sparse crowd was composed of taunting teenagers wearing the Raiders' silver-and-black.

"I started feeling bad for the Jets," said Brown later.

But that was hardly the first time nor the last that Jets fans demonstrated fickle natures. Indeed, they have always seemed on edge during good times, as if they are afraid to revel in success.

Several years after Boomer was unceremoniously dropped, he reflected on what happens to the Jets in front of that roaring, gnawing crowd of turncoats:

"It's real, and it happens only in New York. It would never happen anyplace else. At the first sign of a problem, there's this giant sucking sound from the crowd, and you can feel all the air being pulled out of it. I've discussed this with Dave Brown on the Giants, with Phil Simms, they'll admit it. What they do to you is like what no other fans do to you. And you've got to try to pull yourself and your team together while the fans have turned against you. It's when things are bad that you need them on your side."

A ranking Jets official saw this many times.

"I have never seen this anyplace else," he says. "At halftime, people are leaving to beat the traffic, even in a close game."

"When it's bad, there's also the effect the media has on your family," contends Boomer. "It doesn't stop. My first year here I had 50 season tickets, then 40, then 30. In another city, the fans might have some respect for your privacy, especially if you haven't done well in a game. But in New York, it's 'Hey, what's-a matter with you guys?' It wears you down. I could take it, but there's guys who couldn't accept it."

The fans' reaction to the Oakland loss capped an awful week. For six days earlier, Dick Steinberg had died. He had been such an unassuming man that many people were surprised to learn that he was married, and that he was Jewish. That private side of him didn't surprise me. Once, I changed one word of his in a quotation. He had used the word "we," and for purposes of clarity I changed it to "I." The next day he called me and said, "Just so you know for the future, I never use 'I' when discussing what I do. It's better to say 'we.'"

Dick's lingering illness had frozen much of the front office into inaction. Worse, when they made moves, they were flawed.

Kotite and his staff weren't through with personnel surprises as the pain of the Vance Joseph–Tim Brown confrontation faded.

To match up against the man who was one of the great pass-rushers in football history, the Bills' Bruce Smith, the Jets found another rookie. His name was Everett McIver, and he had never played offensive tackle in a game before.

But the Jets were benching Matt Willig, a journeyman, in favor of someone they believed had a future. Esiason couldn't believe it —that they were going to try to protect him from the great Bruce Smith by using an untried converted defensive lineman.

Speak to Boomer even today and he has a tremor in his normally cheerful voice when he recounts his worst memories: "The Everett

McIver situation—I went to Richie Tuesday, Wednesday, and Thursday and told him, 'This won't work.' And he said, 'Yeah, it'll be good. He's a good kid.' "

Esiason didn't recall much about what happened. I'll remind him: He was unconscious for two minutes and forced to lie on his back for two more when he was leveled by Smith in the second quarter. The defensive end raced around McIver, who had jumped in his eagerness, committing a false start. But the officials blew the whistle too late, Smith claimed he never heard it, and was at full speed as his helmet rammed into the lower part of Esiason's face mask.

Smith had been fired up even more than usual, for McIver had unwisely tried a trash-talking game plan. He told Smith he would blow him off the line of scrimmage. No wonder Smith went for Boomer's head.

If there were to be a fine, Smith told Tim Smith of the *Times,* he would appeal. "Unfortunately," wrote Smith, "there's no penalty for what Kotite did to Esiason yesterday."

Boomer tried biofeedback techniques in an attempt to return, while Bubby Brister took over the team in the following weeks. Boomer went to a therapist who used imaging techniques, in which the quarterback focused his thinking intently on making lines converge. He was healthy enough to return late in the season.

By then, Kotite had made a decision. He thought Esiason's career was winding down, and why not get a look at Glenn Foley, a last-round draft pick of 1994 who had played in only one game in his two years?

"Let's see what the kid can do," Kotite told me privately before Game 10 against New England. "If he does well, then maybe we can start him the rest of the season, and maybe we have a quarterback for the future."

The move irritated Boomer, who felt he was ready to return. Boomer realized then he was soon to be an ex-Jet.

Foley had to wait for his Jet moment. In his first start, he got by almost until the end. He completed better than half his passes and he was intercepted once. The Jets were about to lose to the Patriots. On the final play of the game he was hit by Aaron Jones and suffered a dislocated shoulder. So much for the Foley experiment.

So many things that Kotite tried that season failed. He acquired, with much fanfare, Dexter Carter, a Pro Bowl returner with the 49ers. Carter fumbled three times before going into the doghouse. The Jets also unloaded or lost to free agency three veteran offensive linemen from the year before. They waived the versatile, heavy-duty running back Johnny Johnson and traded Moore, the productive receiver.

Jeff Lageman, their top defensive lineman, opted to take the same amount of money the Jets were offering and head for the first-year team in Jacksonville. He wanted a club that had a commitment to winning, in his view. In their second year in the league, Jacksonville went to the playoffs.

Kotite's first draft pick was Kyle Brady, the tight end out of Penn State. He had caught only a few passes, and was a forgotten man, when he opened up to me one day. It became one of the bigger Jets stories of the year, and many people were incredulous when they realized that Kotite, the former tight end, had never bothered to get a tight-end coach for the Jets. And he had a pair of players who needed coaching, badly.

Brady said he was confused in his first year in the league, that he had always had a coach, but that when he came off the field and headed for the sidelines he didn't know whether to stand with the offensive line and their coach, or the wide receivers and their coach.

"No one corrects me when I come in off the field," said Brady, a very religious young man who would have been the last player on the team to ever complain.

He got so confused, he used to call his old tight-end coach at Penn State for advice. The coach mailed him videotapes of his better games so he could see what he was doing when he was doing it right.

The next day's story didn't help Brady, at least not at that moment (the next season the Jets hired the experienced tight-end guru Pat Hodgson). Kotite berated Brady for talking to me. And, oh yes, there was another tight end on that team.

"They didn't even have a tight-end coach at all for the most volatile player on the team," recalls a rueful Boomer, reflecting on Johnny Mitchell. "And he needed direction the most. I roomed with Johnny Mitchell on the road that season. I thought it would give him a chance to be successful and for us to be successful."

Mitchell and Boomer. What a combination. The year before Mitchell had complained about not getting the ball from Boomer, and Boomer had complained that Mitchell never was where he was supposed to be. But Boomer, bless him, knew that Mitchell was potentially his most talented and potent weapon. Perhaps by rooming with him he could keep him focused. They could talk football. They could . . . they could . . . be successful?

"He was a guy who needed constant attention," Boomer explains. "You can't tell him something once. You've got to tell him over and over again."

Mitchell's back injury ended that plan.

Meanwhile, Boomer's relationship with Kotite and Bratkowski deteriorated.

"I sat in those meetings and I saw what was going on," says Boomer. "When Frank Reich was signed the next year as backup quarterback, I told him, 'Frank, you better make sure your guys know what's going on when they get on the field because they're sure not going to get it in the meetings.' "

The '95 Jets stumbled along. Their record was 2–9 as Thanksgiving approached. Hess took the practice field for his 19th straight Thanksgiving Day pep talk.

The 81-year-old refused to sit in the plastic chair they brought for him on the sidelines. So, wearing his green-and-white knit Jets hat, and bundled in a gray topcoat against a wind that whipped across the field, he stood and watched stoically as the team rehearsed for the following Sunday's game in Seattle.

At the end of practice Kotite told the players the old man wanted to talk to them. They surrounded him, towering over him.

He complimented them on how close they had come the previous game against the Bills. But the season was winding down, and there wasn't much they could salvage. Well, at least they weren't quitting like the '94 bunch; at least there wasn't finger-pointing.

"You didn't quit last week," he told them in his growly voice. "You came back and learned you can do a hell of a job. Let's go out with dignity—and show them we're not a bunch of horses' asses."

When those of us on the sidelines heard that, we asked one

another, "What did he say?" For Hess seemed to have defined exactly what the franchise had become, and he seemed to know it.

"Hear, hear," some players shouted. Then Hess hugged Kotite and Boomer and shook hands with everyone he saw, including someone from the maintenance crew.

The Jets won the following Sunday at Seattle. And then they dropped their final four games.

When Richie's first year as the head of the Jets' family ended, he had presided over a 3–13 team. It was the worst record in pro football, and the poorest in club history, too.

What they got for going 3–13 was the number-one pick of the 1996 draft. But obviously, that wouldn't be enough to rebuild the team. They had to plunge into the new world of free agency to get well quick, and that wouldn't be easy. Still, the Jets gave Kotite whatever he needed in money. Would that be enough, though?

"No one wants to come to the Jets," one of football's top agents told me. "You have a successful free agent, he's usually made it big with a good team. Why would he want to come to New York? What is the Jets' commitment to winning? That's the problem the Jets will have—to convince the good players that the team is serious about winning."

They were. They worked feverishly to sign free agents. Gutman and personnel maven Pat Kirwan and Haley and James Harris and Kotite told all those good players out there that 1996 would be different. We know what we need and we'll pay to get it, they said.

It worked. In a month of wheeling and cajoling and needling, they acquired a pair of bookend tackles (David Williams of Houston and Jumbo Elliott of the Giants), a Super Bowl quarterback (Neil O'Donnell of the Steelers), and the Bears' top receiver, Jeff Graham. They got Ron Erhardt, the Steelers' offensive coordinator, and he brought along their tight-end coach, Hodgson.

When the draft arrived, and Keyshawn Johnson, the Southern California megareceiver, was plucked off the top, the Jets felt they were set on offense. They had committed more than $70 million in contracts in the richest acquisition splurge in sports history.

"We have done," said Gutman, "everything that we possibly could do."

I, for one, believed that, and so did virtually all my colleagues and the fans. The Jets suddenly took on an aura of go-getters around the league. I did write a few words of caution, though: With that tricky salary cap, if the Jets didn't produce immediately, or the players they chose fizzled, the team would still be stuck with their expensive contracts counting into the future. Essentially, it froze the Jets from making any big deals for the next two years, almost to the year 2000.

And while there were a few doubters, most people believed the Jets had taken advantage of every opportunity to improve. The doubters, however, could point to the fact that Williams, who had back problems with the Oilers, had been dropped by them during the previous season and had not been picked up by anyone.

Elliott, meanwhile, had a Pro Bowl Giants career, but also suffered a back injury.

O'Donnell signed a $25 million package, fourth-highest in league history. He had been a solid quarterback for the Steelers, but some wondered, Why did Pittsburgh let him go? The Steelers believed their team was so good that they could replace him with an inexperienced quarterback.

"The most disappointing thing about my not being a Jet is that they went out and spent $25 million on my replacement," says a bitter Boomer. "They spent so much money on a new quarterback to make it look like it was me, that all they needed was a good quarterback. At least, that's how it looked to me. But I busted my ass for that organization."

One go-to guy for the media was gone with Boomer's departure. It left us with Nick Lowery, and, for drama, Keyshawn.

Nick was a special guy. That happens when your mother was an Oxford-educated Briton who translated captured World War II German documents, and your father a Fulbright Scholar who worked for the CIA. Nick's next-door neighbor when they lived in Washington was Byron (Whizzer) White.

Lowery was one of the great placekickers in league history. He also was the most altruistic athlete I'd ever met: He ran programs for Navajo children, was a member of President Clinton's White House staff as an assistant to the director of the Office of National Service, spent time and money on the Kick with Nick foundation to combat cerebral palsy, and worked in a soup kitchen.

But he slapped a kid who wouldn't keep his balls warm.

At least, that's how I always wished I could have written it for the *Times*. The Jets were en route to losing to the Patriots late in the season on a cold day in Foxboro, Massachusetts. Don Silvestri kicked off, but complained to Lowery that the ball was rock hard in the 26-degree cold. Lowery walked toward the ballboy, a local 20-year-old who worked for the Patriots.

"Is there someone here keeping the balls warm?" Lowery asked. The ballboy cursed Lowery. Lowery slapped the ballboy.

Later, Lowery said, "He was 180 pounds and 20 years old. This wasn't a Wimbledon ballboy."

Only Nick, once Dartmouth's intramural tennis champion, would use a Wimbledon analogy. I miss him and his insights into the game and his analysis of what the Jets were becoming.

Enter Keyshawn, an extraordinary big-play athlete who believed he was perfection. The Jets had made the rare pick of a wide receiver with the number-one choice in the draft. Keyshawn, though, was universally acclaimed as the top receiver in college. He was taller, bigger, tougher than most defenders he was matched against.

"You're gonna love him in New York," his attorney, Jerome Stanley, said.

Of course, first he had to get here.

The Jets and Johnson did a mating dance more suited to a prenuptial agreement than a football contract. Stanley got Johnson riled up during negotiations, which became very difficult. The Jets had the overall top pick, and they were determined to show the rest of the teams how to negotiate without giving away the store. Here was a novel approach: The Jets had the temerity to offer a contract that was keyed, in significant amounts of money, to performance.

Finally, after weeks of talking and no deal, Stanley got Johnson to do a conference call with a few of us in the press room. There were intimations by Stanley of racism in the Jets' dealings. Keyshawn was truly upset. He did not believe he was being treated right or given the respect other teams had given their top choices. And why was Gutman being so difficult about the performance money? Stanley wondered. Didn't Gutman realize the Jets needed Keyshawn to be in camp?

The 1996 season was one great mistake. From the moment training camp began with the bookend tackles on the sidelines, after they had injured themselves warming up for the first day's activities, everything was off-center.

Keyshawn missed a month of camp before finally signing after the team had played one exhibition game.

"Now," said an upbeat O'Donnell, "we've got everyone."

Johnson received the highest average salary ever paid a rookie —$2.5 million a year. His six-year deal would be worth at least $15 million. But the Jets added two innovations. His $6.5 million signing bonus would not come all at once, as most players get it. The Jets spread it over three years, allowing them to make some money on his money.

And then they added the $2 million kicker: It required Johnson to attain at least two of four very high standards of excellence a year. These were making the Pro Bowl, or catching 85 passes, or scoring 13 touchdowns, or amassing 1,000 receiving yards in one season. The more he accomplished, the higher his salary would go in his last years, up to the $2 million maximum.

How difficult were those figures to reach? Only the 49ers' Jerry Rice and the Cowboys' Michael Irvin achieved all four goals in each of the previous five seasons, and neither had done it as a rookie.

"If he does it," said Gutman, "he'll be worth it."

Well, Keyshawn had a good season but the Jets didn't. They lost their first eight games (to run their losing streak to 12 from the previous year). O'Donnell suffered his injuries. The Jets blew six games they led at halftime. They beat only Boomer's new team, the Cardinals.

These weren't the Same Old Jets. These were the spiritual descendants, the Same New Jets, and worse. They were close, but they would always lose.

Everybody waited for the season to end. Even Kotite's announced departure, on the eve of the final game, was jumbled. He said he wasn't quitting. "I am not a quitter," he explained. "I'm stepping aside."

If we thought the Jets would go gently into that good night of the offseason, we were fooled. It wasn't merely the flap and the drama and the intrigue surrounding the courtship of Bill Parcells and the deal to bring him to the Jets. It was also Keyshawn, the author.

Before he had even caught a pass in the pros, he signed a six-figure deal to collaborate with his long-time surrogate aunt, Shelley Smith. She had helped him get through a remarkably troubled youth in Los Angeles, where he had been arrested and spent time in a juvenile facility for a series of street crimes. Shelley, who was a writer and producer for ESPN, also hired him as a babysitter for her young child once he began to straighten himself out.

Keyshawn was the kind of guy who ingratiated himself with people. He became the mascot of the USC athletic department. He was a bootstraps kid and he had a quick smile and an outrageous ego, which he backed up with talent.

He kept a diary, and during the season he would speak to Shelley most days and she would record and rewrite his thoughts, which were opinionated and strong. If he called offensive coordinator Ron Erhardt "an old fool," so be it. If he called little Wayne Chrebet, the spunky wide receiver from Hofstra, "the team mascot," well, those were his words. Just asking, said Keyshawn, but did O'Donnell fake his season-ending calf injury to protect the job of Erhardt? If Keyshawn wondered if there was racism on the Jets —those were his thoughts, right then, in his rookie season on a 1–15 team.

Keyshawn made some wonderful plays that first year, and he showboated after his first big-league touchdown by slamming his helmet to the ground, which prompted some new rule about happiness displays. He almost snared a Hail Mary pass that would have given them a victory at Indianapolis. He caught a touchdown at Washington that could have tied the game if an official hadn't mistakenly blown the call. In all, he set a team rookie receiving record with eight touchdowns and 844 yards.

His book came out four months after the season ended and all his bitter, often silly, words were there. They came blurting off the pages. Just when the Jets thought they could enjoy springtime under Parcells, this book opened its pages and bit them.

Keyshawn wouldn't apologize for the book, which was called, not so subtly, *Just Give Me the Damn Ball! The Fast Times and Hard Knocks of an NFL Rookie.*

Oh, he met with Erhardt and he met with O'Donnell to explain what he really meant, but they didn't believe him. And Chrebet was still waiting for an apology.

As the weeks went by and I got deeper and deeper into Jets history, I attempted to put this all into perspective by getting other people's thoughts. I was disappointed that my old friend, Rich Kotite, didn't call me back. Nor did Lou Holtz, although I still have his autographed book. Nor did Pete Carroll, who, in the way life laughs at coaches, had now switched to the Patriots. But all the other Jets head coaches did get back to me.

I had actually been around the Jets longer than any of them, although I was merely an observer. I wasn't there for the team's greatest moment, and I have come to realize how difficult it is to get just one, let alone to recreate it. Most teams have never won a championship. I find it amusing when fans in other cities are un-happy with 9–7 records, or when 49ers' followers are upset when their team wins but doesn't do it in style.

Jets fans didn't care any longer about style. Just get them a damn victory.

17

Along Came Bill

Football's laughingstocks; that's what they became in Kotite's 1–15 season of 1996. The symbolism of everything that the Jets ever tried and failed coalesced in a cartoonish kaleidoscope: the number-one draft pick creating problems; a nutty injury to the quarterback; high-priced free agents who didn't help; a record number of no-shows; coaching flaws; fans who did attend quickly turning against their beleaguered erstwhile heroes.

The Jets of 1996 were like so many other Jets teams, only more so. History had distilled the unstable elixir of Jetdom and made everyone drink. How many years in a row can you produce football's worst record? For how many decades can you be the worst team of the decade?

And yet, there was this feeling—and I know you've heard it spoken of before—among fans and players who cried out, "We're not as bad as our record!" In truth, they weren't, and yet they were. For as a former Giants coach likes to say, "You are what your record says you are."

Now, finally, the old Jets had seen enough. The modern Jets were trifling with their memories. Something had to change.

So Don Maynard volunteered to bring back the old glory.

While the Patriots were generating playoff victories as their coach Bill Parcells marched to his inevitable exit, Maynard wrote to Leon Hess. At about the same time, so did Curley Johnson. They wanted to coach the Jets. Maynard, in fact, wanted to become the head coach and he wanted to bring back with him Super Bowl players such as Grantham and Lammons and Baker and Baird as his assistants.

Maynard's emotional display was part of a sudden wave of old Jets reaching out to the new ones, trying to effect a change. That 1996 season was the final straw: Attention had to be paid to Jets history. No one in charge here seemed to give a damn about it. And except for the owner, the equipment manager, the public-relations director, and the doctor, nobody even knew anything about it.

As each coach came on the heels of the previous losing coach, he would say, "I don't care about Jets history." It was a defensive reaction because what he really meant was, I don't care about the *losing* history. What he should have cared about was the brief winning Jets history.

When I spoke to Maynard in El Paso to ask about his unusual offer, he admitted, "I spoke to Mr. Hess after the other guy [Kotite] was gone."

What prompted this interest in running the Jets?

"I coached a long time ago," Maynard explained. "There's seven guys I know real well from the Super Bowl. Look, I played for nine head coaches and 42 assistants and there's only a few things you have to know about coaching. You look when the last winning seasons came about, and they were under Weeb and under Walt Michaels."

I didn't want to quibble that there were also three under Walton, because Walton wasn't in Maynard's frame of reference. That last winning season of Walton's was nine years ago; the 1960s were fresher in Don's memory.

For Maynard a coach merely has to control three aspects of the game, something no Jets coach since Michaels had done:

"Three things can kill you in a ball game," Maynard continued. "Turnovers, mistakes, and calling the wrong play.

"I've been watching even though I haven't been coaching. I chart every game I see on TV. It's simple. When it's third-and-10, you throw it 12. When you're behind, you throw into the end zone." Got that, Jets coaches, whoever you are?

Maynard envisioned himself as the man who could avoid these three killing errors. Then he sought to pull together a coaching staff that would instill the football verities.

"I don't second-guess Mr. Hess," said Maynard. "But why get losers? Go hire me or Larry Grantham or Gerry Philbin. I may run a financial-planning business, but third-and-10—I know to throw the ball."

Meanwhile, Curley Johnson was going bust in the salsa business while the Jets were going bust under Kotite. Johnson had hoped to get his bottles of salsa in supermarkets, but there was some convoluted business problem and suddenly Curley wasn't making salsa anymore. He turned his attention to reviving the Jets.

Although Johnson conceded, "I've never coached," he believed his experience and versatility gave him the necessary background. He was, he explained, the Jets' "fifth running back, second tight end, did all the punting and kicking off."

His letter to Hess, dated January 6, 1997, echoed the feelings of ex-Jets everywhere, especially those who had known the delight of the Super Bowl:

Dear Mr. Hess:

I know the Jets are going through some tough times right now and we all hurt to see this. I am writing to you to ask for your help in the way of a job in some capacity. I know I have been away from football but having played 13 years of pro football you never forget the things you were taught.

I would like to try and help you bring the Jets back. I think I could help in scouting players for the Jets. Having played tight end, fullback and being a kicker I certainly feel I should know a good prospect when I see one. Also, by living in Austin, Texas, I am within driving distance to all southwest colleges as well as

Oklahoma, Louisiana & Arkansas. I know most of the coaches as I play in several NFL golf tournaments each year.

I talked with Coach Ewbank today and he said he would highly recommend me for a scouting job. He said to be sure and give you his number and feel free to call him anytime.

Coach Ewbank once told me you never get football out of your blood. I know now what he meant. I miss being part of the Jets and would love to do my part to help get us back to our Super Bowl days.

Please let me help with our rebuilding program. I love the Jets and think you need some people around that feel the same as you and I do.

I would appreciate any help you might be able to give me. Let me hear from you in the near future. I would love to come to New York and sit down and visit with you. Call me at my home.

Sincerely,
(signed)
Curley Johnson
NY Jets/'60–'68

A subsequent letter to Parcells, three months later, brought only a call from Dick Haley, the efficient, experienced draft and personnel expert and one of the few holdover football people in the organization whom Parcells retained in the same capacity, telling Johnson there were "no openings."

Johnson said he had no quarrel with Parcells, whom he described as "a fine football man." But until the Jets hired Parcells, claimed Johnson, "They've never gotten anyone in there, a general manager or coach, who could get the job done. They didn't take that receiver, what's his name? Yeah, Rice. They passed up Dan Marino. Coach Parcells will do a great job, but I'd like to see ex-Jets help them."

Ralph Baker is one of a coterie of ex-Jets who live near their old team.

"I think everybody is kind of embarrassed the way the team has gone," he says now, "but nobody seems to be able to figure out how to make it better.

"When I came to the Jets we were definitely second-class citizens. Some group would get a Jets speaker—but only if they couldn't get a Giant. I hate to see the Jets now leaning toward the Giants. I hate to see so many ex-Giants in there. I'm sure there are very capable Jets. Why not bring in ex-Jets? Still, I think the team made the right choice with Bill Parcells. He's probably installed the philosophy, 'It's my way or the highway.' "

Ralph was rehired by the Jets for their 1997 season, and was back evaluating personnel. So the Jets did try to keep some memories alive. Memories were virtually all the Jets had.

.   .   .

The Jets wanted one man to stop the madness.

Only Bill Parcells, Gutman and Hess felt, could do something about a franchise that, when it opened the 1997 season, would take the field showing only one victory in the last 642 days.

The Jets were ready to hand over the reins, along with the rest of the farm, to a man who had brought the Giants a pair of Super Bowl victories; who had forced people to stop laughing at the Patriots; who was a bona fide New Yorker; and, most important, who knew how to win.

Oh, they knew he wasn't perfect, all right; they knew how he had left his previous teams under tangled circumstances. The Patriots gig was his 11th different coaching job; in his first 14 years of coaching, he had been with seven different colleges.

He had actually left the Giants twice (once, many years before, when he was an assistant virtually for a day) and had tried several times to quit as head coach before he actually did, leaving the team floundering after its second Super Bowl victory in 1990.

"With Bill," said an NFL team official who knew him well, "it was never about control—it was always about money."

And yet, it was also about winning. What a remarkable record he always achieved, and quickly. This was the man for the leaderless Jets. But Parcells was still under contract to the Patriots, even though he hated the owner, Robert K. Kraft—hated him with a passion—and the owner hated him.

Whenever I think of the two of them, I remember this little scene that played out during Super Bowl week in January 1997 when

Parcells's Patriots faced the Green Bay Packers. The pair had made a show of walking together across the field of the Louisiana Superdome—not quite arm-in-arm, you understand, but talking and even joking.

Later, after Parcells had left their joint press conference, Kraft was talking privately about the contract snare he had tossed over Parcells. With a self-satisfied grin, Kraft whispered, "He's not as smart as he thinks."

Despite this mutual antagonism, the Jets had a problem in getting Parcells. He was in the midst of a playoff run, and who knew how far he could take the Patriots? Why, it could be all the way to the Super Bowl. So the Jets had to wait, and while they waited, the longer they failed to hire anyone to fill the void, the more rumors and nasty innuendos swirled around. The most prevalent was that the Jets were tampering—a charge leveled, not surprisingly, by Kraft. He and Parcells became even more contentious. Their seething relationship dominated Super Bowl week.

Fifteen hundred miles away, the Jets were frozen in place. Three dozen people applied for the job. "Not at this time," Gutman told them. The February free-agency period was approaching. The April draft was approaching. Contracts had to be signed or offered, players searched out. January wore on, and the Pats continued to win in the playoffs, and the Jets continued to rebuff would-be coaches, would-be general managers, would-be saviors from among ex–Super Bowl players.

I spent much of the playoff run hanging around Foxboro, Massachusetts, where the Pats played. After one of his news conferences, I grabbed Parcells alone and asked, "Since your team's winning now, does that change your mind about coming back here next season?"

"Please don't ask me that now," he said, with a pained look.

Meanwhile, Kraft was being solicitous and beaming as New England continued to do well, while back in New York all Gutman and Hess could do was sigh with every Patriots victory.

Kraft was a remarkably successful man, with worldwide financial interests in the paper-goods industry and social involvement that included sponsoring the Boston Symphony and donating money to cancer research. He was a trustee of his alma mater,

Columbia University; he had a business degree from Harvard; he was altruistic when it came to taking care of things for Boston. He had been a season-ticket-holder since 1972, and now he had seen the Patriots filling Foxboro Stadium, had seen their grip on the New England consciousness, had seen the psychic rewards a good athletic team brings to a community.

And Parcells was making him miserable. Kraft wasn't being allowed to enjoy this wonderful moment in time.

The roots of their disagreement are easy to discern: Kraft took over in 1994, a year after Parcells had been hired by an interim owner and told he could run everything. I remember Parcells on a podium that first day sitting with other club officials. Someone asked him whether he would run the draft as well.

"I'm going to run everything," said Parcells. "I know more about it than anyone else up here."

But when Kraft bought the club for $160 million, he wanted it run like a successful corporation. And that meant a place for Parcells and a place for other executives.

Two years after Kraft sank his money into the team, he made an unusual deal with his troubled coach. Parcells was worried about his health; he knew something was wrong, but the doctors told him they couldn't find anything. There was something irregular going on with his heart, yet each time he took a test the result was negative.

"Finally, I said I'm going to find out what this is, even if it kills me," he explained. "I vowed I was getting on the treadmill in the doctor's office and we were going to keep it up until we found out."

They found out. Under the heavy stress, there were circulatory difficulties. He was to undergo three different procedures—two angioplasties and a heart bypass.

Early in 1996, following a 6–10 season, Kraft disclosed that Parcells's contract was being cut by a year. He wouldn't have to coach in 1997 if he didn't want to.

"I've basically tried to build him a support system," Kraft said. "But if a man asks you to alter his contract after a tough season, am I going to say no? If you don't have two willing people in a contract, what's the sense of it?"

Yet when Parcells became the Patriots' commander-in-chief in

1993—a role he seemed to envision as somewhere between dictator and president-for-life—his energy was boundless despite his history of heart problems. He was signed through 1997.

There were other factors in the disenchantment between owner and coach—most notably the 1996 draft-day fiasco. Not only did the Patriots hierarchy (what a terrible word that must have been to Parcells) overrule him on his number-one pick, they soon "undrafted" a player, Christian Peter, whom he had chosen in the fifth round. Peter had a record of abusing women and other loutish behavior at Nebraska, and Kraft was embarrassed when the various police reports came out.

"What we stand for is important to the community," said Kraft in dislodging Peter a few days later.

Of course, Kraft and Parcells already had argued over the top pick: Vice-President Bobby Grier wanted Terry Glenn, the Ohio State wide receiver, while Parcells wanted a pass-rushing defensive lineman. When Parcells learned his choice was overruled, he stormed out of the draft bunker at Patriots headquarters.

Of course, even during the parting dance between the antagonists there was some good feeling. Winning will do that to you. So after the Patriots defeated the Steelers in a playoff game, Kraft was proud that his coach, the most superstitious man ever to win a Super Bowl, had carried a "chai," the Hebrew symbol for life, in his pocket.

That hardly lasted. One day during Super Bowl week, Parcells gave his metaphorical reason for wanting more power:

"If they want you to cook the dinner, at least they ought to let you shop for some of the groceries."

The gist of their final conflict had come down to whether Parcells would be completely free after the game with the Packers, or whether Kraft had an option on his coach for next year, too—so Kraft could at least demand compensation from another team if Parcells left.

Two days before the Super Bowl, Kraft faxed a copy of Parcells's contract to Commissioner Paul Tagliabue, presumably to show that the Pats were, in fact, entitled to compensation if Parcells coached elsewhere in 1997. And after the Super Bowl, when the Patriots, playing gamely, lost to the Pack, Tagliabue announced that he would mediate the continuing battle between the two parties.

This was the third post–Super Bowl controversy on Parcells's resume. After the Giants captured their first Super Bowl title, in January 1987, Robert Fraley, Parcells' agent, negotiated with the Atlanta Falcons for Parcells, but Commissioner Pete Rozelle made Parcells honor his existing contract. After the Giants won the Super Bowl four years later, Fraley was close to an agreement that would have sent Parcells to Tampa Bay. Parcells vacillated, then when he made up his mind he was rebuffed by the Bucs' owner, Hugh Culverhouse.

Quickly, Tagliabue ruled on the Kraft–Parcells affair. The commissioner said that Parcells's contention that he was free to leave New England and coach wherever he wanted next season ran "contrary to common sense." Kraft immediately demanded that negotiations with the Jets start with their offering their overall number-one draft pick.

"You tell me what someone with three Super Bowls is worth on the open market," an ecstatic Kraft told associates when learning of Tagliabue's ruling. Then Kraft added, "I didn't break."

The Jets, meanwhile, had not had a coach for five weeks, nor a general manager since Steinberg's death during the 1995 season.

So the Jets didn't have the coach, and they weren't about to fork over the number-one draft pick for one. But at least they announced they were beginning negotiations to get him. Gutman began talking to Kraft.

Kraft still was seething. During Super Bowl week he complained bitterly to a friend, "This should be a great week for us, but he's sticking the knife in my back and twisting it."

"I've been through hell because of this," Kraft said as negotiations began. "I'm just supposed to hand Bill Parcells to a team in my division? I don't think so."

Five days after he coached them in Super Bowl XXXI, Bill Parcells formally resigned as coach of the New England Patriots.

Now get this: Frustrated by the way negotiations for Parcells were going, the Jets interviewed Bill Belichick for the job they had earmarked for Parcells. So while Kraft was introducing his new coach, Pete Carroll—last seen in the East as the Jets' head coach!

—the Jets were talking to Belichick, Parcells's long-time assistant. Actually, Parcells's alter ego would be a better description.

A beaming Kraft said of Carroll, "He's someone I can relate to."

And Carroll? What had he done since the Jets canned him? He had been the 49ers' defensive coordinator, a chance to look at another side of football life, where the standard of excellence was unwavering.

Meanwhile, Gutman showed that losing had not affected his mind. He conceived a brilliant idea that was to force the Patriots to accept a deal for Parcells, although it was costly to the Jets.

The headline over my story the next day was: "Flea-Flicker Jets Hire Parcells, but Not to Coach."

Yes, the Jets, unable to make a deal for Parcells, executed an end-around: They hired Belichick as head coach for a year and named Parcells as a consultant who eventually would take over.

"A sham," charged Kraft. It didn't get much more bizarre than this.

So Gutman announced not only that the Jets had hired Parcells and Belichick, but that they would elevate Parcells to head coach as soon as possible. In other words, if they could arrive at a deal with Kraft, Parcells would immediately step in.

Thus, the Jets, in a sense, hired their fourth and fifth coaches in a five-year span. But Belichick sounded like anything other than a permanent fixture as he contemplated taking over the team. He said he would create an environment of discipline and physical toughness. He also said the Jets' series of injuries in 1996 were something he might be able to control with a better strength and conditioning program.

The idea of Bill Parcells being hired as a "consultant," while serving as the coach-in-waiting, evoked bemused reaction. "What is he going to do, walk around the halls and not talk to the players?" wondered one general manager.

So one day after the Jets named Parcells as their 1997 consultant and their 1998 coach, Tagliabue placed an embargo on him, stating that Parcells was off-limits to the Jets until all the terms of his unusual contract could be reviewed. This caused an equally unusual scene:

The Jets had signed Parcells, but they couldn't make any announcement about it in their little enclave at Weeb Ewbank Hall on the grounds of Hofstra University in Long Island. Use of the hall could be construed as "football-related," and the Jets had been warned that Parcells could do no football-related work for them until the deal had been approved.

So the Jets announced it in the parking lot. We all turned out in the great outdoors and there came Parcells, with Gutman, while Gutman's wife, Carol, waited in the Mercedes, motor running, for the press conference to end so she could spirit her husband out of there.

In Parcells's head-coaching career, his teams had gone to the Super Bowl every four years. If that pattern continued, the Jets might actually be playing in the big game in 2001—and wouldn't that be symbolic?

Finally, one of pro football's more confounding legal scrimmages came to a conclusion. Tagliabue brokered a deal that freed Parcells to coach immediately. He got the combatants together in a midtown office building and spoke sweetly to the Jets. He said they wanted Parcells, didn't they, and wouldn't they rather he spend the year coaching the Jets than at his other home in Jupiter, Florida?

Then he told Kraft, "Look, you've just been to the Super Bowl. Don't you want to revel for a while in this good feeling instead of having controversy? And anyway, in a few years you're going to start losing some of these players to free agency. Take a deal I've put together. You'll get draft picks, you'll still have something."

So it was done. Instead of getting the Jets' top pick of 1997 the Pats got the Jets' third- and fourth-round picks for that year, their second-round pick the following year, and their first-round pick in 1999.

Now, the work began.

.   .   .

I showed up at 8:00 A.M. in the parking lot to see the beginning of the Parcells era. One of his first acts was to fly in the entire team for a meeting and tell them the law.

"This," he said, "is where you work."

And this was where they would begin their voluntary offseason conditioning program. It was voluntary because according to the union contract a club had to give players the entire offseason off, with the exception of some minicamp time. "Voluntary" to Parcells meant do it or be fired.

So I stood bright and early in that damned parking lot waiting for the players to come in and begin lifting weights and perhaps I'd get a glimpse of Parcells and Keyshawn.

But the coach had arrived at 7:00 A.M. So had Keyshawn, who had just come in on a redeye from Los Angeles. The only media guy in the lot at that hour was Anthony Fucilli of the Madison Square Garden Network, with a cameraman, and Parcells greeted him with, "What the fuck are you doing here?"

When Fucilli asked for an interview, Parcells told him, "The wall is going up." In other words, we were to be barred from the parking lot. And we were.

Parcells instituted a host of rules designed to keep the Jets safe from outside forces—that is, the prying eyes and poison pens of wretches like me. We could not interview any of his assistant coaches without his permission—and that rarely came. We could not interview players once the locker room was closed. He told his players not to accept phone calls from us at their homes. His assistants' contracts stipulated they were not allowed to talk to the news media without his approval.

He had ways of making his points. After one practice, Neil O'Donnell, an avid golfer, sought out the *New York Post*'s Mark Cannizzaro, who also covered golf. O'Donnell, standing 15 feet away from a group of youngsters, started to chat about golf when Parcells spotted them.

"You're breaking the fucking rules!" he shouted at his quarterback, perhaps traumatizing a bunch of first-graders.

And yet, through it all, I found the guy fascinating. Never once in that first year was he anything but courteous and open to me—and to most of the regular beat writers. Usually, when his press conferences ended and the guys with the microphones and tape recorders had left, Parcells hung around. He loved baseball and he loved trivia and he also enjoyed talking about players, saying things off the record he didn't want to utter in the glare of television lights.

Immediately, the whole place changed. "Everyone's walking around here faster," said a secretary. People were accountable.

Parcells put up an all-weather practice bubble. He tore down one practice field and put up another. Public-relations director Ramos marveled at Parcells's knowledge of grass; he understood which types grew in the Northeast, which were better for football fields.

He kept tabs on players' workout habits. Never again would Mo Lewis have someone else sign in for him while he was out having a hamburger. Parcells brought in his old staff of coaches, led by Belichick as his unofficial defensive coordinator and sounding board. Several Jets coaches were kept, but many players soon found the door.

Players would ask me about him. "Does he tell you anything? What are his plans for me? Is he going to make any trades?" Somehow, there had been a perception that Parcells, the man who had taken three teams to Super Bowls, was not a great front-office mind, that he couldn't judge personnel. But he shook up everything and everyone.

A new strength coach arrived. A young negotiations and salary-cap guru named Mike Tannenbaum took over contract dealings from Gutman. Carl Banks, the former Giant, came aboard as an adviser to young players who never had opened their own bank accounts and didn't know which tunnel to take to get to New Jersey. Lowery, the senior Jet in point of service, was gone; Kyle Clifton was asked to retire; half a dozen players were dropped.

With a pair of predraft and draft-day deals, the Jets converted their overall number-one pick (which they earned by having football's worst record) into a total of seven choices. They moved down to sixth with a trade with the Rams, then down to eighth by trading that choice to the Bucs. And with their first-round pick they plucked James Farrior, the University of Virginia linebacker.

And then the new and the old learned to become Jets in the Parcells mold. In minicamp, and in the grueling summer heat, he was on top of them. In fact, he suddenly started to act fidgety during the second workout in July; he began to go over to each unit and shout that he wasn't happy with what he saw. He yelled at Belichick. He yelled at Romeo Crennel, his defensive-line coach. Then he barked for practice to stop.

He called over all the coaches and made them gather round him. He faced them and began yelling, while just a few feet away stunned players listened.

I could hear words like "shit" and "fuck" coming out as Parcells's jaw moved furiously, obviously unhappy with his coaches. Or so he wanted everyone to think.

Was this just for effect? Was he letting coaches and players know this was not the same old Jets team, that it wasn't business as usual, that there would actually be accountability here? Probably. But what the heck—whatever you'd say to a team that was 1–15, you were right, weren't you?

"You don't tell me what to do!" he screamed one day at Hugh Douglas, the only Jet defensive lineman of any significance. Douglas looked at him perplexed. Parcells wouldn't stop. "I tell you what to do!" Parcells shouted at the impressionable Douglas.

Often, as a rookie two years earlier, Douglas would be near tears because of blown assignments. He had come out of Central State of Ohio, wherever that was, and had produced 18 sacks in his first two seasons. He could get to the passer, but he had trouble remembering alignments. He often stayed after practice, his nervousness getting the better of him when the full team was around. Parcells showed him no mercy. (And, after the season Douglas was traded.)

Even for the coach's old student Jumbo Elliott, who had helped take Parcells to a Giants' Super Bowl, there was no letting up. Parcells ragged Elliott, an offensive tackle who had been to the Pro Bowl, on his stance, or for jumping offside, or for his technique.

He seemed to be able to see what was going on behind him. When Dedric Ward, the unknown returner from the unknown school (Northern Iowa), who had been a third-round draft pick, dropped a pass as Parcells was coaching another unit, the coach took him aside. He showed him how to position his feet, how to hold his arms.

One summer morning Parcells came over to me, smiling. It was not yet nine o'clock and he was about to get his guys ready for the first workout of the day. He had been with the team about a week.

"Well, it's not all that bad, is it?" he said. And he walked off to the field quite happy.

He came over to me another time during the final week of open practice—that is, where he allowed the news media to watch. "So," he said mischievously, "this is your last practice." As always, he had the last word.

Over the summer we had several conversations about his insistence on keeping players isolated from us. He didn't do this with the Giants, although he had started the practice with the Patriots. Why was he so single-minded about keeping the media at bay?

"It's a different media business now," he explained. "Everyone's looking for a story and it can only come out bad. It can't help us." No matter what I said, he wouldn't budge. No matter how many writers and television and radio complaints went to Tagliabue or the Football Writers Association, he never changed his stance.

The Jets I had covered for more than 20 years had been famous for their open-door policy, access that began under Ewbank. I used to stand behind Namath in the huddle on the practice field, I was elbow-to-elbow with players on the sidelines during Holtz's workouts. I used to walk to the back of the plane to schmooze with Todd. I used to walk in unannounced to Michaels's office, to the locker room, to players in their dorms in the summers.

No, these weren't the Jets of those days any longer. And I suppose you could say, if you were a Jets fan, what a good thing it was, too. Parcells changed the culture of the locker room as well as the newsroom. Certainly it worked in the locker room; he got their attention.

Adrian Murrell fumbled twice in the second exhibition game, against the Ravens.

"My backs don't fumble," Parcells told him. "If they do, I don't play them."

A week later, against the Giants, Murrell fumbled again. Yet after the game Murrell did something that impressed Parcells: The player was the first one to gather in front of the coach for the postgame talk. Parcells liked that. Adrian didn't hide.

That game marked the third straight Jets preseason victory. And although I had learned in my very first year of covering them that exhibition games don't matter, this time they seemed to. Even the pregame shtick he pulled on the Giants in their exhibition was impressive.

This was his first meeting against his old team as a Jets coach. The Giants had massed early in front of the tunnel leading to the field. Outside, 50,000 fans screamed. The Giants tried to pump themselves up. Dave Brown repeated over and over, "Let's go!" Tight end Howard Cross jumped up and down.

Suddenly, they grew quiet. For the Jets—the Bill Parcells–led Jets—were coming down the hallway from the other side of the tunnel, heading straight toward them. He marched in front of his players with a somber look. The Giants said nothing as Parcells's troops came almost face-to-face with them, then suddenly veered to the right and to the tunnel.

"Hey, Tuna, where ya been?" a fan shouted as Parcells walked by.

Well, the Jets went undefeated in the preseason for only the third time in their history, and they went on to trounce the Seahawks in the season's opener at Seattle.

They were overcoming their history—a history that decreed they didn't win on the road, didn't win at home, couldn't hold a lead, couldn't win in December, couldn't . . . couldn't do anything right.

Tuna continued to set the tone in that opening victory. They came in at halftime leading by 27–3. They had been awesome.

Bill was pissed at them.

"They say you can't hold a lead. They say you blew six games last year after leading at halftime," he scolded. "Let's see what you're made of."

They won 41–3.

As the season evolved, the old phrases disappeared. "Same Old Jets" never made its way into a headline. The sobriquet "Gang Green" no longer implied a disease but rather a killer collection. Even Parcells's nickname of Tuna came to have some class.

That name, he explained, was tagged on him in his first incarnation with the Patriots back in 1980 as linebackers' coach. The players were trying to put something over on him, and Parcells blurted out, "You guys must think I'm Charlie the Tuna," evoking the naive character in the Starkist commercial. Since Parcells was sort of rounded in the middle, the nickname stuck.

With each passing week, it was apparent what was happening. I recalled a conversation from that summer.

"Can you change them mentally?" he was asked.

"Yeah, but you have to win before you change," he said. He cautioned, though, that you could still begin to take on a new persona even if you were losing.

"I think people from far away just assume that because you don't win nothing's changed. But after we were 1–10 at New England we knew it was different. The team has to see it. It can't be because I say it. It has to be genuine."

He wanted his players to understand winning and losing just as much as he wanted them to understand their roles. He would quiz them on coverages and he would suddenly halt a practice and say, "Okay, we're up by four points, there's 30 seconds left, we've got the ball on our 20 and it's first-and-10. What's the call?"

These Q and A sessions were extremely important to the team.

"What causes you to lose—you have to understand what that is. Because until you do, you'll never understand how to win."

So I came to understand that for Parcells, it wasn't winning he was obsessed with—it was not losing.

The midpoint of the Jets season saw them beat the Patriots before more than 70,000 fans at Giants Stadium, elevating their record to 5–3. Now the place was routinely packed. No one wondered anymore about performing in a stadium named for another team, or playing across the Hudson.

After the game, Keyshawn Johnson was walking outside the stadium, still in a glad daze. He spotted Parcells in front of him, getting into his Cadillac.

Parcells shut the door, stuck his head out of the window, and with a big grin, shouted to Keyshawn, "I told you we'd get this thing turned around."

It had been apparent not only in victories, but in losses. There was the third game of the year in New England, a theatrical circus with Parcells facing his old team. The Jets lost in overtime after John Hall's 29-yard field-goal attempt was blocked in the closing seconds of regulation time. A victory in this game, Parcells felt, could have propelled the Jets into a different class. Instead, it took time, but it was apparent the Jets were competitive.

Parcells was forever tinkering. Even after the big opening-game victory, he switched from a 4–3 defense to a 3–4 so he could use the rookie Farrior, but doing so detracted from the single great skill of Douglas's—rushing the passer.

Still, Parcells was back with his four-linebacker alignment, with Marvin Jones playing healthy, with Lewis, who a few years earlier had been the best football player in New York, and with old standby Pepper Johnson.

Lewis in particular was revived. He had grown fat and lazy during the Jets' woeful 1995 and 1996 campaigns, in which he was highly paid and poorly motivated. But Parcells had told him how great he could be again only if he wanted to be.

Despite winning, Parcells also messed around with his quarterbacks, taking out O'Donnell at New England and bringing in Foley, who led the Jets to victory. A week later, O'Donnell started again—but again came out for Foley. The Jets won in overtime and Foley became the starter.

But not for long. Foley started only twice. Inklings of the Jets' past failures crept in as he was lost for the year in his second start against the Bears. O'Donnell, in whom Parcells had lost faith, was the starting quarterback again.

The Jets went into the final game of the season with a playoff berth in their hands. They were 9–6 and playing at Detroit. They even had an outside chance at first place in their division. Keyshawn had thrived even though he still wasn't getting the damn ball as often as he wanted. O'Donnell had put up respectable numbers. Chrebet was still making clutch third-down catches. But what kept the Jets going was a pretty decent defense—and an extraordinary special-teams collection.

Parcells early on had identified the special teams—his kicking and kick-defense units—as the ones who would provide a difference on a team with many marginal players. He had a rookie returner from North Carolina named Leon Johnson, whose high-school nickname was "the natural." There was Hall, the rookie from Wisconsin who had been recruited by Donna Shalala when she was the school's president and hadn't yet joined the Clinton cabinet. In his first big-league attempt, he booted a 55-yard field goal, second longest by a rookie in NFL history.

The suicide squad tacklers were led by Corwin Brown, who played chess in the locker room and was proud of the way his chessmen outflanked and outfoxed the big and benign Ernie Logan, a Muslim who wore a watch with a compass so he could face northeast. He needed to pray in that direction every evening.

Another key special-teams guy was a Parcells favorite, Ray Lucas. He had been a quarterback at Rutgers and made his way to New England, where Parcells tried him at defensive back one day, receiver another, quarterback a third.

"I don't know what to do with you," Parcells told him, "but I want you."

Lucas had followed Brown from the Patriots to the Jets to be with Parcells again. They were players searching for someplace to play, and until they settled down, they were going to be on the special-teams squad. Indeed, Parcells had told them this might even be their destiny—that some guys are just not good enough to be starters. But they hoped.

The mostly young and inexperienced special teams were among the league leaders in returning kicks and pinning back opponents' kick returners. It was a terrific combination and kept the Jets in every game.

The Jets' implausible dream in their first Parcells year lasted until the final minutes of their final game. But they still could not avoid a Jets moment or two.

What else would you call it when Leon Johnson, the rookie full-back, throws an option pass in the final quarter that was intercepted deep in Detroit territory, when a chip-shot field goal might have propelled them into a tie and a playoff berth? Or when Parcells fell in love with the inexperienced Lucas at quarterback after he brought the Jets close to the goal line with his running and passing, only to throw another costly interception.

Neither of these players had ever thrown an NFL pass before the season; each was intercepted at critical moments while the former Super Bowl quarterback O'Donnell could only watch in frustration. The Lions won by 13–10, and the Jets' season ended.

Later, Parcells confided to at least one person that he had been wrong to call so many passes by inexperienced passers.

Still, the 9–7 won-lost record represented one of the great one-season turnarounds in league history. They had been a gambling club all year, depending on hunches and risks and surprises; if they fell short of the playoffs because of such risks, at least they were staying true to a tone set by a single man, and a strong football man at that. Losing because three different players throw interceptions for you in the same game was many things, but it was certainly not Same Old Jets. At long last, as the thirtieth anniversary season of the Jets' one great triumph approached, something new was in the air.

So was something old. The club announced that in the 1998 season it would return to the green-and-white uniforms sported by Joe Namath when he raised his index finger skyward three decades before. A link to the best days of Jets past would be reestablished. Everything old—not Same Old—would be new again. Perhaps, just perhaps, the long strange saga of the New York Jets would have a happy ending. No one—from Don Maynard and Curley Johnson to Leon Hess and the suffering multitudes in the far reaches of the green-draped "Meadowlands" Stadium—could feel they deserved anything less.

Index